WOMEN IN CHANGING INDIA

WOMEN IN CHANGING INDIA

Rameshwari Pandya

SERIALS PUBLICATIONS
NEW DELHI

First Published - *2008*

ISBN: 978-81-8387-126-6

Published by

SERIALS PUBLICATIONS
4830/24, Prahlad Street, Ansari Road
Darya Ganj, New Delhi-110002 (India)
Phone : 23245225 Fax : 91-11-23272135
E-mail: serials@satyam.net.in

Dedicated to
My Mother

Content

Preface

Development of "Women" has emerged as an important area of scientific work. But its very nature is interdisciplinary in nature. Considerable public opinion and public funds has been invested in the cause of development of women. Each and every aspect of women's life is discussed in a systematic and rational manner. The major objectives of writing this book is to equip everyone with enough fundamental issues related to women. To furnish the reader with all practical and necessary information related to women.

In *"Women in changing India"* emphasis is placed on presenting the subject matter in a very simple and explicit way. The book is a sincere and modest analysis of the real position and status of women in today's changing Indian society. It is hoped that the book may prove to be useful to the post graduate students of Education, Sociology and of the courses of Women studies as well as the research scholars who have their interest in this field. The social workers, politicians, social planners and many others may find the book informative and useful. This book is intended to serve as a basic text book for students, University and College teachers.

The Author tries to put together the concerns at various levels with the grass roots level realities. From decentralized planning, poverty eradication, income generation it goes up to the wider issues of policy formulation and implementation. It is this neat arrangement of different chapters that make the book a practical guide to researchers and teachers alike. Also, the book demonstrates how action projects can be successfully carried out.

The book focuses on two sections. The Section I contains research studies conducted by the author. Whereas the Section II contains chapters on perspectives.

The first section focuses on need of women empowerment to match with the changing Indian scenario. In the first chapter author discusses the important issue of empowering women by imparting legal education. The chapter presents a research study which was conducted to find the effectiveness of video films in imparting legal education. Seven educational video films were developed and undergraduate students were taught with the films in a quasi experimental style. The findings suggested "Women and law" subject needs to be included in the curriculum of studies. The law, courts, parliament, assembly alone cannot solve the problem of crime against women but spreading legal awareness can help in promotion of women's empowerment.

In the second chapter author discusses the problem of Reproductive health in rural areas of Baroda. This was an action project which was funded by ONGC and Bank of Baroda. The author along with her research team trained "dais" - the traditional birth attendentors in a village. It was a very challenging project as the topic was such that initially women were very shy in joining this project but with good planning and support from the local lady sarpanch the project was very successful. The findings suggests that if there are initial hurdles in reaching the target group and in developing rapport with beneficiaries then they need not get frustrated. The final outcome suggests that there is lot of scope, gap in the area of Reproductive health which need to be addressed by educationalist, doctors and social workers. Education is universally established as an effective medium for social development and reform.

The third chapter attempts to focus on the role of income generation as an instrument for promotion of women empowerment. It is found from experience that entrepreneurs from traditional dominant business castes and communities come forward to avail the business opportunities and incentives provided by various promotional agencies. This income generation project was carried out in slums of Baroda. It shows an effective mechanism and can sought to enlarge the pool of new entrepreneurs from traditional groups who can be trained and guided to establish new ventures.

The fourth chapter reveals the dynamics of "gender" and "sex". This research study was conducted and couples were asked to give their opinion about Role of Men and Women. It is very encouraging to note that with education, women are coming out to work leaving home front and families to make practical arrangements for themselves. Women's dual role, position and place of women can be located in the attitudes of male in general and policy-making in particular. Society change cannot be brought about without participation of women in every sphere of life. A clear framework of practical support and value system that believes that everyone has to offer and greater potential to fulfill if given the opportunity and appropriate environment. Empowerment is therefore about helping everyone to be their best.

The fifth chapter in the Research section is a Research study, it was conducted in Baroda, Gujarat. The objective of the research study was to find out the effectiveness of slides and exhibition in promotion of awareness regarding non conventional fuels and stoves like solar cooker, Priyagni Chulhas etc. The study was conducted with school children from urban as well as rural areas. It was found that girls and boys equally learnt through both the teaching aids, this indicates that these children when take up adult roles of men and women will be conscious of the fact that environment needs to be protected for better tomorrow. Through education the goals for planned change can be achieved.

Sixth chapter explains how women can be empowered by systematic Extension Education. The Extension service has the role and responsibility of bridging the gap between research and users of technology by developing linkages on one hand with institutes of higher learning and on the other hand with the field and community. It also helps in the two way communication process, i.e. transferring of knowledge and technology to the field through demonstration, talks, workshops and collecting feedback. Home Science extension aims at helping people specially women to change their knowledge, skills and attitudes.

Seventh Chapter titled "Refocus Home Economics to change the status of Women". It is the need of the hour to change the contents to meet new needs, several new specializations as part of home economics. Home economics must stress upon cooperative, supportive housekeeping and liberate women from over glorified mother hood and self damaging subservient wifehood. Home economics contents must be increasingly vocational so that women gain economic freedom. Economic freedom is a prerequisite to development of self and family.

In Chapter eight author highlights the importance of health and how different dimensions like physical, mental, social, spiritual, emotional and vocational health makes complete health. The notion of positive health plays a vital role in our lives. In India people who are illiterate, less aware about the various promotive and curative dimension of healthy practices. Women health remains an insufficiently tackled social issue. When resources are limited, the governments cannot provide all the needed health services. Under these circumstances the aspirations of women should be satisfied by giving them equal right to available health care services. It is important to value our health as our "valuable asset". It is in our hand to maintain our health as only a healthy person can lead a healthy and productive life.

Chapter nine titled as the "World of Advertisement and women". The author has given the analysis of advertisement as an art. The concept and use of advertising is as old as civilization itself. The face of advertising has changed since 1990's. Advertisement is a part of our economic fabric as they inform, influence, conveniences and reaches people by entering new geographical market and attract new customers. In advertisements women are shown as attractive and sex objects. The world cannot afford to waste the great resources, abilities and talents of women. Welfare of women is a subject of great concern for the society and media has a major role to play in enhancing this aspect.

The tenth chapter titled as "Women administrators : Myths and Realities" analyse the barriers and attributes of women managers. Recent studies reveals that the stereotype of the notion regarding women that they lack the abilities and personality traits required for managers is widely held and has contributed much to the lack of progress in the area of employment. However, on the other hand, if she demonstrates assertiveness, initiative or ambition, many men and women see her as hostile, maladjusted and over controlling. The chapter further examines the areas were training is needed by the women administrators in order to perform the managerial role effectively. There are certain myths which can be discarded by the success stories of women managers such as women cannot take decision, due to her higher position she may lose her tenderness and family responsibility is a major barrier. The women can overcome this by dreaming and putting the dream into action.

Chapter eleven is titled as "Population issues and women". In this chapter author describes the very important issue of population education and reproductive health. The gender ratio, of number of females per thousand males was low in India to start and it continues to fall. In India the position of women is still worst and they are marginalized within the society. The cause of women's ill health are necessarily rooted in the economic and social realities of their existence. Providing information, education and communication services to mobilize public opinion to persuade couples to avail of health and family welfare activities, engagement of women can get fruitful results.

Author in the chapter twelve "Environment Education a Tool to Protect Mother Earth" describes how women and environment are inextricably linked and no longer is environment education is the sole concern of scholars of biological science only. Scope of formal environmental education has four integrating and interrelated components like awareness, real life situation, conservation and sustainable development. They can be at primary, lower secondary, higher secondary as well as at University level. Similarly environment education ca be imparted through non formal as well as Adult Education programmes.

Women are primarily responsible for the health, nutrition, hygiene level and comfort of their families. In this context women's access to natural resources like water and firewood is of extreme importance. Thus their involvement and interaction with their environment is intimate and immediate.

In order to both conserve the environment and promote the advancement of women, it has become necessary to give the issues of ecology and development an intellectual analysis from the view point of women.

In Chapter thirteen, the author describes the need to understand the importance of consumer education. As we have experienced in the last decade of the twentieth century the process of globalization. In theory globalization means free flow of goods, ideas, individuals, capital and information. It has changed the quality of products and even the value system of man kind. It is important to mention that globalization to be successful it requires great foresight and systematic planning.

The new concepts calls for effective networking with formal and non formal education. Some important strategies for promotion of consumer education could be (1) Public Education (2) Training Programmes (3) Extension Programmes (4) Research (5) Technical Advices (6) Knowledge transfer (7) Literate environment (8) NGOs as an interface (9) Strengthening the capacity building initiatives (10) Capacity building in the communities (11) Home Scientist can play important role in promotion of consumer education. With the world rapidly becoming a global village, the role of teacher becomes a more responsible one. They should recognize and rearrange the curriculum to build the future generation more capable of utilizing the global network for the benefit of mankind. Appropriate strategies should be evolved for improving interaction between journalist and consumer forum. Out reach of folk media needs to be expanded through involvement of NGOs.

In the fourteenth chapter "Health and Nutrition Education for Women" the author describes the concept of nutrition and health education. The main aim of health education is to help women to achieve health by their own action and efforts. This would make them understand health as a valued community asset, help in promotion of proper use of health service, participate as community representatives. Health and Nutrition education can be imparted very successfully both by formal as well as by non-formal education. A module for imparting health and nutrition education. This module can be followed where gender as a determinant of health can be taught.

The author in chapter fifteen has given a detailed description how women can be empowered if they are trained to be entrepreneurs so that they can venture into new areas. Women can be successful at entrepreneurship and get higher economic status and get empowered. Characteristics of women entrepreneurs are hard working, desire for high achievement, independence and good organizer. There are several organizations in the service of women Entrepreneurs. Author based on her own action projects and field work experiences have suggested some simple products which can be taken by women for income generation activities. The model explains each steps of the entrepreneurship project very systematically and clearly.

The chapter sixteen is titled as "Women and Development: A complex interrelationship" on examining the policies and programmes of government one would find that the approach has shifted from a welfare to a development and to an empowerment approach. Yet the role of women and development has not been understood properly. The real development can only be assessed by the criterion of active participation of people at all levels of national development, including essentially women, who are the neglected group. In order to integrate women into national development the following strategies like more control over their own lives, education, life skills, income generation, rural development with women at the focus. The women need to raise their status and collaborate with men on an equal footing in achieving national development goals.

Author in chapter seventeen "Functional Literacy for women" highlights the importance of education in general and adult education in particular 'As it helps in improving the status of women, family and society as they are the vital National Resource, National Adult Education programme stressed the incorporation of Universities and NGOs in spreading the literacy which is relevant to learner's need, flexible in terms of time and location. In order to give women their rightful position in the main stream of national development, it is essential they should be empowered psychologically, economically and politically. Adult and functional literacy plays an important role in Women's Development. Social and familial restrictions and responsibilities on women and girls inhibit them from taking up adult education. To make the adult education programmes successful several practical suggestions from authors personal experiences have been listed. These suggested activities are very easy, practical yet result oriented. Author is incharge of the Adult Education Center "PRAGATI" where in different adult education programmes are conducted through out the year.

Acknowledgement

This book is the result of my work and interest in women and women related issues. I am grateful to my guide and mentor Prof. Arvinda Chandra, whose intellectual strength, and critical approach has given me all the confidence in taking and facing challenges. I am grateful to her and hope she will be happy to see this work.

I am extremely grateful to Prof. Veena Gandotra, Former Dean, Faculty of Home Science for writing the Foreword for this book. She has been very supporting and encouraging throughout.

I would fail in my duties if I did not thank Prof. Prerna Mohite, Dean Faculty of Home Science for her constant support, encouragement and motivation. She deserves a big Thank You for everything.

I am thankful to all my professional and personal friends with whom I shared my joys and academic experiences. The comments and suggestions of several people have seen this book into its present form. I am grateful for all their comments and help.

To my husband Dr. Mahesh Pandya, I owe a special debt. He was not only tolerating my self imposed isolation and oscillating moods, but also helped me with computers. I would also wish to place in record my affection to my sons Siddharth and Shrikanth. Inspite of their not knowing much about this work but they kept inquiring about the progress of my work.

At this important moment of life, I wish to remember my mother and mother in law for their blessings. They have been source of motivation and guidance to me.

Baroda 2007 *Rameshwari Pandya*

Foreword

The development of women as the human resources of the country has been recognized as a crucial factor in the national progress and development. In recent years there has been growing awareness in the country of the need to involve women in development programmes in a systematic way. Women being nearly one-half of the population are the important human resource of any country. India in its present changing and developing stage has to give its due share to women if it has to reach the status of a developed nation.

Empowerment has become the key solution to many social problems like high population growth rates, environment degradation, low status of women. The concept of women's empowerment appears to be the end result of a number of important article discussions, dialogues, generated by women's movement throughout the world. Feminists are increasingly investigating the shifting boundaries between the public and private spheres in different societies and how issues of concern to women can become part of public debate. Social change, advancement in education alongwith the economic need to supplement the family income has brought forward women as a potential labour force in the economy.

Empowerment of women is empowerment of family / household and in turn development of a nation of a country. Women are a significant part of all development be it education, employment, health, environment protection of consumerism. They are the key decision-makers in the family and are thus vital resource for the family as well as country.

Dr. Rameshwari Pandya has in the past published several articles in reputed journals and has published books also. Being a true academician Rameshwari has interest of student at heart and has contributed to knowledge base in Home Science.

The present book is also one such endeavour in which she deals with women in India in the changing scenario. The chapters are covering varied aspects of life and the role of women in it.

There are various key national issues directly proportional to women empowerment, like health, income, population, legal education, infant mortality, adult education, status of women, environment. These critical issues requires woman as policy makers, implementer and controller and calls for understanding dynamics of women in changing India.

I wish Dr. Pandya success in her efforts and wish she continues the good work.

May 2007
Baroda

Veena Gandotra

Section I

EMPIRICAL STUDIES

1

Empowering Women by Imparting Legal Education

Introduction

Women have been idolized in India and yet they have also been exploited and denied social justice. This is seen in the increasing incidents of violence on women. In recent years, violence against women has become increasingly visible and an important social issue. Police officials, lawyers, social workers, policy makers and educationists are of the opinion that only a small number of incidents, especially those involving severe injury or death, get newspaper and media coverage. There are social, cultural and economic factors which combine to compel Indian women to play the role of silent victims of violence. All Indian laws get their sanction from the Indian Constitution which guarantees justice, liberty and equality to all citizens of India. The preamble speaks of equality of status and of opportunity for all citizens. Article 14 of the Indian Constitution states that "The State shall not deny to any person equality before the law or the equal protection of the laws within the territory of India".

The Constitution, however, is a document at a high level of abstraction. It is the guiding document of the State. The Indian Constitution is remarkable for its clear-cut emphasis towards justice and equality for all. Women in particular, are recognized by the Constitution as weak and vulnerable, therefore are to be given special protection. The Constitution has guaranteed equality to women not only before the law, but also in education, in providing equal opportunities and in public appointments. Women have been made an integral part of the constitution so that the goals of justice - social, economic and political equality of opportunity for all, can be achieved. Furthermore the Constitution makes special provisions for women to help them improve their social status in society. In the Planning process, under the trickle down theory, it was expected that women will equally benefit along with men. The Five year Plan Document recognizes that "in spite of the Constitutional legal equality given to women, they have lagged behind in almost all sectors". In the past decade, there have been various forces and pressures which have pushed women in to a low and inferior place. These forces have been more dominant than those which should have tried to bring up women towards growth and development.

Whether legislation exists or does not exist, the benefits are virtually zero. For many women the laws are non-existent or, if existing, insignificant, ill-conceived, delayed or simply not implemented for the women. Though several ameliorative legal provisions have been passed for the welfare of women, they continue to suffer. There is a big gap in the enactment of legal provisions and the benefits reaching the women. Lack of awareness of the rights and lack of knowledge of law is the reason why women continue to be mute victims of an unjust and irrational society.

In short, despite the amendments in laws over a period of time, the advantages of laws have not been used to its fullest which can be attributed to the lack of proper understanding of the law by the women. That is the reason crime rate is on an increase. It is indeed sad that whatever changes and amendments have been made, for the improvement of the legal status of women, have not reached them. The benefits have not reached due to lack of awareness of the beneficiaries as stated in several studies. To a lay person a law is very strange - something distant and incomprehensible. If the law says so, it is irrevocably right and just, even though apparently it may not be so. In the case of women, basically there is injustice built into the system, or justice which has not been brought out forcefully, nor often enough. It is not enough to pass a law. There should be continuous education of the people, for the real purpose behind the various laws so that they themselves can become the epitomes of law and justice.

The laws are seen to remain a dead letter until there is pressure for its implementation. There are many examples all over the country where progressive laws exist but have had no impact because they remain unimplemented. The findings of the various studies and the observations made by the Joshi Committee on software, confirm the invisibility of women. T.V., the medium which is supposed to educate and inform, has very little information about the actual condition of women. (Sharmskati 1987, p. 189). Women are provided beauty tips, but no advice is given to women who are unhappy in their marital home, on how they should take help from the law. Advice is given on how to be a good wife and a good mother by making adjustments within the family situation. Doordarshan repeatedly portrays women as house bound engaged in homemaking entirely dependent for their existence and fulfiilment on their husbands and children. The sıruggle that women are facing for economic and political autonomy, legal rights and identity is almost completely ignored.

> *Laws relating to women are rarely covered in the media and issues related to women are let out. It rarely receive the necessary exposure, so that at least through word-of-mouth, information may trickle down from one literate, informed women to another. Women's plight, hardly seen newsworthy matters. Even when media attention is given they are usually sensationalized with headlines such as 'Minor raped in K.E.M. Hospital'.*
>
> *Sharmskati 1987, p. 179*

There is an attempt in print media to maintain the status quo, and counteract good articles on women with negative ideas and images. For example, an article on harassment of women may be subsequently trivialized by a light-hearted account on 'eve teasing' highlighted by a cartoon. However, lately radio, television and other mass communication media have exposed the women to information and knowledge about legal provisions. However, such exposure have not yet resulted in creating consciousness to the desired extent among women, nor have they succeeded in loosening the hold of tradition-oriented thinking of the masses. Over the last two decades, due to the constant campaigns of women's groups and the overall impact of the women's decade, which was declared by U.N.O., there has been a steady increase in the serious coverage on women's issues. This is also because women themselves are becoming articulate bold and expressive. Issues such as violence, dowry and sexual harassment, which were at one time dismissed as the problems of an individual woman, are being seen within socio-political structural context. The result is that, there is an awareness in the print media with women wishing to discuss problems such as gender insubordination, social and sexual exploitation, legal disabilities and wage discrimination. Committed individuals and groups are leaving no stone unturned to get the message to the concerned persons.

> *By and large, women have been ignored or treated as sex objects. Attempts have been made by free lance, journalists, activists, academicians and concerned staff to counteract these features.*
>
> *Sharmskati 1987, p. 202*

Some research organizations also produce journals and newsletters wherein information about women in the organized sector is disseminated and for the first time, attention has been drawn to the oppressive conditions of women in India.

> *The Commission strongly recommends a special drive for imparting legal literacy to women so as to enable them to be aware of he existing legislations and the methodologies through which they can take benefit under the legislation.*
>
> *Sharmskati 1987, p. 293*

The struggle for legal equality has been one of the major concerns of women movement all over the world. Whether in the internal situation of her position in the parental or matrilineal home or in the external situation of acquiring education, skills, profession, employment, all these involve law. Even best of the intensions to generate an atmosphere of equality can not easily overcome the thousands of years of social distance perpetrated by caste, class, community and gender differences. Women themselves need to develop a self identity so that they can lead a life of security and dignity. This can be achieved by making them aware of their legal rights and potentials. A number of social enactments have been put on the status books for removing various constraints which hinder women's progress. Inspite of these measures, women have been lagged behind by men in different spheres. Home science, today is inadequate without inclusion of legal knowledge in its curricula. The University Grants Commission has also emphatically recommended guidelines for restructuring and reviewing courses so that new ideas, concepts, content and structure can be incorporated. It has suggested that the courses at college should have more application-oriented components. The National Policy of Education (1986) has also laid special emphasis on the education of women and suggested reviewing and reorganizing the educational activities to ensure that it makes a substantial contribution towards women's equality. Therefore, by introducing a course on women and law, which will make students aware of their legal rights. The investigator reviewed the literature in the form of reports of Government of India, Seminar and workshop reports, research reports, books, journals and newspaper articles. All these confirm the fact that there are various laws for the benefit of women but because of lack of their awareness, women are victimized.

Today's girls are going to be future women and they may have to face the world where the crime rates are progressively increasing. It, therefore, becomes very important to educate these young girls about their legal rights. This would also help to create awareness, understanding and sensitivity among them. Moreover, the home scientists must use their foresight to prepare women for the time of crises. The general observation and practical experiences of the investigator is that the legal knowledge and awareness among

Home Science students is very poor. The results of the feasibility study conducted by the investigator with a sample of first year Home Science students in March 1990, revealed that students have a positive opinion towards legal education as a course in Home Science. More than 90 per cent respondents agreed that legal education is desirable for Home Science students. Further, the findings showed that, there were only about 40 per cent girls who had correct awareness of the different laws concerning women. The remaining 60 per cent either did not have any awareness or had incorrect awareness. The feasibility study also supports the need for legal education to be given to Home Science students, because only 10 per cent of the respondents had a course on legal education in school or outside the school by any other agency. This highlights the need for a formal education system to impart legal education to the girls so that it could be of some help at the time of distress.

Generally one avoids reading about the laws as it is assumed that legal jargon is too difficult to understand and that laws are not pertinent to our lives. Therefore, an introductory course could be planned in simple and understandable language, highlighting the issues relevant to women. Women in India suffer from a variety of society and economic disabilities which prevent them from exercising their human rights and freedom in society. During the last few decades, a number of legislations have been passed with a view to ensuring equality of status and opportunities for women. In practice, however, it seems it has eluded women. Therefore, it is important to educate the women about the radical changes in the law. Reviews of the studies conducted established that awareness of women regarding laws is very poor. It was further revealed that a change was creeping slowly and steadily in policies of government, women's organizations and need to spread legal education is felt.

A sizeable theoretical literature was available on effectiveness of T.V. and Video but very limited literature was found on teaching college students through video.

There is a need to develop systematic video film on "Women and Law". The amount of investigation, research on video film is limited which necessitated further exploration in this area. It is established that the law related course are strongly recommended for women. Although need to educate women about law is felt, a systematic beginning has not been done. Therefore, undertaking a study to develop the content of "Women and Law" to teach Home Science students assumes significance. Thus, it is obvious that course "Women and Law" can play a catalytic role in bringing about social change which is also one of the ultimate aims of Home Science education.

Legal education in Home Science should be considered more seriously than anything else because in recent years crime against women has assumed giant shape. Even facts related to figures on crime serve as an eye opener for Home Scientists whose activities are geared towards betterment of family, community and nation, keeping the women as their focus. Undertaking a study to develop the content of course "Women and Law" in relation to the curriculum of Home Science assumed significance and should be given appropriate priority. Keeping the above justifications in mind, a study on "Developing a course and video instructional package on "Women and Law" and measuring the effectiveness of package with the students of Faculty of Home Science, Baroda", was undertaken.

The very nature of investigation necessitated undertaking multidimensional study revolving around those aspects of "Women and Law", which were not investigated in the past. The study was carried out using content analysis, experimentation and survey methods. Developing course, producing video films, experimentation with the video films on "Women and Law" formed the nucleus of the study.

MAJOR OBJECTIVES

1. To develop an effective introductory course on "Women and Law".
2. To develop video instructional package on "Women and Law".

3. To study the effectiveness of video package to teach "Women and Law" to the first year Home Science students in terms of performance of students on knowledge test.

FEASIBILITY STUDY

The investigator conducted a feasibility study in March 1990 in the Faculty of Home Science, M. S. University, Baroda. Sixty First Year students were selected in such a way that there were twenty students, each representing Art, Commerce, Science streams. Such a selection permitted a comparison between the awareness of students regarding laws pertaining to women and enabled the investigator to know whether the type of school education and characteristics of the students affected the awareness and opinions of the students. The purpose of the feasibility study was to find out the data and background information of the students, source of legal information, their opinion about legal education being given to the girls and the correct knowledge about laws related to women like age for marriage, divorce, dowry, rape, eve teasing, inheritance, maintenance, etc. It was intended that the findings of the feasibility study will help the investigator to crystallize her problem, to determine the feasibility of the doctoral study, to draw a meaningful sample and to select the relevant variables. The data were collected with the help of questionnaire.

An encouraging observation of the feasibility study was that the girls had very favourable opinions about the need for imparting legal education. Thus, if a course on "Women and Law", is initiated it would be well received. The variability of different characteristics of Home Science students confirmed certain assumptions and helped the investigator to formulate hypotheses like relationship between personal and demographic variables with awareness regarding laws and opinions about legal education to be give to Home Science students.

POPULATION OF THE STUDY

The population of the present experimental study consisted of 306 First Year students of the Faculty of Home Science, M. S. University of Baroda, in the year 1992-93. However, in reality only 279 students were attending the classes and the others dropped out. In other words, the population consisted of 279 students.

SAMPLE

The following summary shows the number of student viewers and absentees for each video film.

Summary of number of viewers and absentees for seven video films

Video Film	*Class Strength*	*Viewers*		*Absentees*	
	(N)	*f*	*%*	*f*	*%*
Introduction	279	207	74.2	72	25.8
Eve Teasing	279	225	90.6	54	19.4
Inheritance	279	184	65.9	95	34.1
Marriage	279	217	77.8	62	22.2
Dowry	279	237	84.9	42	15.1
Divorce	279	233	83.5	46	16.5
Rape	279	215	77.1	64	22.9

It was decided to let the whole class of the Ist year view all the seven video films. But as the whole population did not remain present to view the video films, selective sample were only available for each video film instead of the population. Upon checking the attendance at the viewing of each film it was found that some students were absent at each viewing. Therefore, the numbers of viewers and absentees is presented in the summary. 306 students paid the fees in the Faculty office, but only 279 students attended the classes. From the total number of 279, different number of students were absent at the viewing of the video films. Thus, the selective samples for each video film had different number, as shown in the summary.

TOOLS FOR DATA COLLECTION

A battery of tools was prepared by the researcher to collect the required information. The data collection tool for each purpose was as follows.

Purpose	Tool
1. Background Information	Questionnaire cum Checklist with structured items.
2. English language competence	Examination office records
3. Academic Achievement	Office records
4. Socio-economic status	Standardized Socio-Economic Scale prepared by Desai (1987).
5. Modernity	Scale to measure level of modernity adapted and standardized by Mehta et al (1974) from the original 'OM' Scale of Modernity for Indian conditions
6. Personality	The personality inventory by A. Hafeez and V. S. Shantamani (1974)
7. Gain in Knowledge	Seven tests on "Women and Law" having recall and recognition items, True and False, Fill in the blanks, multiple choice.

SCORING AND CATEGORIZATION

For scoring and categorization of data, different procedures were used. The weightage was given to all the items of the questionnaire. The total number of respondents which might fall in each category was divided by the scores which they received. The scores of the respondents were considered for deciding the range of each category.

The first part of the questionnaire contained questions regarding background information of the respondents of the study. No scoring had to be done for this part and the variables were categorized directly according to the questions.

Variable	Categories	Range of Score
1. Stream in Higher Secondary	Arts, Science, Commerce, Any other	-
2. Medium of instruction	English, Gujarati, Any Other	-
3. Place of residence	City, Town, Village	-
4. Choosing Major	Related to Science, Related to Social Science	1, 2
5. Legal education in family	LL.B., LL.M.	0-1, 0-1
6. Family's social work background		0-1
7. Involvement in Legal cases		0-1
8. Mother's occupation		0-1
9. Exposure to television and video		

Scores were given to the students for this variable. The possible scores ranged from least (0) to maximum (37). The respondents were divided into two categories under this variable as follows.

Criterion	*Range of Score*	*Category*
Below mean	0-18	Less exposure
Mean and above	19 and above	More exposure

Second part of the questionnaire had items to measure socio-economic status of the respondents. The scoring was done according to Desai, scoring pattern, 1987. The categorization was done as follows:

Variables	*Category*	*Range of Score*
Socio-economic status	High	26-35
	Middle	21-25
	Low	0-20

Third part of the questionnaire had items to measure level of overall modernity. The scoring was done according to the Alex Inkele's scoring pattern, 1974. The categorization was done as follows:

Criterion	*Range of Score*	*Category*
Overall	Modern	8-13
Modernity	Conservative	4-7

The fourth part of the questionnaire had items to measure personality of the respondents. The scoring was done accordingly of the respondents. The scoring was done accordingly to A. Hafeez and V. S. Shanthamani scoring pattern, 1974. The categorization was done as follows.

Range of Score	*Personality traits*
8-10	High extroversion
5-10	High introversion
below 8 in extroversion	Ambiversion
below 5in introversion	

For the variable Academic achievement, the office record was used by the researcher by obtaining the percentage of the marks secured by the First Year B.Sc. (Home) students in the Board examinations of twelth standard. The categorization was done as follows.

Variable	*Categories*	*Scores*
Academic achievement	High	60-75 Ist division
	Low	45-59 IInd division

For the variable of competence in English, the student's previous semester's grade in English subject was taken as an indicator of their competence in English. The grades for the English course were collected from Faculty examination office. The respondents were divided into two categories according to the grades secured by them in English subject in first semester in the seven point scale.

They were as follows

English grade	*Category of competence*
B and above	Good
C and below	Poor

Knowledge Tests : As discussed before, the knowledge tests were completely objective in nature. Each correct answer was given a score of one and the incorrect answer was given zero score. The maximum obtainable score for one knowledge test was 20. A key was prepared for scoring the tests. Thus, seven tests were made to check the knowledge gian from seven video films.

METHOD OF PROCEDURE

Developing Outline For The Course "Women And Law"

In order to develop the outline of the present courses, content analysis of the course outline of the related courses was done. An outline was drawn in light of broad objectives of the course "Women and Law". The developed outline was validated by the experts and was revised according to their suggestions.

Planning For Experimental Teaching

The units for the experimental teaching were selected and five libraries were consulted for collecting subject matter for teaching. The subject matter obtained for the course "Women and Law" was then organized. Unit plans for teaching the experimental units were developed and were validated by the experts.

Preparation Of The Video Films

For preparation of the video films full length of scripts with a complete list of visual illustration and accompanying sound was made ready.

Mode Of Presentation

The mode of presentation of the content was as follows

Topic of the Unit	*Title of the Film*	*Format*	*Type of the Film*
Introduction	Introduction to Law	Documentary, Interview	Informative
Eve Teasing	Are you Eve teased ?	Documentary, Interview	Informative
Inheritance	Law of Inheritance	Interview, Illustrative talk	Informative
Dowry	Is Dowry legal ?	Dramatization, Illustrative talk	Persuasive Information
Marriage	Marriage made easy with law	Dramatization, Illustrative talk	Persuasive Information
Divorce	Law of Divorce	Interview, Lecture	Informative
Rape	Trauma of Rape !	Lecture, Illustrative talk	Informative

Mode of presentation of video films were decided mainly in such a way that it achieves the objectives and yet presentation is done in interesting and practical manner. Since the films were made to impart information about various laws related to women mainly informative approach was used in writing the scripts.

Experimental Teaching

Experimental teaching with the video film was done after conducting the pretest for all seven video films.

Administering The Posttest

The posttest was administered immediately after the video teaching. The researcher personally with the help of two assistants took the classes of First Year for experimentation. One theory class of 55 minutes was taken for one session of pretest, experimental teaching and posttest. Thus, each group had seven classes of teaching of the selected units of "Women and Law" through seven video films.

The Experimental Teaching and Data Collection

The questionnaires were printed in different colours, one for each law. The experiment was conducted with 279 First Year Home Science students in the month of March and April 1993. For data collection, the groups formed by the Faculty office were used. The experiment was conducted by administering pre-test, experimental teaching and post-test on the students. Personality, Modernity and Socio-economic scale were also administered. Data thus gathered, were scored using the predetermined keys for the respective research tools.

Analysis of Data

The analysis of data was done in IBM-PC/AT 386 compatible computer system. The various statistical procedure were used for the analysis of data. Keeping in view the objectives of the study, the following statistical methods were used for analyzing the data.

1. Frequency and percentage distribution
2. Mean Scores
3. Paired 't' test
4. Analysis of covariance

MAJOR FINDINGS

1. Majority of the students were from general stream having urban background with social science

inclination and majority did not possess legal and social work background.

2. Majority of the respondents were modern and extroverts although their mothers were housewives.
3. Nearly equal percentages of respondents were having high as well as low exposure to TV and video.
4. Majority of students were form high socio-economic status and nearly 60 per cent had high English competence, but low academic achievement.
5. All the seven video films were effective as there was considerable increase in the mean scores of the students achievement on post-test for all the seven video films.
6. Overall, the film "Trauma of Rape!" was found to be most effective and film on "Introduction of Law" was least effective.
7. The Science stream respondents gained significantly higher than the general stream respondents for all the seven video films.
8. There was significant difference in gain in knowledge of students from English medium school as they learnt more in comparison to the students form vernacular schools.
9. Respondents who had science inclination learnt significantly higher than the respondents having social science inclination.
10. The presence and absence of legal exposure had nothing to do with the knowledge gain. However, in some cases, the previous legal exposure of student's family raised this awareness.
11. The respondents from city learnt significantly higher from the film 'Are you eve-teased ?' For rest of the films variable place of residence did not play any role.
12. The film 'Marriage made easy with law' was found most effective by the respondents whose mothers were housewives.
13. The effect of variable 'English competence' was found to be significant for all the seven video films.

14. The respondents form high socio-economic status gained significantly higher from the video films in comparison to students from middle and low socio economic groups.
15. There was no significant difference in learning, in relation to Social work background, TV and video exposure, Modernity, Academic achievement and Personality.

CONCLUSIONS AND IMPLICATIONS BASED ON FINDINGS

In order to use video films in teaching a course "Women and Law", certain conclusions can be drawn on the basis of the findings of the present study. It is difficult to conclude with maximum certainty on the basis of this study, because it is the first study of its kind, and has built-in limitations of the sample and the nature of the experiment. It can be said from this first multidimensional study, that the developed outline of the course "Women and Law" is learnable and acceptable by students and yet there is a wide scope for its expansion. The course outline was developed logically as a 'Model' was adopted to develop the course and precautions were taken to assure that no psychological gaps in learning occurs. As this was the first attempt, the content was deliberately simplified and the evaluation of learning was also simple. May be later on some advanced course can be planned.

However, it can be concluded from the present findings that the detailed outline of a course "Women and Law", was feasible for learning as there was apparent gain knowledge of the students after viewing the video films based on such a course outline. The trends of findings of quasi-experiment further supported learning theories which postulate that the increased reinforcement, recapitulation, cumulative sequence, and psychological arrangement of the topics enhance learning, as a significant gain in knowledge was found for all the seven video films on "Women and Law". Therefore, it can be concluded that well balanced and systematically organized films can be produced by teachers. The teachers should be encouraged to use such video films for teaching instead of lectures alone.

As the films tried to include most of the required teaching resources which are not always possible in the class room situation, they added to the clarity and understanding regarding the topic. For example, the 'Drama' shown in the video film may not be brought to the classroom in the live situation. Thus, video films tried to overcome the limitations of a lecture method and thereby helping the students to gain more knowledge. It is said, 'seeing is believing' and these videos have visuals with the commentary on the subject matter, to illustrate this principle. Illustration and motion in the video films held the attention of the learners and helped to score high in the knowledge test.

Considering the wider, and modern concept of the Home Science Education, the course on law becomes very much a part of its content. Therefore, teaching laws through video films will prove very useful in Home Science colleges. The delivery of content through the video films was direct, simple, open, down to earth, which facilitated learning of law. The entire positive findings can be attributed to ease, simplicity and directness of the video films. Along with this finding, the investigator took great care of making everybody comfortably seated while viewing. The whole class was divided into small groups, close to the video which helped the students in internalizing the content.

The laws which were selected were for young women regardless of their characteristics. The teaching of laws through seven video films concretely showed that women need to know these laws related to women. However, significant differences were found in the gain in knowledge regarding "Women and Law", in relation to stream of study, medium of instruction, social science inclination, and English competence. Thus, these variables were found to be very relevant. Although some other variables were relevant from a social point of view, very small portions of the sample were having variables namely, Legal Exposure, Social work background and place of residence. The effect of these variables could not be found because of sample size was very small. It is also possible to describe and operationally define these variables in a totally different manner in a future study, and to discover about their relation to learning of laws.

On the other hand, there may be some other variables which could help in learning of law. The Home Science students perceive the need to learn laws related to women. Perhaps today's college students face situations of crimes against women like disregard of property rights, marriage and divorce problem. Therefore, their sensitivity to learn laws could have developed. The present students thus, can be considered more motivated to learn laws. It is the prime time for them to be taught laws. The need to become more independent, more self protective and more knowledgeable, seems to have developed in college students. Therefore, it is justified to teach laws.

In the video films the laws were described in a straight forward informative manner and the content on law was simplified for the undergraduate level. There were not many analytical situations regarding the use or knowledge of laws. The test was simple and it lacked the use of analytical power. It was a direct test having only recall and recognition items, and, therefore, much discrimination among the students was not possible. This was deliberately done as there was no precedence for teaching of laws. Moreover, there is a general feeling that teaching of law is dry and boring. So to overcome these difficulties, investigator purposely made such video films and tests. No special method to teach and evaluate learning of laws was found by the investigator in her literature search. Hence, teaching and testing of knowledge both were rather simple. In future it could be tougher than this.

A more clear picture may be derived when a tight experiment is employed by exercising control on the variables and randomizing the sample. The methods of teaching and evaluating the learning can be more specific in a future study.

RECOMMENDATIONS

The investigator on the basis of her experience during experimentation and findings of the study recommends that:

1. A similar type of study can be conducted including control group and retention test.
2. A similar type of study can be conducted with other variables related to media utilization.
3. Production and validation of the video films on more laws related to women other than included in the present study can be tried out.
4. A comparative study of the effectiveness of the present video package in teaching formal and non-formal group of women can be conducted.
5. A similar type of study can be conducted with other samples like, students form different levels and specializations.
6. A study can be taken up with other instructional strategies on the same topic.
7. The strategies having both software and hardware components can be developed and tried out.

REFERENCES

Agarwal, B. C. and Chandiram J. Towards Equality, Women in Indian T. V. Media Asea 1982.

Anderson, H. R. Selecting and developing media for instruction. Van Nostrand Reinhold Co. Inc. 1976.

Barbro, O. H. Violence against women. Women and Health 13 (3-4) Studies on Women Abstracts, Vol. 7, No. 3, 1989.

Bhagat, R. Impact of mass media on farm women, a study *Kurukshetra* August 1988.

Bhoite, A. Sex ratio and the status of women in India. Ahfad Journal 5(7) 1988.

Chandra, A. Introduction to Home science, New Delhi, Metropolitan Book Company Pvt. Ltd., 1978.

Chatterji, S. A. The Indian women's search for an identity, Delhi, Vikas Publishing House.

Decade for women-world conference Nairobi Kenya, July 1985. Report by Centre for Women's Development Studies, New Delhi, 1986.

Dosi, J. K. Television for Development, *Journal of the Council for Social Development,* 13(4), 1983.

Dowry Deaths, *Hindustan Times* (Delhi) 12 Aug. 1989.

Dua M. R. Themes in Indian Communication, Metropolitan Book Co. (P) Ltd. New Delhi, 1980.

Gore, M. S. Education for women's equality, New Delhi. Centre of Women's Development Studies, 1988.

Women's Religion and Family Law" *Asian Women's Conference report.* Bombay, Dec. 16-20, 1987.

Haksar, N. and Singh N. Demystification of Law for Women, New Delhi, Lancer Press, 1986.

India Ministry of Human Resource Development, *National Policy on Education,* New Delhi, May 1986.

Joshi, V. Menon, G. Research on Women's education in India, A review, Perspectives in Education, 1986, Vol. 2, No. 2.

Majority of women unaware of rights, (Hindustan Times, Patna, 7 Dec. 1987) in *Legal News and Views* 1987, Vol. XII (12).

Mittal L. N. Women's studies in curriculum development. *University News* April 20, 1992.

Sharmaskati, Report on the National Commission on Self-employed women and women in the informal sector, 1988.

2

Equipping Dais For A Healthier Tomorrow

Introduction

The information of health service planning in India was laid by the Bhore Committee report in 1946, which had prioritized health needs of women and children. India was the first country to launch a National Family Planning Programme in 1951 and the Reproductive and Child Health Programme (RCH) was launched in 1997. The major objective of this RCH programme was to improve the health status of the most neglected sections of the Indian population, women and girls of socially disadvantaged groups, particularly those living in remote, rural settlement.

Reproductive health implies, that people are able to have a satisfying sex life and that they have the capability to reproduce and the freedom to decide when and how often to do so. It also includes sexual health, the purpose of which is the enhancement of life and personal relations and not merely counseling and care related to reproduction and sexually transmitted diseases (World Health Organization, 1994). Reproductive health is a crucial part of general health. It is not only a key element of health during adolescence and adult hood, but also sets the stage of health beyond reproductive years for both women and men has its effects. Women's health status varies widely both within and among countries because of factors such as local disease prevalence, health related behaviors, and women's educational attainment, exposure to health information, influence on decision making and access to health care, poverty, environmental degradation, civil conflict and migration also influence women's health.

Whereas agriculture and animal husbandry get priority, sanitation and personal cleanliness are neglected. There is no proper health care facilities. The health of rural woman is often impaired due to frequent child births, ignorance and superstition in which she has to live and work. Most often, they go without medicine and doctor's consultancy, but go to the local 'vaid' and get herbal mixtures to cure themselves from diseases and illness. In the absence of any health centre and trained doctors, they are deprived of the basic medical facilities and in consequence remain ignorant and unhealthy. For pregnant women, the only hope is the untrained village midwife, who backed by her long experience is bold enough to meet any emergency. The Indian Primary Health Care (PHC) system has an extensive nationwide network with more than 20,000 primary health centres staffed by doctors and over 1,00,000 sub-centres staffed by female and male health workers. 1,31,000 village level sub-centres has been set up to provide primary health care including maternal care and family planning services. Unfortunately, the PHC system has primarily focused its attention on family planning, and to some extent, on immunization. All the other components of primary health care have been neglected. Women are only recognized by the health system in the context of maternal and child health (MCH). Their general health and reproductive health needs are ignored.

The fundamental issues concerning women and their health are nutrition, sanitation, infections, overwork, work hazards, stresses, mental tensions, pregnancy, child birth and sexual harassment. Women face high risk of malnutrition, retardation in growth and development, disease, disability and even death at three critical stages in their lives – infancy, early childhood and reproductive phase. India is one of the few countries where there are fewer women than men : only

93 women for every 100 men. In 1901 the sex-ratio was 972 women per thousand men. In 1991 it was declined to 927 per thousand men. The main reason of this declining sex-ratio is high mortality rate among females in all age groups. It is noteworthy that in India about 15 million girls are born per year but almost one fourth die before 15 years of age, despite being considered biologically stronger than boys. Mortality indicators show that upto the age of 35 years more females than males die at every age level.

Table 1
Death Rates

Year	*0-4 Years*		*All ages*	
	Male	*Female*	*Male*	*Female*
1970	51.7	55.1	15.8	15.6
1985	36.6	40.4	11.8	11.8
1990	24.8	27.9	9.7	9.6
1991	25.6	27.5	10.0	9.7
1992	24.9	28.2	10.0	10.2

Source: Sample Registration Service, Fertility and Mortality Indicators for respective years, Registrar General and Census Commission, India New Delhi.

The table 2 offers the state wise estimates of Maternal Mortality Rate. The maternal mortality rate in India is unacceptably high. The maternal mortality rate is a measure not only of poverty but also of priority society gives to a problem that is of life and death concern to women. According to National Family Health Survey 1992-93, about 1,25,000 women die in India each year due to causes related to pregnancy and child birth.

The survival of mothers and babies is closely correlated with the care and attention received at the time of delivery. Gynaecological and reproductive morbidity among women is high in India. At the time of delivery, no more than 20 percent of all women have some contact with medical or paramedical personnel. Deliveries are largely conducted by untrained personnel and in unhygienic conditions, both of which contribute significantly to poor maternal health. All deliveries must be managed by trained birth attendants. Normal deliveries can be managed at home or at the institution but in all cases infection must be prevented by ensuring clean delivery practices. Because complications can develop without warning, it is critical to put in the plan effectively to ensure timey referral and management of emergency complications. Death from haemorrhage, for example, can occur within two hours of the onset of bleeding. Establishing effective referral systems for life threatening complications is therefore, critical for saving women's lives. Communities should be involved in organizing timely transportation for women needed care to the referral facilities.

Table 2
Maternal Mortality Rate

Sr. No.	*State*	*Maternal Deaths per 100,000 Births*
1.	Kerala	87
2.	Maharashtra	336
3.	Punjab	369
4.	Tamil Nadu	376
5.	Gujarat	389
6.	West Bengal	389
7.	Andhra Pradesh	436
8.	Haryana	436
9.	Himachal Pradesh	456
10.	Bihar	470
11.	Assam	554
12.	Rajasthan	550
13.	Uttar Pradesh	624
14.	Madhya Pradesh	711
15.	Orissa	738
16.	India	453

Source: NFHS, 1992-1993 and Indirect estimates of MMR from League Table.

Two decade ago, in 1981, no more than 15% of all rural births were performed in an institution and as many as two thirds were delivered by untrained workers and others. And in such states in Bihar, Jammu and Kashmir, Madhya Pradesh, Orissa, Rajasthan and Uttar Pradesh more than three out of four births are delivered by an untrained attendant. And what is disturbing is the evidence than over the 1991 to 2005 period, the picture has hardly changed. The proportion of births conducted institutionally increased from 8 to 15 percent in rural areas and from 32 to 47 percent in urban. The proportion of births delivered by untrained attendants fell from 81% in 1971 to 68% in 1987 in rural areas and from 43% to 39% in urban areas. Even so, there are rural areas of the country where 9 out of 10 births are delivered by an untrained attendant. (Khan et al. 1986 for U.P., Kanitkar and Sinha 1989 for Bihar, Rajasthan and Gujarat). In such circumstances, the role of the estimated 5 lakh traditional birth attendance in India-about 1 per 1000 population-becomes especially important (Singh and Paul 1988, Planning Commission 1985). However, the vast majority of births in India takes place at home The National family health survey shows that in 1992-93 only 25.6 percent of all births and 16.1 percent of all rural births were conducted in institutions and as many as 65% were delivered by traditional birth attendants.

An immediate priority therefore, is to ensure safe home delivery by trained birth attendants. Traditional birth attendants must be trained to recognize danger signs and ensure timely referral to the hospitals. Collaboration between the health sector and the traditional birth attendants is an important way of bridging two very different cultures concerning reproductive health, but this link has not yet been effectively implemented. The little evidence which is available suggests that trained attendants do in fact have significantly better health care knowledge and can better recognize high risk conditions, suggesting the importance of training of traditional birth attendants. As a part of the safe motherhood initiative, first level referral units (FRUs) with specialists and equipment are now being established to treat complicated pregnancies and obstetrician emergency in selected states and districts. Innovative approaches needed to attract specialists to work at these rural units and expand their reach so that peripheral level institutions can be upgraded to provide specialist care.

VILLAGE

- Village Health Guide
- Sub Centre (SC) (For every 5000 population) with ANM/Multi purpose female worker (MPW-F) Multi purpose Male worker (MPW-M) Primary Health Centre (PHC) (For every 30,000 population) with Medical Officer and His Team of Para Medical Staff
- Traditional Birth Attendant (TBA) (Dai)
- Aanganwadi worker (for every 700 persons in Tribal Areas and Every 1000 persons in Non-Tribal Areas)

Hence understanding need and importance of training Dais, was recognized. This area of research attracted the attention as the review of studies reveal that women are victimized more than men in the matter of poor health.

REASONS FOR TAKING UP DAI PROJECT WITH ONGC-BARODA

At the stage of initial conceptualization of the project, it came to the knowledge of the project worker the ONGC was funding some projects and Centre for Adult and Continuing Education was taking up these projects which were:

- Literacy awareness programme
- Health and Nutrition awareness
- Dai Training programme
- Child care
- HIV/AIDS awareness programme

The project worker decided to take up Dai Training programme as it seemed more challenging a task to work with women's health.

- Since last few years UBS/UCDS agency have also expressed needs in terms of training paramedical under the community development programmes.

- Health is one of the aspect under the community development which is carried out by this department. Health means covering each and every dimensions that is children, mothers and family. The students who work as community volunteers find children and mothers health to be considered most neglected.
- Even the Department of Home Science Extension and Communication, M. S. University, Baroda is working for community development since past many years and has been focusing on health aspect widely.
- Dai Training is an important training through which women or dais trained will successfully deliver child and help low percentage of death of child and mother.
- Teaching aids are the most effective means of communicating and the use of teaching aids for village or community people makes it very much effective and easy in passing on a message.
- Thus to make the experiment successful, teaching modules helped in dai training classes as a means of communication.
- Thus as a researcher of Extension and Communication and understanding the need for trained Dais in villages for controlling death rates of women and child this project was undertaken.

OBJECTIVES

1. To study the need for trained Dai.
2. To study the Job chart / performance of duties by Dai in various Nursing homes and hospitals private and government, small and big and those in urban and rural setting.
3. To identify the concepts and generalization or content to be promoted through Dai training programme.
4. To study the Government approved syllabus for Dai Training and update it.
5. To develop teaching modules for promotion of Dai Training.

6. To promote awareness regarding personal hygiene, reproductive health and family life education amongst the women of village Dabka.
7. To train the women of village Dabka for "Dai Training" through the use of various communication strategies and materials.

METHODOLOGY

Research Design

At the stage of initial conceptualization of the project, it came to the knowledge of the project worker that ONGC, Baroda is funding some projects. One of the five projects was on "Dai Training". All the villages identified by ONGC were surveyed for this specific purpose with other team members. It was decided to take up village Dabka.

Firstly, the project worker contacted the Sarpanch of the village, Ms. Kailashben Jadav. The project worker, sarpanch and the team members visited the village to make the women aware about the Project.

Several initial visits across two months were made to the village to enable the investigator to get familiar with the setting and build rapport with the women. During this period, the purpose of the study was reiterated. While meeting women in the village the style of asking questions was informal and conversational. The sequential steps followed in data collection were as follows:

- Initial visits were made by the two research investigators on a number of occasions in order to get acquainted with the local people.
- Simultaneously, there were informal introductions of the two investigators to the local doctor and Traditional Birth Attendant (Dai).

SAMPLE

Analysis of data obtained through structured schedule. Out of 89 households which were surveyed only 23 women were selected. The criteria for selecting the women was as follows.

Age range of 20-45 years and was ready to attend the 21 days training. A list of women was prepared after building a good rapport with them. All the women were selected from the same area. A dialogue with them showed that main concern was that training would increase their prestige in the community. At the start of the training, 17 women enrolled but later that number increased to 23. The most promising feature is that three daughter-in-laws of old Dais came forward to undergo training to carry on their traditional occupation.

Figure 1 shows the complete plan of the Project.

PLAN OF THE PROJECT
Figure 1

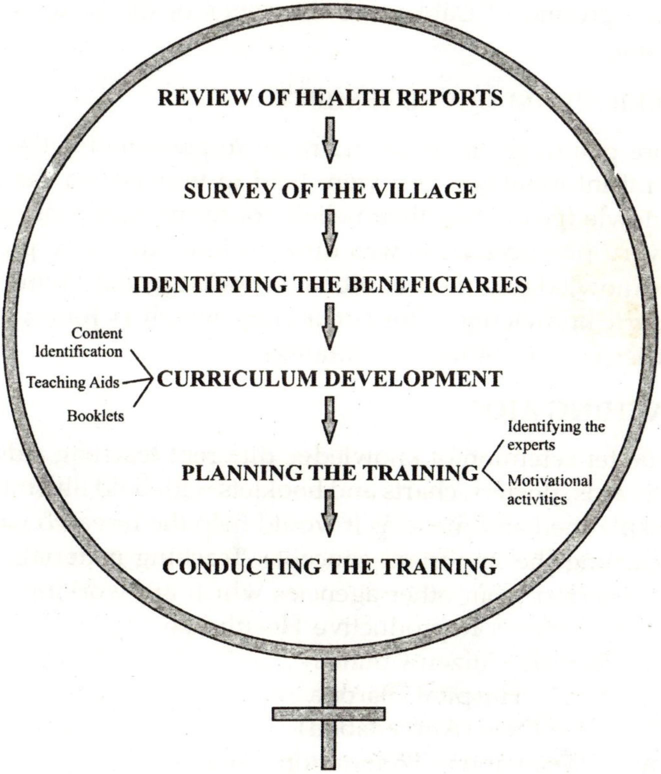

INAUGURATION OF THE PROJECT

A formal inauguration of the Project was done on 8th December 1998 in the village Dabka were all the women from Dabka village were invited. The Vice-Chancellor of The Maharaja Sayajirao University, Dr. Anil Kane, The Regional Direction ONGC, WBRC Shri N. Lal, DGM-Drilling Shri Gupta, Manager Public Relations Mrs. Narayani Mhail, Hon. Director of the Centre for Continuing Adult Education and Community Services Dr. Kalpana Parlikar and the staff from the Faculty of Home Science along with important village leaders were the invited guests. The function started with a prayer, followed by speech of chief guests and introduction of the Project was given. An exhibition was also arranged in which different charts, posters, flash cards were displayed. The PTC college ground of Dabka was the venue of the inauguration function.

CURRICULUM DEVELOPMENT

Before planning the actual training programme for the Dais several informal sessions were held to understand the level of knowledge of Dais, their beliefs concerning pregnancy and delivery practices. This was done to have two-way process of acknowledging the traditional knowledge and giving new modern knowledge. The curriculum which is followed by District Health Office was followed.

TEACHING AIDS

For better retention of knowledge different teaching aids like flash cards, posters, charts and booklets with bold illustrations were planned and made as it would help the research worker in teaching the important concepts. Teaching materials were also collected from other agencies which are working in the area of Women's Reproductive Health like

1. Baroda Citizen Council
2. S.S.G. Hospital, Baroda
3. CHETNA (Ahmedabad)
4. Tribhovandas Foundation (Anand)

PLANNING THE TRAINING

1. Identifying The Experts

The effort to collaborate with government PHC was planned but it had to be abandoned due to lack of support from District Health Office. The next alternative was to utilize local resource persons and private doctors from Baroda City who were well-versed in rural obstetrics. We also took help of Dais who have access to the women in the community. We were initially reluctant to choose the option because the Dais are very old and have physical limitations. Nevertheless, we thought if given a situation we could utilize, the Dais as the key persons and also as master trainers. The different experts from Baroda were taken to Dabka village to impart training.

2. Motivational Activities

Different motivational activities were planned by the project worker to ensure good attendance throughout the training. The motivational activities on various topics like Food, Health, Legal education etc. Activities which were planned and carried out were as follows:

1.	Slide show	-	Care during pregnancy, Deficiency diseases, Healthy and unhealthy living conditions, supplementary income generating activities.
2.	Film Strips	-	Why small family ? Immunisation schedule for your child. Food we eat.......
3.	Video Films	-	Meena Hasi Kali Kem Mari ?
4.	Illustrative Story	-	Importance of education, Small family happy family
5.	Food Demonstration	-	Khajoor Roll, Chocolate Burfi, Palak Pooda, Nan Khatai, etc.

Table 3
The daily plan of work during the project was approximately distributed in the following manner

Activity	*Time (Minutes)*
Casual talking	15
Motivational activities	50
or	
Expert Talk and Discussion	60
Attendance and instructions for the next class	15
Total	Nearly 1.½ hrs.

TRAINING OF DAIS

The objective of the programme is to impart correct information on pregnancy and delivery in a very simple manner so that Dais, who are mostly illiterate, can understand the basis of why they have to change certain practices. First they were exposed to the basics of human anatomy and physiology and modern concepts of obstetrics and gynaecology. The next step was to train them the diagnosis of problematic pregnancy. As majority of the Dais were illiterate the training was participative and conducted according to their capacity. Different topics were covered by the experts during the training. The Dais were not only given the facts, but also given ample opportunities for discussion and clear their doubts and share their experiences. Several practical sessions on How to wear the gloves ?, Process of Sterilization were conducted so that, hands on experiences are given. They were taught the use of ready kit for delivery, how to do per vaginal and per speculum examination.

A field visit was arranged to give enriching learning experience. During the training in S.S.G. Hospital they were taught about scientific medicine, and micro organisms by looking through microscope, Functioning of Auto-clave Room. Practical tips of how to handle emergency during pregnancy, visit to labour room and modern operation theatre. This helped them understand the rationale behind the practice of sterilization. The practical traiing as well as the visit to the gynaecology ward of S.S.G. Hospital was crucial as it improved their knowledge and gave them confidence.

VALIDICTORY FUNCTION

A Validictory Function was organized on 30th March 1999 for all the Dais who had successfully completed the training programme, after the training programme was over. Dr. Kalpana Paralikar was the chief guest and Dr. Mukesh Bhatt and Ms. Kailash Ben Jadav were the special invitees for the function. The venue of the programme was PTC college Dabka. The dais had not received any salary or honorarium for getting the training so along with the certificate, Ready Made Delivery Kit and a Steel Box along with cash of Rs. 75/- as a token money was given to all the 23 Dais in a public function which was attended by the village women and students of P.G. Diploma in extension from the Faculty of Home Science, Baroda.

RESULT AND DISCUSSION

Description of the Study Setting

The present section describes the study setting and the demographic and socio-economic characteristics of the population and sample. The locale of the study was Dabka village, Padra Taluka of Baroda.

DABKA : Where Training Was Done

Dabka is a village situated about 38 km away in Padra Taluka of Baroda District. It has a population of nearly 15,000 people. An alarming 40 percent of the population live in poverty. The project worker along with other team members surveyed all the villages adapted by ONGC namely Vadu, Mufpur, Karkhadi, Chokari, and Dabka in Padra Taluka.

Village Dabka was selected because of various reasons which were:

- No Government PHC in the village.
- Lady Sarpanch in the village.
- The women were motivated to learn about women's reproductive health.
- Women belonging to the age group of 18-45 years were available for the project.

Health facilities in the area are limited. The few health services that exist focus on family planning and maternal and child health. Pressure to meet contraceptive targets set by the National Family Planning Programme has resulted in poor quality of services. Government assistant nurse-midwives (ANMs) are not properly trained for reproductive tract infections (RTIs). In this area, there are hardly any women doctors. While women's general health is neglected, her reproductive health is even more deplorable. Poverty, women's low status and ignorance contribute to women suffering from a variety of reproductive health problems and high prevalence of reproductive morbidity among women. The above conditions prompted us to conduct an Action Research on Dai Training.

Background of Dais

The Social Status of women is low, female literacy is only 30%. Generally, women's workload in this area is very heavy. Many have to rise at 4-5 a.m. and work throughout the day till 7-8 p.m. The usual work includes farm work, which is backbreaking especially during the harvesting season and household work, which includes collecting firewood, cooking, washing and caring for the children. Due to heavy burden of work and relatively poor diet, most women are malnourished. In this area the total fertility rate is high. Almost 44.5 percent of birth takes place at home and are attended by traditional birth attendants. Four of them were trained by the Government but the training was negligible. Antenatal care (ANC) is generally very poor and only restricted to tetanus immunization and iron supplementation through government PHC system.

The highlights of demographic and socio-economic characteristics of all the women who attended the Dai training programme are as follows:

- Majority of the women (56%) belonged to the age of 40-50 years.
- Little less than half of them were educated till primary rest of them were illiterate but could read and write their names.

- Majority of the women (69%) were living in nuclear family have 5 or less than 5 members in the family.
- Majority of them had less than 4 children.
- All the women were Hindu by religion and had Gujarati as their mother tongue.
- Majority of the women (67%) of the women reported that they had two or more than two family members working in the family.
- For little less than fifty percent of the women had monthly income between Rs. 1000 to 1500 per month.
- Majority of the women were engaged in unskilled jobs such as domestic help and farm labour.
- More than 40% of them were living in Kutcha homes but had electricity in their homes but no water connection, so they were using community water tap.
- Treatment of minor illness (80%) of them used home remedies and few only (4%) reported that they go to Bhoova for treatment. All 100% said they go to hospital to seek medical help in case of serious illness.

The Dais in Action

After training, the Dais were given the basic Delivery Kit for attending deliveries, so that they could conduct delivery hygienically and safety. The Dais are to conduct antenatal examinations, identify and refer high-risk cases to the Referral Hospital.

The Dais are also able to examine women internally, diagnose pregnancy and related symptoms. This is no easy task as Dias encounter many barriers to learning, since all of them are not equally fast learners. They have difficulty with the lessons. In most cases, village women are not willing to be examined internally even by the Dai. Dais do make occasional mistake in treatment. But by and large they know the way to safe delivery. The Dai training provided them with a whole new experience. Their roles have expanded from that of a mere attendant and scavenger to a community health worker who provides a range of services to women and children. This would bring new meaning to their lives. Because of the new skills and additional roles given to the Dais, the villagers would give them more respect and recognition. An old woman in the village commented that the Dais have become the first contact for health care of pregnant women. This recognition from the community would significantly enhance the self esteem of the Dais. As a result of this Action project, which was a new experience, the dying tradition of Dai, is being revived Younger women, particularly daughter-in-laws of the Dais who earlier did not see any prospect in this field came for training.

Problems Faced During the Project

1. The place where the training was planned and started initially as it was a open verandah, so young boys and men used to come and gather around the place which was disturbing, so women showed hesitation in coming to attend the training. So the place was shifted to interior of village in one of the village leaders house.
2. When only talk or lecture session were arranged the attendance used to be very thin, to make the sessions more interesting use of more teaching aids were planned and incorporated.
3. Distance was always one of the main constraints as the village Dabka is 38-40 km away from Vadodara and there is no direct link in terms of transport facility.
4. Initially project worker decided to work with all the women of the entire village who were from 18-45 years age. Due to the social stigma attached to this profession only women from Harijan Vas came forward for the training.
5. The topic "Dai Training" is very personal to women's health, so it was very difficult to convince the women to learn about it and so it took little longer time.
6. A major problem during the training programme was irregular attendance. This was checked by planning and using variety of motivational activities and food

demonstrations. The motivational activities were selected with dual purpose of providing recreation and education.

CONCLUSION AND SUGGESTIONS

Women patients are usually brought to the hospital when it is an emergency. Poverty makes the situation worse and women and children are the hard hit. Today 80% of health care is in private hands which provide for quality health care for those who have the purchasing power According to the Human Development Balance Sheet of South Asia, 1997, in India there is only one doctor for every 12,500 people, 135 million people are denied access to primary health care. The Report added that 88% of all pregnant women aged between 15 and 45 suffer from anaemia. Research studies have shown a definite link between low socio-economic status and lack of knowledge and utilization of preventive health services. This is the reason that although we have family welfare, safe motherhood and child survival programmes, yet maternal mortality rate continues to be embarrassingly high. As women are unlikely to seek health personnel in time, health personnel must seek them. Women need health care at the door step. More attention to a woman's health needs can prevent the serious problems which undermine her position and capacities. Women are the providers of health care, yet they have little or no control over the priorities of health services, environment or research. The emphasis here should be on direct participation.

Drawbacks of the Rural Health Care System

1. Lack of proper health services due to problem of distances, transportation and communication facilities.
2. Lack of and shortage of supplies of medicines.
3. Non-availability of medical and para medical staff.
4. Doctor and medical staff overburdened with administrative work of completing paper work.
5. Lack of refresher courses of training for 'Dais' who play a very' important role in women's health care.

What Will Work? Suggestions

1. The undergraduate curriculum in the medical colleges for teaching maternal and child health should be reviewed and modified suitably particularly to deal with health problems of women and children in the rural areas.
2. From time to time refresher training on following topics-
   - Health education
   - Preventive health care like ante-natal care, immunization of children, promoting use of preventive equipment like gloves and mask.
   - Referral to large hospitals
3. Improving women's nutrition through "Shakti Packets".
4. The real challenge before us is to tackle the careless attitude which most women have towards their health needs and nutrition. Too often, especially in rural areas, females eat last and least. This neglect of health needs of women leads to serious problems and in further undermining their position and their capacities, so, there is a need that this practice must be discouraged by convincing them that the women's health is as important as that of other family members.
5. Maternal mortality is a very severe problem, it can be checked to some extent by providing such Dai training at different places under such Action Project.
6. Post Graduate and Undergraduate students can take up assignment and projects for developing Information Education and Communication (IEC) materials related to "Dai training" as people specially in rural areas do not know the complications which can arise during home delivery.
7. Suitable incentives should be offered to make the training acceptable to the Dais.
8. Para-professional and semi-professional workers from the community should be trained to provide simple promoting, preventive and curative health

services needed by the community. Young persons, elementary school teachers, educated and willing house-wives should form part of the pool and these services should be planned to cover the entire country.

9. Conducting Research on :
   (i) Effectiveness of Training of different para medica staff in terms of duration of training.
   (ii) Problems of Dais and other para medical staff in the rural areas.
   (iii) Studies are also required to assess how the trained Dais are performing their roles.
   (iv) Study of logistics and management problems of "Training Programmes".
   (v) More methodological studies are required to evaluate the usefulness of the "Training programmes".
   (vi) Studies into attitudes, beliefs and practice of traditional birth attendants (Dais) should be made to improve upon the training programme now designed for them and to obtain their greater participation in maternity and family planning services.
   (vii) To assess the access of village women to the traditional and modern Reproductive Health Services.

The institutions of higher learning have a very useful and practical role to play. They have genuine contributions to make both in the spheres of policy making and implementation. The university system should undertake evaluation, research and documentation of projects related to women's health. The university system can be more focused in environment building and motivation. The local level bodies, such as Panchayati Raj institutions, political leaders, women's activities and religious leaders should be meaningfully involve in advocacy, motivation and programme implementation. Women are an active part of our work force making up for more than half of world's population. They bear the burden of "paid work" as a part of the work force and "unpaid work" in the house. It is sad to see that development has not benefitted men and women equally. This means that customs, habits and other social traits of the community are to be considered.

The combined demands with the fact that Health of women is a necessary commitment to social development of the country calls for a focused visionary approach to women's health. The attainment and acceleration of our national goals in terms of economic development, strengthening of social infrastructure gender equality, health and education of women is a must.

REFERENCES

Bang R. A., Bang A.et al. "High Prevalence of Gynaecological Diseases in Rural Indian Women, Lancet-1 (8629), 1989, 85-88.

Baroda, M. S. University of Baroda. WOHTRAC and WSRC. "Workshop Report on Qualitative Research Approaches and Women-Centred Health Care" Baroda, Centre for Operation Research and Training, 1997.

Bhadauria, Mridula, Some Issues of Women's Health, Social Welfare Vol. 46 No. 1 April 1999.

Bhadauria, Mridula, Women in India, Some Issues, APH Publishing Corporation, New Delhi 1997.

Black M. The Health and status of women-girls and women, New York UNICEF, 1993.

Burisch, Mathias and Edith Marx, Humanising Development Training, Development and Cooperation No. 6, Nov.-Dec. 1983.

CHETNA 'A Decade of Health Education', Ahmedabad, Chetna, 1993.

CHETNA 'A Workshop on Women and Occupational Health', June 1-3, Ahmedabad, Sardar Patel Institute of Public Administration; Chetna, 1995.

CHETNA. 'Wah! - Women and Health Training Programme, India'. Ahmedabad, Chetna 1993.

CHETNA 'Women's Health Mela, An Innovative Training Approach for Women', 5-7 April 1990 Ahmedabad; Chetna, 1990.

Dhanu, A. Networking for Adolescent Reproductive Health, CHETNA News, Jan.-March, 2000.

EPW Research Foundation Poverty Levels in India, Norms, Estimates and Trends, Economic and Political Weekly, 28 (34), 748-68, 1993.

Evaluation of Traditional Birth Attendant Training Scheme in India, A Collaboration study New Delhi, National Institute of Health and Family Welfare, 1983.

Florence M. Tadiar, G R. Malayang and A Baldemore, Her Story. The International Council on Management of Population program, Philippines Oct. 1998

Friedmann, J. Rethinking Poverty; Empowerment and Citizen's Rights, International Social Science Journal Vol. XLVIII (2), 161-172, 1996

Gopalan, S. Fourth World Conference on Women-Country Report, Department of Women and Child Development, Ministry of Human Resource Management, 1995.

Khan, M.E. et al (1985) "Health Practices in Uttar Pradesh" A Study of Discrimination Against Women, (Working paper no. 45), Baroda, Operation Research Group, p-44. 1985.

Khan, M.E. et al. " Nutrition and Health Practices among the Rural Women - A Case Study of Uttar Pradesh India', (Working paper No. 3), p. 26. 1990.

Mahajan P. Mani and Siby K, Josep, "Human Resource Utilization" Musing on an Alternative Development, Pardigm Kurukshetra, Dec. 1996, p - 11.

Mittal, D.N., Women and Education Development Process, University News, 31(3), Sep. 1993, p. 3-4.

Ninth Five-Year Plan (1997-2002), Vol.-II, Govt. of India, Planning Commission, New Delhi, p. 8-9.

Prasad C. 1994 Training for Agricultural Development, A Basic Functional Area, Journal of Rural Reconstruction 27(1), 1994.

Rodin, J. and Ickovics, J.R 1990, Women's health, Review and research agenda as we approach the 21st century, American Psychologist, 45, 1018-34. 1990.

Srinivasan, S. and Prasad P.D., Reproductive and Child Health Programs and Women's Health-Problems and Prospects. Social Welfare Vol. 47, No. 1, 2000.

3

Income Generation and Women Empowerment through Home based Enterprises

Introduction

The common old belief that women dedicate their lives solely to look after their homes and in bringing up children is either set aside altogether or partially and now women are going in for self employment and entrepreneurship. Women entrepreneurs are overturning the stereotyped image as being passive and subservient to their men folk. Instead of taking preparatory and supportive roles, women are venturing to independent creative roles. Women represent over half of the world's population. They also make a substantial contribution to national development. Hence they should be given access to necessary inputs required for enhancing their productive ability and for their equal share in the benefits of development. In order to achieve this, in recent years the percentage of women beneficiaries in development programmes is increasing. Thus in self-employing areas the need for training of women is necessary.

Indian people know that "when you educate a woman, you educate a whole family" and they are fully aware of the fact that her learning will go into the bloodstream of the generations that will follow her. She can bring grace and dignity to the place where she lives, she can build a new nation and can mould a rather new era in the history of mankind.

Her role and effectiveness has been fully realized and accepted. Women can now choose from many new careers. They have a vast choice before them, they can enter any field, which previously was the exclusive domain of men. They can hold the highest position which men have been holding. Women can even become industrialists, entrepreneurs, exporters, beauticians, craft-persons, electronics technologists and so on for which they would need proper training.

Women can be successful at entrepreneurship or self-employment. Women get a higher economic status through self-employment. This is the basic requirement for raising their status. They are regarded as "inactive labour" or "secondary workers" or "dependents". Only women themselves can change this situation. Self employment will give them money, power and status, both in the family and society. For those women, who would like to remain at home and earn, having self employment at home premises will serve the purpose. This self employment promotes the idea of a flexible work time, helping women to work in the hours that suits them, giving women a chance to do something other than the household work, which can make the lives of many women pleasant and satisfying.

For the past three or four decades, employment of women is becoming an important issue at national level in India. This trend has made it more essential that women who have the potential to develop certain skills, get the right kind of training to join the work of employment with all the confidence and faith. So with the help of training only, women's earning power can be developed. Training programmes provide training in selected vocations to the women with skills which would enable them to earn through self employment.

Enterprise has forever been mentioned in relation to a men. But the male bastion has already fallen under the on slaught of female persistence, industry and perseverance. Entrepreneurship among Indian women cuts across barriers of affluence and education. Today there are Indian women entrepreneurs at the grassroots level who can put little capital but have a lot of courage to start small enterprises on their own.

Enterprise among women is no longer confined to manufacture and marketing of women centric products catering to a female market alone. The most important problem before the country today is to reduce the burden of poverty and inequality which history has put on the Indian masses. Despite decades of planning majority of Indian population lives below the poverty line. For the development of any society the status of women is the key factor, they are the ones who give vital input to the future generation. The nation today enfolds an era for reconstruction to enhance the quality of life of Indians. Emancipation of women is one of the generators of economic development and social progress. Developing entrepreneurial opportunities among women are the need of the hour because entrepreneurship.

- Helps women to supplement family income.
- Gives scope of women to express urge for independence.
- Proves mettle of women as a potent economic factor.
- Offers scope for development and diversity of choice as a career.
- Bring good impact on women's social position and status.

Organizations in the service of Women Entrepreneurs

1. Entrepreneurship Development Institute (EDI)
2. National Small Industries Corporation Limited (NSIC)
3. Government Stores Purchase Programme
4. Prototype Development and Training Centre (PDTC)
5. Small Industries Development Organization (SIDO)
6. State Industrial Development Corporation (SIDC)
7. Delhi State Industrial Corporation (DSIDC)
8. Industrial Consultancy
9. State Financial Corporation
10. NAYE (National Alliance of Young Entrepreneurs)
11. Voluntary Organizations

Entrepreneur

An entrepreneur is a person with a dream, originality and daring, who acts as the boss, who decides as to how the commercial organization shall run, who coordinates all the activities and other factors of production, who anticipates future trends of demand and supply and prices of products. According to Higgins, 'By entrepreneurship we mean, the function of seeking investment and production opportunity, organizing an enterprise to undertake a new production process raising capital, hiring labour, arranging the supply of raw materials, finding site, introducing a new technique and products, discovering new sources of raw materials and selecting top managers for day to day operations of the commercial organization.

An entrepreneur of every business enterprise invents and introduces new ideas, new products, new processes or revolutionary machinery and who, in general, carries out new activities in his business organization. Due to these reasons in modern times, the role of an entrepreneur is recognised as an important factor of production for every business organization. Economists have identified entrepreneurship as the essential element in generating investment opportunities in an economy. Entrepreneurship comprises of all these productive functions that are not thought to be rewarded by wages, rent or interest. It is not associated with routine human efforts, it does not involve the use of indestructible natural resources and it does not imply the provision of capital funds.

Status of Women Entrepreneurs in India

Nature has made a division of labour of the responsibilities of man and woman for betterment of process of evolution. In this division of labour, the women have been endowed upon with gift of motherhood and upbringing of the future generation. The women, the mother, has been the symbol of continuity of culture, tradition and religion, being the binding force of the family system. Quality of life indicated how well or how badly women performed her duties. Gradually women withdrew to the four walls of the home to take care of the children, while men worked outside forging for food. With the advancement of science and technology, an increasing number of women wanted to participate in economic activities of the nation. Thus, we find the emergence of women entrepreneurs.

Categorization of Women Entrepreneurs

1. Entrepreneurs in Large and Medium Sectors
2. Entrepreneurs in the small sector
3. Entrepreneurs in cities and slums

JUSTIFICATION OF THE PROJECT

We all know that an entrepreneur is a decision maker, who performs various functions to run the enterprise or to settle entrepreneurship. Thus, in short, the attempt here in this project was to make each beneficiary or participant of the programme into an entrepreneur and thus bring in the positive change of empowerment in our women through developing the potential of entrepreneurship. Further, this could be justified by the shift in approach towards women's issues and concerns, which is very clear from the plan documents, that is from -

Welfare oriented approach during the First Five Year Plan to- Development approach and 'Empowerment' during the Eighth Five Year Plan. This is further brought out more strongly by the Government of India and Ministry declaring '2001' as the Women's Empowerment Year'.

In the project of empowering women through entrepreneurship the thrust and focus was on :

- The determination of those objectives of the enterprise and the change of objectives as required, due to change in the market demand. It has been felt and researches are available that in due course of time, the job market for women will be scarce, especially for women who do not have proper training. So, women belonging to low socio-economic status can be trained for income generation through building their small enterprises.

In the Department of Home Science Extension and Communication, Faculty of Home Science, The M.S. University of Baroda, Vadodara, there are Master Level dissertation studies to prove the importance and need of developing the potential of income generation in low socio economic status women of Baroda through training and entrepreneurship.

- It has further found that women get lost and do not have any direction for securing financial resources for such enterprises. So, an attempt will be made to train and bring in an awareness regarding this very important factor.
- Women also do not have knowledge regarding market for their goods or services and devising new products or services to meet the demand of consumers or market. It is here that this training programme would focus on getting the feel of the market and thus meeting the changing and growing needs of the market.
- In the present times, the entrepreneur should be well versed with the efficient and the latest technological equipment and the revision and maintenance of it as and when necessary and should keep abreast of new knowledge and technology.

It is important to define some important characteristics of an Enterprise as:

1. It consists of people working together primarily for the purpose of production, sales, purchases, etc.
2. It consumes other valuable resources to produce output, that is, raw materials, workers time and energy, shop space, utilities, fuel, etc.
3. An enterprise is a continuing entity. It is not an adhoc effort to produce a single product or output, but rather a recurring and continuing effort to produce a stream of products or services.
4. Every enterprise carries out some sort of final net profit or loss calculation.

NEED FOR INCOME GENERATING ACTIVITIES

Illiterate women are mostly in the low income group and do not have much attraction for literary education alone, therefore, it is necessary that income generating activities (handicrafts) are planned for the workshop. Income generating activities will not only help in motivating, but also in sustaining their interest in continuing with the 'Women's Empowerment Programme'.

This is one way by which women can contribute to the family income. These activities will enable women to give a better income to the family. These activities will thereby :

- Improve women's social status
- Make them economically independent
- Can make them fight against the ill treatment rendered towards them by the family and society.
- Will be able to utilize their leisure time productively and avoid boredom.

NEED FOR SELF DEVELOPMENT

A fruitful and purposeful utilization of leisure time is necessary for making life happier and fuller. There is the need to initiate the work of organizing people for self development through better utilization of their time. The society and the family still do not expect women to be socially active in community affairs or civic problems and prefer that women should remain confined to their homes. Such workshops will enable women to work collectively in groups, and make them socially active. It will bring them out from the confines of their houses, make them financially independent, giving them immense self confidence and will also earn the respect of their husbands and in-laws when they pool additional finance into the family income.

Keeping the above justification in mind, the following project was undertaken.

METHODOLOGY

To help women set up their own business from scratch either individually or in partnership, time has witnessed the birth and growth of several organizations all over India. The Faculty of Home Science has also taken up several Action projects to help women cope up with problems of finance, labour, how to prepare project report, whom to contact for finance, how to choose a product, marketing. Through these projects attempts have been made for economic and social betterment of women. These action projects have helped in opening direct communication line with women from slums. Women were organized into local neighbourhood groups and training was given in the following manner -

The training package included mix of both theoretical information as well as practical workshops.

Workshop with Urban Slum Women of Low Socio Economic group of Baroda

Activity	*Teaching Materials*	*Teaching Aids*
• Moti Earrings and Necklace	Demonstration Workshop	Charts, Flashcards
• Candle Making	Demonstration Workshop	Flashcards
• Artificial Flowers	Demonstration Workshop	Booklet specimen
• Showpiece	Workshop	Flannel Board
• Bandhni (Tie and Dye)	Demonstration, Expert Talk	Booklet specimen
• Pot Decoration	Demonstration	Exhibition
• Glass Painting	Workshop	Exhibition
• Toran Decoration	Demonstration	Specimen
• Decorative Piece	Expert Talk /Demonstration	Chart, Flashcards
• Tissue paper flowers and popcorn tree	Workshop Film Show	Specimen, Flashcards

In order to make any programme effective and successful, the first essential step is of drawing up of a plan of activity since planning is an intentional effort carefully designed to attain the goals. It does not indicate priority and design, but also helps in carrying out the work successfully.

The steps that were followed during the workshop are :

1. Planning the activities (curriculum planning which includes - small scale activities such as batik printing, block printing, fabric printing, tie and dye, ceramic work, moti earrings and necklace, candle making, artificial flowers, showpiece, pot-decoration, glass decoration, toran decoration, tissue paper flowers and popcorn tree and decorative piece, which would help them in income generation and skill development. The demonstration of the productive

art will be given by the experts. The demonstrations will be followed by workshops.

2. Conducting the actual project by
   (a) Publicity
   (b) Carrying out the workshop
3. Distribution of booklets

ASSUMPTIONS OF THE PROJECT

1. Women have skills to learn handicraft activities.
2. Non-Formal education helps the women in improving their standard of living.
3. Women of urban low socio-economic status are interested in learning self employment activities.
4. Women want to earn to increase their standard of living.
5. Women of the urban low socio-economc status are creative in nature.

Time

The training programme was conducted from 1 noon to 4 pm.

Place

The 'Pragati Centre' for Non Formal Education at The Department of Home Science Extension and Communication, Faculty of Home Science, M.S. University, Baroda. It has a big hall with big tables and cooking range and facilities for use of audio visual aids.

Target Group

Adolescent girls and women from urban slums of Baroda. A total of fifty women took part in the workshop.

FINDINGS AND RECOMMENDATIONS

This section gives a brief sketch of the background information of the beneficiaries who attended the Training programme conducted under CDIP.

Background Information

Table 1
Percentage Distribution of Respondents according to Age N=50

Sr. No.	*Age (In years)*	*F*	*%*
1.	15-23	19	38
2.	24-31	15	30
3.	32-39	11	22
4.	40-47	2	4
5.	48-55	3	6

Table 1 indicates that 38% of women were between the age group of 15 to 23 years. The table further shows that 30% of women were between 24 to 31 years and 10% of women were between 40 to 55 years.

Table 2
Percentage Distribution of respondents according to the educational level N=50

Sr. No.	*Educational Level*	*F*	*%*
1.	Illiterate	6	12
2.	Upto Primary	13	26
3.	Upto Secondary	18	36
4.	Upto Higher Secondary	10	20
5.	Upto Graduates	3	6

Table 2 indicates that 20% of women were educated upto the higher secondary level and 6% of women were graduates. The table further shows that 12% of the beneficiaries were illiterates.

Table 3
Percentage Distribution of respondents according to their marital status N=50

Sr. No.	*Marital Status*	*F*	*%*
1.	Unmarried	32	64
2.	Married	18	36

Table 3 indicates that 64% of beneficiaries were unmarried girls and 36% were married women.

Table 4
Percentage Distribution of respondents according to the Reasons for attending the Training Programme N=50

Sr.No.	*Reasons for Attending*	*F*	%
1.	To become economically independent	44	88
2.	To utilize their free time	6	12

Table 4 indicates that 88% of the beneficiaries reported that they attended the training programme to become economically independent, whereas only 12% reported that they attended the training programme to utilize their free time.

Suggestions for the development of women entrepreneurship

1. Access to information on entrepreneurs should be provided in a large measure for all women throughout the country.
2. Associations of women entrepreneurs should assume responsibility of creating a greater awareness among young women. This programme can be linked up with youth programmes of education.
3. Programmes on continuous basis have to be designed, planned and implemented for the benefit of women students in all universities in our country to attract young women to take up entrepreneurial activities.
4. Women Entrepreneurs Associations and all other Non-Government Organizations (NGOs) interested in the course of promotion of economic empowerment of women should play an active role in the implementation of income generation schemes evolved by the central and state governments.
5. Serious efforts should be made for maximum utilisation of all viable informations and technologies for promoting the course of women entrepreneurs.
6. Efforts should also be made in the direction of starting diploma or certificate courses.
7. National organizations such as NRDC, National Small Industries Corporation (NSIC), Small Industries

Development Bank of India (SIDBI) etc. should assist the University authorities in establishing centres for training, counselling and production of woemn entrepreneurs.

8. Central and State governments should assist women entrepreneurs to participate in international trade fairs, exhibitions and conferences.
9. The family members of women entrepreneurs should also actively participate and extend all possible support in the matter of managing units setup by the women entrepreneurs.
10. Adequate insurance coverage should be provided to the industrial and business risks in order to safeguard the interest of enterprise as well as the employees in the enterprise.
11. Rural women entrepreneurs should be provided with special training facilities for their talents and skills.

IMPORTANT RECOMMENDATIONS

1. There should be better support for voluntary agencies from the government.
2. There should be state advisory committee for development of entrepreneurship among women.
3. There should be a better coordination between developmental agencies, voluntary agencies and financial institutions in putting together entrepreneurship development programmes.
4. Awareness and Sensitization programmes should be organized.
5. A Federation of Women entrepreneurs need to be strongly advocated.
6. Appropriate Technology need to be developed.
7. Education and Training is the most important factor to be taken note of, if we want to make women independent.
8. Credit facilities should be made easily available.
9. Marketing network should be women friendly.
10. Research Priorities and Strategies should be made keeping women in the focus.

Specifically, for solving the problems that women face to become an entrepreneur -

1. Separate cells for women should be established so that women entrepreneurs have easy access to credit.
   - Women co-operative banks should be established.
   - Those women who have been successful can help other women with advice and giving facilities to see that the percentage of failure in the scheme is kept down to the minimum.
   - To develop a greater degree of mutual confidence between bankers and women entrepreneurs, separate institutions should be set up for women.
   - Larger financial institutions should have separate cells for women.
2. Multiplicity of laws and regulations and their different connotation in different state of India limit the market especially for non-traditional products.
3. With the technological advancement India has to face many problems like:
   - Developing countries have merely sold technologies to India
   - Some imported technologies are not suitable for India
   - India needs some technologies which can help small and medium industries to increase the production using the labour intensive method which will be beneficial.
4. Easy access to infrastructure is also important. Women entrepreneurs have to face many hurdles in obtaining power and licenses wherever necessary, to set up an industry.
5. In spite of the progress that women entrepreneurs have made, there is still a lack of awareness among women entrepreneurs especially in developing countries. It is obtaining knowledge essential for identifying projects as also for credit, for marketing and training.

6. There is need for co-operation amongst women entrepreneurs with limited resources to group together to set up an industry.
7. Another problem women entrepreneurs face is due to mental reservations and attitudes of policymakers, planners and administrators.
8. Most of the women entrepreneur are handicapped and cannot continue with their business or trade activity for want of guidance on consumer demand, market mechanism, designing and resources for producing capital and raw materials apart from managerial and training support.

CONCLUSION

India being a developing country, is on its way to industrialise the economy. This would need an opportunity for entrepreneurs to participate in the economic activity of the country. Women constitute half of the population. We have seen that Indian Government is providing various incentives and measures for promoting women entrepreneurship. By proper utilization of these measures and incentives and also by motivating the women, we can achieve development and thereby growth of the economy as a whole. In short, we can conclude that women are in no way inferior to men and can contribute much to the economic prosperity of a country by an active participation in industrialization through entrepreneurship - viz women entrepreneurship. Hence, the development of women entrepreneurship would raise the status of women in the society.

BIBLIOGRAPHY

Anuradha G. and Sinha B. P., "Trainee under TRYSEM" Kurkshetra No. 12, Sep. 1985.

Chetana Kalbalbagh, 1991, Women and Development, Discovery Publishing House.

Desai, F. Promotion of income generation through production of decorative candles, among the women from Peon Quarters of the M. S. University, Baroda 2000-01. M.Sc. Thesis, M. S. U. Baroda.

India, K. Women Entrepreneur in the slums of Hyderabad and Secundarabad, Social change 20 (2) 1990.

Jose Paul and Ajith Kumar, 1999, Entrepreneurship Development, Himalaya Publishing House.

Lalitha Rani, 1996, Women Entrepreneurs, A.P.H. Publishing Corporation, New Delhi.

Mattu, A. and Pandya R. A guide to an Action Project. Faculty of Home Science, M. S. University Baroda 2000.

Nayak Madhab. Women entrepreneurs need for supportive service. Social Welfare, May 1991. No. 38.

S.S. Khanka and S. Chand, 1995, Entrepreneurial Development, New Delhi.

Swarajyalakshmi, C. 1998, Development of Women Entrepreneurship in India, Discovery Publishing House.

Vasanth Desai, 1996, Entrepreneurial Development Vol. 1. Himalaya Publishing House.

Vasanth Desai, 2000, Dynamics of Entrepreneurial Development and Management, Himalaya Publishing House.

Verma and Verma. "Development programme and Women Emplyment" Journal of Extension Education No. 3, 1985.

Verma S. K. and Saida V. Self Employed women in Gujarat. Social Welfare 38(2) 1991.

Vinze M. D. Women enterprise in India. Mittal Publication Delhi 1987.

4

Shifting Roles Redefine "Men's Work-Women's Work"

During the past few decades, women groups and development experts have worked to raise the status of women in society and to increase their education, income, decision making authority, and ownership rights. Experts are asking : how can men be more supportive and involved in family life ? Programme of Action of the 1994 International Conference on Population and Development that men and women should have the opportunity to share equally in child rearing and house work, as well as breadwinning. But how many years - or generations will be needed to put this principle into practice? The programme of Action promotes a concept of responsible fatherhood that includes sharing in child rearing and house work and encourages men to participate in ensuring proper nutrition and health care for their wives, their children, and themselves. It urges men to support their wives in seeking greater economic and political power, and advocates that daughters and sons be raised equally.

Women's active participation in all spheres of public and private life through a full and equal share in economic, social, cultural and political decision-making. This means that the principle of shared power and responsibility should be established between women and men at home, in the work place and in the wider national and international communities. Equality between women and men is a matter of human rights and a condition for social justice and is also a necessary and fundamental prerequisite for equality between women and men is a condition for people-centered sustainable development. A sustained and long term commitment is essential, so that women and men can work together for themselves, for the children and for society to meet the challenges of the twenty-first century.

The women of today, seek equality in all spheres of life. Many of the rights implied in the concept of legal, civic, or even economic equality can be legislated upon in theory. But, it is always doubtful whether in practice, the extent to which women exercise these rights, actually attain equality. Seeking and getting this equality depends on their own value frame work, their readiness to assert the rights available to them, the degree of social mobilization of the issue and the immediate familial and social content in which they function.

The problems of integrating women in the development process are now engaging the attention of planners and policy-makers all over the world, not so much because of the International Women's Decade and the United Nation's Call for action plans for this purpose as because of increasing realization of the social imbalances that development itself has created.

Several studies have suggested that the mother's participation in the world of work has brought about structural and functional alternations in the family and other social institutions. Society does not expect men to raise their children and work at the same time, underestimating men's ability to do something that is commonly expected of women. This indirectly relieves men of a responsibility that is theirs-often by law, and definitely by nature and by reason of being human-leaving men with few reservation.

Without exposure to information, a changed role in the status of women, increased education opportunities, and financial independence, it is unlikely that the traditional allocation of family roles is going to change. And without change on the family level, the majority of women are unlikely to advance to equal the role of men in society. Women joining the labour force weaken the traditional division of labour under which men have been earning money, while women's labour is mainly devoted to producing goods and services for home consumption.

Problems are faced by both men and women in homemaking, because women have accepted employment The employment of women requires them to stay away from home for long hours, like their husbands, and hence, home responsibilities demand a number of facilities like division of labour between husband and wife, paid help etc.

Several studies established that employment gave power and prestige to women. They developed positive attitude towards outside agencies. They also seeked cooperation and equality like the employed women of foreign countries. It further revealed that a change was creeping slowly and steadily in the minds of Indian husbands whose wives were employed.

The boundaries of the gender division of labour between productive and reproductive roles are gradually being crossed as women have started to enter formerly male-dominated areas of work and have started to accept greater responsibility for domestic tasks, including child care. However changes in women's roles have been greater and much more rapid than changes in men's roles. In many countries, the differences women's and men's achievements and activities are still not recognized as the consequences of socially constructed gender roles rather than immutable biological differences.

Rath (1987) commented : Nowadays men and women do not live in two watertight compartments of breadwinning and homemaking. The women helps in keeping the family, society and life together..... She is no longer a mere housewife. She is an economist nutrition expert, sociologist and educator.

In a literature review conducted by UNESCO, surveying 204 articles on the subject of the family in Latin America, only the articles addressed the issue of fatherhood or the role of the man in the family. International Planned Parenthood Federation says "Giving women total responsibility for their children results in the exclusion of men from the family and makes men less likely to behave in a responsible manner".

The rational of a sharp division of tasks between male and female gradually disappears as economic development moves some tasks from the home and transforms them into specialized occupation. In order to attain status and economic independence women started working outside their homes. They began to realize that career and marriage can be compatible as it is always with men. This new role of bread winning of women forces the husband, children and other family members to perform some homemaking activities, which they did not have to do previously.

Women make a great contribution to the welfare of the family and to the development of society, which is not recognized or considered in its full importance. The upbringing of children requires shared responsibility of parents, women and men and society as a whole.

Special measures must be taken to ensure that young women have the life skills necessary for active and effective participation in all levels of social, cultural, political and economic leaderships. This new generation of leaders must accept and promote a world in which every child is free from injustice, oppression and inequality and free to develop her/ his own potential. The principle of equality of women and men must therefore be integral to the socialization process.

Reducing the problems of employed women and increasing the number of women in gainful employment should be the priority given in all spheres for the progress of the country. In this context Agrawal (1989) commented "No country has developed rapidly over a long period without having been to some extent liberating women from their traditional household chores and without their close association in various socio-economic productive oriented programmes".

The roots of men's lack of participation depends in social "gender conditioning", the roles and responsibilities that men and women learn as children, from parents and other roles models, in the mass media, schools and other social institutions. To keep physical and psychological worlds of man and women balanced, the women should be equally respected and treated as an individual. Recognition and appreciation of women's housework as well as professional tasks, can accelerate the women's proficiency of work, both at home and in work place, and thereby reducing the problems they faced.

In Indian Society, Women's role traditionally has been of child bearing and home making while men performed the activities concerned with relations of the group to external situation including goal achievement. This arrangement served our society admirably for centuries. Now infact, the whole pattern of male-female roles are undergoing a considerable change. The changes in the social conditions and patterns of living have been responsible for women going out for job and this is responsible for the shift towards greater involvement of men in the activities at home. Although the term 'role' denotes a set of expectations and obligations associated with a vertical status position within a group or social situation. In the present study the term 'role' has been operationally defined as the dimension reflects the "ought to do or should do" part of the concept and was obtained by the couples in relation to their position in the household.

METHODOLOGY

Sample

The sample for the present study, which was randomly selected from Baroda city comprised of sixty couples.

Tool

The questionnaire contained activities related to household task performance of the respondents and social demographic characteristics, age, sex, education and employment status of women.

RESULTS

The major findings of the study were as follows:

1. Social Demographic Characteristics

(a) Age

(b) Education

(c) Employment status

The information concerning age and educational level of the respondents given in Table-1. The highest percentage of the respondents both men and women were in the age group of 31-40 years. The least percentage of women were in age group of 51-60. There were more older men than women.

Almost equal percentage of men and women were graduate. The male and female respondents were atleast educated upto secondary and primary level education respectively.

Table 1
Percentage and Frequency Distribution of the Respondents According to Their Age and Educational Level. (N = 120)

Age Group Respondents	*Men (60)* f	%	*Women (60)* f	%
• AGE				
20-30 yrs.	11	18.33	15	25.00
31-40yrs.	29	48.33	27	45.00
41-50 yrs.	13	21.66	11	18.33
51-60 yrs.	5	8.33	6	10.00
61 and above	2	3.33	1	1.66
• EDUCATION				
Primary	-	-	2	3.33
Secondary School	4	6.66	11	18.33
Graduation	36	60.00	33	55.00
Post Graduation	20	33.33	14	23.33

Employment status of respondents as given in Table-2. 100 per cent of male respondents were employed whereas 65 per cent of the female respondents were working outside the home and 35 per cent of the married women were housewife.

Table 2
Percentage and Frequency Distribution of the Respondents According to Their Employment Status (N=120)

Respondents	*Gainfully Employed* f	%	*Not Employed* f	%
Men	60	100.00	-	-
Women	39	65.00	21	35.00

II. Association between household task performance roles of respondents and their

- Sex
- Age
- Education
- Employment

Table 3 shows the association of household task performance roles and the sex of the respondents. The calculated value of Chi Square is less than the tabulated value. This means that there is no significant association of sex roles of the respondents in the areas of household and their sex.

Table 3
Association Between Household Task performance Roles of the Respondents and Their Sex (N=120)

AREAS OF HOUSEHOLD	*W*		*M*		*MW*	
	f	%	*f*	%	*f*	%
CLOTHING & TEXTILE						
Men	35	58.3	3	5.00	22	36.66
Women	38	63.3	1	1.60	21	35.00
HOUSEKEEPING						
Men	14	23.3	15	25.00	31	51.60
Women	16	26.6	12	20.00	32	53.30
FOOD PREPARATION						
Men	34	56.6	11	18.30	15	25.00
Women	43	71.6	3	5.00	11	18.00
CHILD AND FAMILY CARE						
Men	9	15.0	2	3.30	49	81.60
Women	5	8.3	3	5.00	52	86.60

x^2 Cal = 2.4 x^2 tab = 5.99
x^2 tab > x^2 Cal It is insignificant at 0.05 d.f.

In the traditionally Indian society roles were associated with sex. But in the present sample there is no significant association of sex roles and sex of the respondents.

Although statistically there was no significant association of roles and sex, high percentages of both the sexes reported that foods, clothing activities should be performed by women only.

Table 4 gives the association of sex roles of respondents and their age. As there were very few men and women in some of the age groups, the age groups were mixed up to calculate the Chi-Square values. The two age groups thus formed were 40 years below and 41 years and above.

As shown in Table 4 Chi Square value is less than the tabulated value. Hence, there was no significant association of sex roles of the respondents in all the areas of household task performance and their age.

In the present study majority of the respondents had the same opinion regardless of their age. Regardless of age, most of the respondents were of the opinion that activities related to food preparation like cooking, serving and packing food, cleaning and storing grains and activities of clothing and textile should be performed by women only whereas activities of housekeeping, child and family care should be performed by both the sexes.

Table 4
Association Between Household Task Performance Roles of Respondents and Their Age (N=120)

AREAS OF HOUSEHOLD	*Women*			*Men*		
	W	*M*	*MW*	*W*	*M*	*MW*
CLOTHING & TEXTILE						
20-40 yrs.	24	2	16	22	3	15
41-60 yrs. and above	9	-	9	10	2	8
x^2 Cal = 0.41		x^2 Cal = 0.51				
HOUSE KEEPING						
20-40 yrs.	8	9	25	10	10	20
41-60 yrs. and above	4	4	10	6	4	10
x Cal = 0		x^2 Cal = 0.2				
FOOD PREPARATION						
20-40 yrs.	29	1	12	19	2	19
41-60 yrs. and above	12	-	6	12	1	7
x^2 Cal = 0.42		x^2 Cal = 1.68				
CHILD AND FAMILY CARE						
20-40 yrs.	7	7	28	8	2	30
41-60 yrs. and above	3	2	13	7	2	11
x^2 Cal = 0.91	x^2 Cal < x^2 tab			x^2 Cal = 1.64		
x^2 Tab = 5.99						

Table 5 gives the association of roles with education of the respondents. As there were very few respondents in certain age level therefore age groups were mingled to calculate the Chi-Square values. The educational levels were primary, secondary, graduate and postgraduate education.

Table 5
Association Between Household Task Performance Roles of Respondents and Their Education

Household Task	*Women*			*Men*		
	W	*M*	*MW*	*W*	*M*	*MW*
CLOTHING & TEXTILE						
Secondary / Higher	8	2	3	3	-	1
College graduate and Post graduate	18	2	27	35	2	19
x^2 Cal = 0.8		x^2 Cal = 0.92				
HOUSE KEEPING						
Secondary / Higher	3	2	8	2	1	1
College graduate and Post graduate	10	9	28	13	12	31
x^2 Cal = 0		x^2 Cal = 1.91				
FOOD PREPARATION						
Secondary / Higher	8	2	3	3	1	-
College graduate and Post graduate	29	3	15	28	4	24
x^2 Cal = 4.1		x^2 Cal = 1.00				
CHILD AND FAMILY CARE						
Secondary / Higher	38	-	10	2	1	1
College graduate and Post	9	2	36	9	4	43
x^2 Cal = 3.2		x^2 Cal = 1.6				

As shown in Table the calculated value of Chi Square is less than the tabulated value of Chi Square in all the four areas of household task. This means that there was no significant association of sex roles of the respondents with their educational level. This implies that there was no change in the opinion about sex roles of the respondents regardless of their education. Table further reveals that majority of the respondents of both the educational levels were of the opinion that activities related to food preparation and clothing textiles activities should be performed by women only. Whereas high percentage of both the age group were of the opinion that housekeeping and child and family care should be performed by both the sexes. The opinion regarding sex roles did not change with education. Therefore, it implies that once the opinions regarding sex roles are formed it does not change. From the childhood there should be such books which teach egalitarian sex roles. Pictures in story books and school textbooks should show egalitarian sex roles.

The Indian women today has multiple roles. After many centuries, the middle class women is once more becoming a productive member of society. In addition to her traditional roles as wife and mother, guardian of the household and keeper of cultural traditions she is now fast becoming a professional.

Thus we find that there has been considerable role expansion of women. The findings in the present study show that women were accepting the dual responsibilities of employment and household task too. As home is the responsibility of the couple, both husband and wife should do the home making roles.

Table 6 gives the association between household task performance roles of women and their employment status. There were in all 65 per cent married women who were employed. As shown in Table 6 the tabulated value of Chi Square is more than the calculated value of Chi Square. This implies that there was no significant association between sex roles of married women in all the areas of household and their employment.

Majority of both employed and unemployed women were of the opinion that food preparation and clothing textiles activities should be performed by women only. Whereas the both employed and unemployed women were of the opinion that housekeeping and child and family care activities should be performed by both the sexes.

This implies that employment is not changing the opinion married women regarding sex roles. The traditional concept of a women's role is gradually changing and the economic pressures are making the traditional prejudice against women working outside the home is disappearing.

Table 6
Association Between Household Task Performance Roles of Women and Their Employment Status (N=60)

Women Group	*W*	*M*	*MW*
CLOTHING AND TEXTILE			
Employed	27	1	11
Unemployed	18	-	3
	x^2 Cal = 0		
HOUSE KEEPING			
Employed	8	9	22
Unemployed	6	3	12
	x^2 Cal = 1.5		
FOOD PREPARATION			
Employed	29	1	9
Unemployed	17	-	4
	x^2 Cal = 0		
CHILD AND FAMILY CARE			
Employed	8	5	26
Unemployed	9	2	10
	x^2 Cal = 1.9		

x2 tab = 5.99; x2 Cal < x2 tab
It is significant at 0.05 level

SUMMARY AND CONCLUSION

Apparently what is actually happening is that wives carry an overload of roles. The role relationships between husband and wife involve both orientations and abilities. If more equitable time is put in the work by the women, husbands may need either role re-education or skill training for the work of the home or both. A distinction between man's work and woman's work in respect of household jobs will have to be removed. This attitude needs to be built into the socialization process of children both in the home and in the school. A happy partnership can exist between the home and the working world only if men would realize that they also have to help in the house if both are to work. Men and Women who are free of stereotypes may be more secure and thus provide better models for children of both sexes. Perhaps it is the stereotypes that we cling to in hopes of happiness that are the sources of the problem. Admittedly, the present study was exploratory with a small sample and provides no definite answers to queries about actual working of couple.

Equal rights, opportunities and access to resources, equal sharing of responsibilities for the family by men and women, and a harmonious partnership between them are critical to their well being and that of their families as well as to the consolidation of democracy. Encourage men to participate fully in all actions towards equality. It is important to have equal responsibilities and equal opportunities and to the equal participation of women and men in all national, regional and international bodies and policy making processes, the establishment or strengthening of mechanisms at all levels for accountability to the world's women.

Women's empowerment and their full participation on the basis of equality, in all spheres of society, including participation in the decision-making process, and access to power, are fundamental for the achievement of equality, development and peace. Education is the key to breaking the mould of stereotyping. And if education can put a woman into the pilot's seat and send her into space or enable her to discuss nuclear physics at an international seminar, then education can free men from the inhibitions that straight jacket their emotions about their families. So let us redefine "Men's work - Women's work".

REFERENCES

Agarwal, V. Stress and Multiple Role of Women, International Workshop on Woman Studies, New Delhi, NCERT 1989.

Brahmbhatt B. (1974), The Study of Home Making Activities of Married Male Members Residing on University Campus in the Year 1973-74, (Master's Thesis), Baroda, M. S. University of Baroda.

Chunha, J.D. Why Domestic work should be considered Productive. New Delhi, Times of India, 1990.

Coverman, E. Explaining Husband's Participation in Domestic Labour. Sociological Quarterly, 26, 1985.

Devi, M.I. Conjugal Role Performance and Decision making among urban Hindu Families, Study of Educated couples with Employed and Unemployed wives, A Quarterly Journal of ICSSR Vol. XV No. 1, Jan-March New Delhi, ICSSR, 1986.

Jeries, N. (1977), Wives perception of marital decision making, Home Economics Research Journal, 5, 146-153.

Kamal, A. Women's Plight, New Delhi Indian Express, 13 Sept., 1990.

Larson L.E. (1974), System and subsystem perception of famiy roles, Journal of Marriage and Family, 36-123.

Mascarenhus, N.M. Women in Multiple Roles, Journal of Social Welfare Vol. XXXV No. 5 Aug. 1988.

Newland, K. Women, Men and Division of Labour, Washington World Watch Institute, 1980.

Nye, I.J. Emerging and Declining Family Roles, Journal of Marriage and the Family, 1974.

Rath, S. Working Women in Cuttack. Journal of Social Welfare Vol. XXXIV No. 1, April 1987.

Smith, B.M. Division of Household labour and Marital Adjustment in Two Earner Families, International Dissertation Abstract, Vol. 48 No. 10, April 1988.

5

Promotion of Non Conventional Energy- An Experiment in Baroda

Introduction

In the face of the man's relentless and indiscriminate plundering of nature more and more people are beginning to appreciate the vulnerability of our planet's life support system. Indeed, conservationalists warn that unless action is taken in the near future, our children will inherit a barren, polluted and decimated world. On a global basis an ecological threat to human well-being is undermining of the productivity of the land itself through soil erosion, increasing severe flooding creeping deserts and decreasing soil fertility.

All these problems are accounted by deforestation. This has attracted the attention of development planner, rural technologists, scientists and others to look for new sources of energy as well as to conserve and use the existing resources more efficiently. Wood is the primary energy source for more than one third of the world's population. Perhaps as much as 80 per cent of wood cut in developing countries is used as cooking fuel. More than half of world's kitchen uses simple wood burning stoves for cooking. Some domestic energy consumption pattern studies by Tata Energy Institute of India show that 90 percent of the households in rural areas and 75 percent of the semi urban and 25 percent of the urban households use fire wood stoves.

The use of wood as a raw material for industries and other urban uses like packing etc. is rapidly expanding at the cost of limited forest resources. This has denuded whatever little trees cover that exists in the villages.

In many location around the world the general environment, workplace and even individual dwellings are so badly polluted that the health of hundreds of millions of people is adversely affected. This is inter alias due to past and present developments in consumption and production patterns and life styles, in energy production and use, with little or no regard for environmental protection. The ability of countries to tackle pollution and health problems is greatly restrained because of lack of resources, pollution control and health protection measures have often not kept with economic development. The immense impact of environment pollution on women's daily lives have been too dangerous. Because of the technological development, the desire for materially well being of man has increased. Man is trying to become the master of the environment by using natural energy to decrease the workload and making his day to day living more comfortable. In the process of doing so he has disturbed the balance of the nature by polluting environment, destroying the forest, which took millions of years to create.

HISTORY OF DEVELOPMENT OF NON-CONVENTIONAL CHULHA

Efforts to improve the traditional methods of cooking over open fire began about six decades ago. India has the Magan Chulha developed in 1947. Hari chulha in 1953 and so on. Chulhas were developed outside India like Lorena stove and Gautemela, and New Nepal chulha at Katmandu.

India is a fast developing nation with its prime objective of improving the quality of life. Therefore, its main concern is to bring about desirable social change in the family. It is a challenge for the homemakers and family members to solve day to day problems. One such major problem is that of managing of fuel for cooking. Due to the scarcity of fuel, on one hand and explosion of population on the other hand, the problem has become very complexed.

It is observed that several research projects and studies have been conducted to promote non conventional energy sources. But due to lack of education, awareness and motivation the non conventional energy source for cooking did not get the required response.

PRESENT PROFILE

At present Government is giving priority for the development and utilization of new and renewable source of energy. Review of Literature suggests that growth of commercial energy in Asia is much faster and on the other hand non-commercial sources are vanishing fast. This crisis has given rise to many committee and commissions to look into this important and challenging issue. Ministry of Energy was set up in 1974. India was one of the first few countries to set up Commission for Additional Sources of Energy (CASE) 1981, followed by Department of Non Conventional Energy sources 1982.

Similarly different, states developed their nodal agencies to formulate policies and programmes for development of new and renewable source of energy. Planning programmes for developing different devices and disseminating information regarding them through programmes like seminars, workshops, demonstration, training programme for all new and renewable sources of energy such as water, solar, wind, Biogas, improved cookstoves and solar cooker. However because of environmentalists and researchers hue and cry for safer and cleaner environment, people have started looking for energy conservation mechanism. This energy is required for industries, agriculture, transportation. The energy consumption patterns are of two types one is for non-commercial energy which is normally used in rural areas with the use of firewood, animal manure, agricultural residues and the other type is commercial which is used for industrial and commercial work.

The Department of Non-conventional Energy Sources has taken up a countrywide programme of demonstration of various new types of chulhas. Government is trying very hard to see that the non-conventional chulha is adopted by the villagers. The new cooking stoves use less fuels, save cooking time and avoid fire hazards. But still these chulhas are not capable of auto diffusion because a large majority of potential beneficiaries are women who are more familiar with open fire cooking. Inertia of people and women in particular towards change results in resistance to the adoption of improved stoves.

CONCERN OF HOME-SCIENTIST

The kitchen is an important section of a household. The cooking of food falls under the women's domain and as such any change from traditional to improved practice must involve the women. Since the maximum number of hours per day are spent by them for cooking it is necessary that the cooking appliances (chulha) are of comfort to the homemakers and should enhance speed, save time and energy.

Most of the fuel is collected by the women and children. With the increasing scarcity of the fire wood they have to spend more time and cover longer distance for meeting the daily needs of the family. The traditional method of cooking has health hazards particularly for the housewives and children who are exposed to the smoke most of the time. It has been estimated that 100 million women spend a quarter of their lives in a gloomy kitchen. A report says (the Stateman March 18, 1983) that the rural housewives using traditional stove are exposed to as much Benozo (A) pyrene in three hours as they would inhale it, if they smoke 20 packs of cigarette a day. In fact the Benzo (A) pyrene and total suspended particles received from smoke during cooking are so much that an average women runs high risk of lung cancer or seriously damaging her lungs.

There has been effort on the part of the government for health reconstruction by expanding medical and health facilities. Many specific programmes for the improvement in health situation have been launched by the state and central government. Voluntary organizations too have come forward for support. But the situation is worsening. The issue of women's health is associated with a number of observations such as health problems of men and women are vary considerably due to their biological make up and also their position in the socio-cultural valuation, their reproductive role exposes them more to infections and disease's resulting in morbidity or death. They are socially discriminated against from time to time.

It is important that a conceptual framework for gender-sensitivity research and policy analysis should be done which centres on women's interaction with the biophysical environment and the implications of that interaction for their environment health. Introduction of improved cook stove may fulfill two important needs:

1. Reduction of fire wood for cooking by seeking cooking efficiency improvement.
2. Improvements in the cooking process and environment by providing mechanism for control of the fire intensity and in many cases smokeless operation.

The improved chulhas while helping conserve energy are also expected to be less damaging to the health of women using them.

THROUGH EDUCATION GOALS CAN BE ACHIEVED

"The destiny is now being shaped in her class room" cited Kothari Commission. Education is very powerful instrument of social, economic and cultural transformation so necessary for the realization of our national goals. Through education and school curriculum it is easy to fasten the process of modernization with the enforcement of free and compulsory elementary education act more and more children have come to school even in rural areas.

India is in a period of transition from a tradition oriented to a modern society. This change is mostly to be brought about by the youth whose values are being redefined and modified through the process of education. Further education is expected to have a progressive influence, so it would be fruitful to add in the school curriculum about the non-conventional stoves and fuels which will have positive effect on the values of girls and boys in future. Education influences in the opening of new avenues of thoughts, actions and experiences for them to observe, learn and adopt.

Visual aids form an integral part of any educational programme. These aids are used in learning situations as well as in communicating ideas. The inherent problem before educationalist is to find out the most effective medium of instruction and subsequently a technique for the effective use of such media. Such audio-visual aids include both projected and non-projected aids. One does not always succeed in giving a real picture through words. Through audio-visual aids a real understanding of things and a correct accurate concept is formed. By using these aids the teacher can bring different senses of the students into use. The true image can be formed through effective communication. Therefore, a teacher should understand how attention is gained, how meaning is transferred from one subjective field to another.

Home Science comprises all those factors and fields which cater to the physical, psychological and emotional needs of the pupils and influences their development and life in the family and community. Through the pupils, home scientists help families to establish values, which are foundation for the health, happiness and well being.

Therefore the Home Science teacher and Extension worker must know which will be the most appropriate Audio-Visual aid or mechanism to achieve a desired change in cognitive and affective or manipulative behavior of the people. During early seventies many programmes were initiated in developing countries for wide spread use of improved stoves. The experience of some countries in popularizing the technology in rural areas shows need for careful planning for the diffusion and constant vigilance on the performance of the diffusion process.

Fuel wood is increasingly becoming a scarce commodity because of haphazard use of forest resources. There is now an urgent need for efficient use of fire wood. A very comprehensive Seventh Plan (1985-90) document was prepared, which proposes to step up extension and demonstration activities for promotion of Non Conventional stoves and fuels on a scale very much larger than the Sixth Plan. There are different programmes for the promotion of improved types of stoves. Howsoever this is taking place is an unscientific, unplanned, uncontrolled and inefficient manner with the result our forests are getting denuded. The Home Science Education and Extension Department of the Faculty of Home Science has also undertaken many programmes of introducing new chulhas in different villages of Baroda Taluka.

Convincing a woman to use these stoves is very hard as resistance to the new models is common and frustrating for those experts who hope for a technological fix to the complex fuel problem. A massive effort still lies ahead to make culturally acceptable stoves and to convince millions of isolated people to try them. The wide spread adoption of improved cook stoves designs may be an important strategy to help slow the losses of forested areas. This kind of study is done to find out the suitability of different aids in promotion of information of non-conventional stoves and fuel, their effectiveness in promoting information can be established for further use. The findings of this study can be used while implementing any such programmes in future.

The state of the world's environment is of growing concern. Environment is the sum total of all conditions and that affect development of life organisms. Over the past 200 years industrial processes have been responsible for the pollution and degradation of air, water and land. In addition the environment is being degraded as a result of unsustainable exploitation of natural resources and environmentally unsound agricultural practices. Pollution is an undesirable change in the physical, chemical or biological characteristics of our environment.

Women who works closely with their environment are affected by environmental degradation in ways that have not always been acknowledged by agents of change. Women and men have different roles within social and economic structures likewise their assumption and connections with the environment are different. Women live in different and varied environment. Therefore linkages made regarding women's relationship with their environment need to be understood within women's varied social, economical, cultural, political and class contents.

In India, researches have been undertaken to find the effectiveness of different Audio-Visual aids but specifically the relative effective effectiveness of projected aids (slides) and non projected aid (exhibition) in teaching rural and urban children and its comparison has not been done so far. Therefore the present topic was selected by the investigator. To find out the relative effectiveness of two selected teaching aids-exhibition and slides in imparting information about non conventional stoves and fuels to primary school children of Ankodia village of Baroda Taluka and Municipal Primary School No. 4 Fatehgunj, Baroda.

OBJECTIVE

The major objective of the study was to find out the suitability of exhibition and slides in promotion of information on non-conventional stoves and fuels to boys and girls of VI and VII standard students belonging to different categories of achievement from one rural and one urban school of Baroda.

DESCRIPTION OF DESIGN

It was an experiment with no control group. The experimental design was based on pretest, exposure to the exhibition and slides, post test, retention test.

SAMPLE

The sample consisted of the students who consistently took part in the experiment. They were 45 boys and 35 girls from VI and VII standard of one urban and one rural school of Baroda.

PREPARATION FOR THE EXPERIMENT

After the content validation, the exhibits were prepared. Whereas ready slides were selected from the set of slides which were prepared under the D.S.T. Project on fuel management in the Department of Home Science Education and Extension.

TOOL

An objective type test paper was made to check the gain in knowledge. It was same for pre, post and retention test. It contained the items like fill in the blanks, true and false, multiple choice, matching statements and short answers type items, which called for recall and associative learning.

EXPERIMENT

Pretest

Pretest was administered to know the existing knowledge of students.

Conducting the Experiment

After a period of 20 days, the experiment was conducted. Eighty students were in the experiment. Out of which forty students were exposed to slides and other forty students to exhibition.

Post Test

Once the students were exposed to the aids they were given the post test.

Retention Test

After a period of 20 days, the same test was administered for checking the retention of knowledge.

Analysis of Data

The data were coded and different statistical technique like percentage, mean score, paired 't' test were employed for analyzing the data to test the hypothesis.

FINDINGS

The major findings of this study were as per the following:

1. There was significant differences in the mean scores of pretest-posttest and pretest-retention test which showed overall gain in knowledge as well as its retention through instructional aids for both VI and VII standards students.
2. There was significant differences in the mean scores of pretest-posttest, in relation to selected variables such as sex, place of habitation and academic achievement for VI and VII standard students, which showed gain in knowledge through instructional aids.
3. The mean scores on retention test were higher than the mean scores on pretest which showed retention of knowledge through instruction aids in case of VII standard boys, low achievers and urban students.
4. The mean scores of retention test were significantly lower than the mean scores of post test, indicating loss of knowledge, when the students did not see the exhibition and slides.
5. Overall gain in knowledge was more in VII standard students as compared to VI standard students.
6. The VII standard girls gained and retained more knowledge as compared to VI standard girls.
7. The gain in knowledge was found same in rural school students from both VI and VII standards. However, the VII standard students had retained more knowledge in comparison to VI standard students.
8. The VII standard students gained more knowledge as compared to VI standard students in relation to selected variables such as -
   (a) Sex (girls)
   (b) Place of habitation (Rural)
   (c) Academic achievement (High)

9. There was significant differences found in the mean scores of pretest, posttest and retention test in relation to selected variables such as;
   (a) Sex - among boys and girls,
   (b) Academic achievers - among high and low achievers,
   (c) Place of habitation - among urban and rural school students
10. The overall gain in knowledge was more through slides as compared to exhibition.
11. No significant differences was found in the mean scores of pretest, post test and retention test independently due to exhibition and slides for both VI and VII standard students.
12. The gain in knowledge was more in VII standard students through exhibition and slides as compared to VI standard students.
13. The gain in knowledge was more through slides as compared to exhibition for VII standard students in relation to sex.
14. The gain in knowledge was more in case of girls of VII standard as compared to boys due to slides as well as the exhibition.

CONCLUSION

The increased degradation of wood land is a great challenge of the late 20th century. It is causing a great ecological threat to human being as it leads to loss of fertility of land, increase flooding and creeping deserts. Wood is the primary energy source for more than one third of world's population. The traditional chulhas are very inefficient as most of the energy produced is lost and the smoke causes dangerous disease.

Government of India is giving priority for the development and utilization of new and renewable source of energy. There are government departments which plans, initiates, financially supports and monitors research development and demonstrates programmes. The non conventional stoves are cheap, save fuel and cooking time inspite of all this. These stoves are not popular because of beneficiaries who are women and they are resistant to any kind of change in their cooking habits.

Through education the goals for planned change can be achieved as education is powerful instrument of social, economic and cultural transformation. Through audio-visual aids a true image can be formed and it helps in effective communication.

"If I hear, I understand,
If I see, I know"

— *Chinese proverb*

Through the pupils, home scientist can help families to establish values, which are foundation for the health, happiness and well being. Therefore the Home Science teacher and Extension worker must know which will be the most appropriate audio-visual aid to achieve a desired change.

This study indicated that it is possible to impart knowledge through exhibition and slides concerning non-conventional stoves and fuels. It also indicated that exposure to slides and exhibition help in gaining and retaining of knowledge. Exposure to the slides and exhibition help in overall gain in knowledge irrespective of class of study or variables such as sex, academic achievement and place of habitation.

As far as variables, girls and those with rural background, low academic achievement and from VII standard gained more or as much as those with high achievement and who belonged to urban background and VI standard.

Environmental degradation and increasing economic and gender inequality are among the most serious problems we face today. The rich-poor divide is increasing at an alarming rate. The pattern of development adopted by rich societies is leading to increasing pollution and potential changes in climate. The rich billion's unsustainable lifestyle on and unacceptable poverty of another billion co-exist. Structural adjustment is being viewed only in monetary terms and not in terms of adjustment to sustainable life styles. The lack of an educational and health environment, which is conducive to every child achieving his/her innate genetic potential for physical and mental development, leads to the spread of poverty in capability. Education seems to be the only answer to eradicate these maladies of poverty, ignorance and environment neglect.

REFERENCES

Anderson, Steven, Natural resources education through video conferencing. Implications for International Programmes, *Journal of Educational Technology,* Vol. 3 April, 1991.

Chetanlal, N. Relative effectiveness of graphic aids and projected aids enriched with museum experience in teaching and digestion to VIII standard students of Navrachna Higher Secondary School, Baroda, Dissertation (M.Sc. Home), Hansa Mehta Library, M. S. University of Baroda, 1983.

Dale, E. Audio visual methods in teaching, Halt, Rinehart and Winston Inc., New York, 1980.

Dayal, M. Energy policies and the contribution of renewable energies in India, Paper presented at the National Science Academy, Allahabad, 1980.

George, R. Some ways to conserve energy in cooking in domestic sector, Baroda, Gujarat Energy Development Agency, Dec., 1985. *Nimeographed.*

Gujarat Energy Development Agency, Energy Graffiti Baroda, 1988.

India, Ministry of Energy, Department of Non-Conventional Energy Sources. Layman's guide to Solar Cookers' Cooking the natural way. New Delhi, Govt. of India 1985.

India, Ministry of Power and Non-Conventional Energy Sources. Annual Survey of Non-Conventional Energy Sources, *Chemical Weekly,* October 20, 1992, pp. 135-144.

Khan, M. E. and Ghosh, S. K. "Acceptance of community biogas in Punjab". A microlevel study sponsored by Punjab Agro Industries Ltd. Operation Research Group, Baroda.

Khosboo, T. K. Environmental priorities in India and sustainable development. Seventy third session of Indian Science Congress Association, New Delhi, 1986.

Menon, S. B. Relative effectiveness of different instructional media in teaching Physics at Secondary level, Dissertation (M.Ed.) Hansa Mehta Library, M. S. University of Baroda, 1978.

Parlikar, R. K. Comprehension of learning material as a function of visual and auditory presentation, Dissertation (M.A.), Hansa Mehta Library, M. S. University of Baroda, 1960.

Sandhu, N. S. Relative use of non-projected visual aids at the school level. Ludhiana, Indian Journal of Education, 26(5) 40-44, Nov., 1988.

Shah, B. B. An experimental investigation of the effects of selected teaching strategies on the development of creating thinking and achievement in science, Ph.D. Thesis, Hansa Mehta Library, M. S. University of Baroda, 1981.

Section II

PRESPECTIVE STUDIES

6

Inducing Change Through Extension Education

Half a century back the fundamental premise of Home Science was individual and the home and the interface between the two. With passage of time the perspective on Home Science has changed to three pronged approach of individual, home and economically gainful employment. In this direction the curriculum has also undergone changes. The instructions are multi disciplinary in nature with multi-technological and scientific input to improve the status of individual family and community at large.

Home Science extension was introduced in colleges and agricultural universities after the Community Development Programme was introduced in 1952 and it was realized that women played a very important role in national economy and training of women could not be ignored. It's objective is to contribute to national development through socially relevant education.

The Extension service has the role and responsibility of bridging the gap between research and users of technology by developing linkages on one hand with institutes of higher learning and on the other hand with the field and community. It also helps in the two way communication process i.e. transferring of knowledge and technology to the field through demonstration, talks, workshops and collecting feed back.

Extension work is actually performing tasks in helping the people to help themselves in making them self reliant and independent. The emphasis is on helping people to help themselves so that they do not depend on external help for development. The two major aims of Home Science Extension are Human Resource Development and Economic Resource utilization. Human resource is the most important resource in any country. Human resources consist of knowledge, abilities, interests, attitudes, manual skills, communication skills, time and energy. It is estimated that two-third of all work is performed by women who constitute half the population but only share one tenth of the income and one hundredth of the property. Since 1970 there has been a global concern for emancipation of women in general and farm women in particular. Women Resource Development is a development-oriented planning effort which is concerned with the development of women resources (i) for improving the existing capabilities of women (ii) helping women to acquire new capabilities for the social and personal goals. Women Resource goals. Women Resource Development is a must as women have immense potential for growth and this potential can further be developed through systematic and appropriate efforts. Given the right type of opportunity, women can give full expression to their potential, contributing to the achievement of national goals. In our country we have millions of people who have problems of social, economical, health and nutrition. In such a population we are still struggling with ignorance, illiteracy, poverty, diseases malnutrition for which Home Science extension can play its important role by educating the women and the families.

The Home Scientists are well trained in basic knowledge of human needs and environmental factors governing, health, hygiene, Nutrition, management. Economic independence of women accelerate the status of women. The scope can be expanded under the existing programmes of NREP, RLEGP, TRYSEM and promoting their access to credit linkage with marketing and institutional facilities. Home Scientists can study the needs and interests of the groups and develop strategies for communicating with them effectively and enabling them to fully benefit from the schemes offered by the Government and Voluntary organizations.

Extension is termed as bridge between the laboratory and the community. A large number of rural women are unable to enjoy the fruits of technological advancement as these information and knowledge do not reach the beneficiaries. When we use the term "Extension" it is generally referred to rural communities, but, recently we have observed due the multiple factors like globalization, migration a large number of people are shifting from rural areas and settling in urban areas. These families and their issues need to be addressed by the Home Science Extension Educators both in the rural areas as well as in the urban slums. The main target group is women and that too those women who are illiterate, socially and economically needy and those who are living in underprivileged environment.

It is very important that the curriculum of Home Science extension be refocused and revised so that it fits well to the changed social scenario. The world is facing problems of malnutrition, poverty, pollution, inflation, breaking of families, conflicts. These issues can be solved by application of knowledge by the Home Science Extension workers, and bring about change in the conditions of the individuals, families and communities. It has been a long time since UGC workshop (1984) which had emphasized that until unless the research is geared to meet the national needs and challenges we won't be able to progress, UGC workshop had identified the following thrust areas in Home Science extension research

(a) Science and technology as applied to rural household.
(b) Technology transfer.
(c) Intermediate/appropriate technology.
(d) Socio/cultural/political changes taking place in the rural areas.
(e) Changing role of and status of women.
(f) Impact of improved farming on family system.
(g) Impact of the various national programmes on the target groups.
(h) Differential communication networks for adoption of home improvements.

(i) Utilization of mass media in the innovations - diffusions process in the context of better home and family living.

(j) Studies on rural institutions and organizations and their contribution to rural development.

(k) Developing and testing indices to measure rural development.

(l) Impact of Home Science training.

The aim of Home Science extension is not only to make families aware of all their resources but also to make them aware of opportunities for increasing and fully utilizing these resources. The aim of Home Science extension is to help families to increase and fully utilize their existing resources for family and community development.

Home Science extension education is concerned with educating the home makers not in letters and alphabets but in the techniques of managing home in a better way, rearing children scientifically, taking care of health of the family etc. In short Home Science extension education is bringing about desirable changes in the knowledge attitudes and skills of women.

Home Science extension aims at helping people specially women to change in these three aspects.

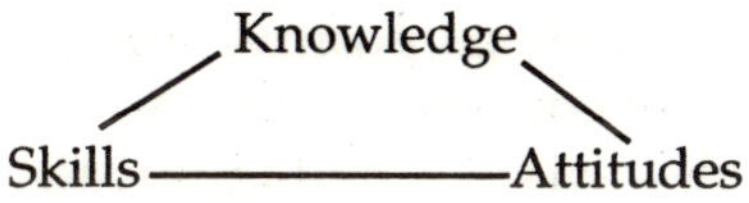

The change in knowledge regarding rights and laws safeguarding her, different government schemes and policies, health services, preventive measures which she can take, similarly about the opportunities for her and her children and how the social, political and natural environment is playing its role in her life.

Similarly how she can improve her status if she improves the skills related to vocational or income generating activities, her good management skills will help her to develop as a leader, and her training skills for various categories of personnel for multiplier effect.

Women can change their status if we can bring change in the attitudes of women regarding family planning, size of the family if she has a say and her attitude is positive towards controlling family and she is not biased with male female child syndrome, her own self esteem as well as towards females at large is very important component which needs to be addressed than only we can see the nation progressing. Rural female population are basically the home makers and the torch bearers of the socio-cultural heritage of the rural communities. Inspite of extension programmes why we are not able to bring about a desired change or reinforcing change in the women folks. It is important to understand and work on the basis of appropriate Education Extension. It means that it should have the following characteristics.

What is appropriate Education and Extension ?

1. Appropriate Curriculum:
   - that develops vocational and/or professional competencies in teaching, communication and extension.
   - that develops awareness of available employment opportunities.
   - that develops awareness of available employment opportunities.
   - that develops positive attitude and philosophy towards the specialization.
   - that is pedagogically-instructionally, psychologically and morally sound.
2. Appropriate Community Reach Out :

2.1 It comprises of:
   - Non formal programmes for urban people.
   - Extension inputs for rural people.
   - Faculty/University services.

2.2 It aims at :
   - Removing or reducing imbalances in :
   - Nutrition
   - Child Survival
   - Resource Utilization
   - Men-women Role Enactments

- Enhancing formal and non formal education in urban and rural sectors.
- Division of labour in family
- Upbringing of girl child
- Preparation for employment

2.3 Suggested Thrusts for Community Reach Out :

- Applied, action, survey, correlational designs rather than fundamental research only.
- Local, block and State level samples rather than national samples.
- Samples of women alone or both men and women for an integrated approach, rather than a mechanically conceptualized sample of women alone.
- Issues relating to women, stratified according to employment, education, community rather than only urban and rural women.
- Possibility of follow-up of findings rather than sterile recommendations reaching nowhere.

4. Appropriate curricular structure of education and extension for Asian Countries:

SUGGESTED NOMENCLATURE

↓

COMMUNICATION AND EXTENSION

↓

4.1 Educational Communication

- Teacher Education
- Distance Education
- Educational Technology

4.2 Developmental Communication

- Legal structures for empowerment of women
- Women's issues pertaining to education and employment

4.3 Extension

- Extension Education

- Programme Planning, Monitoring, Evaluating
- Networking with Government and Non-government organizations in Developmental Activities

Chandra (1992)

Policy and programme approaches need to be derived from an understanding of women's role in development. There are several factors which influence and neglect the women and acts as hinderance in the path of progress and development. Why women have been ignored by extension programmes ? Why women have not been getting their due in developmental process ? These are the questions which demand immediate answer. Some important reasons of the neglect of women in developmental planning are:

1. Self limitation
2. Decrease mobility
3. Lot of time in routine activities
4. Lack of land resource in the control of women
5. Attitude of development officials
6. Low literacy
7. Less jobs for women

1. One of the lacunae for slow development of women is the self limitation of developmental potential that is people tend to think that "this is all for me and I cannot go further". This tendency is very much traced among women, for example higher education is felt to be for men only. Since this type of self limitation is definitely an hindrance to growth, it is necessary to tackle this problem appropriately for bringing about mental orientation to change ?
2. Under the situation women need to undertake activities mostly restricted to their own village. Since, their mobility is limited, so it is necessary to identify the specific income generating activities and projects which can be operated by women in their situations ?
3. The general observation at the village level is that women spend a lot of their time in routine activities like bringing fuel wood or water etc. Though these

activities are routine and simple much of the time is spent on this the time spent on these activities is essential but not productive in terms of economic benefits. Hence, to make productive use of the time would it not be better if these facilities are provided in the vicinity such that the same time could be used for other productive use ?

4. One of the basic lacunae in the development, process related to the role of women is the lack of land resource in the control of women. All the property rights related to land are passed on to the male members in the family and women are only passive on lookers. Since property is the main production oriented resource, it is high time to demand equal rights on the property for both men and women in the family, may be by way of joint ownership.
5. The attitude of the development officials at all levels is generally biased towards men. This is not purposive but the culture in which we are brought about has typified this attitude. It is necessary that we modify this attitude favourably towards the developmental needs for women.
6. Low literacy is one of the major contributors to slow development of women and the slow pace of development. Since the situations in the rural areas are not favourbale, it is necessary that informal or non formal education systems need to operate to build up literacy level.
7. Various jobs or activities are undertaken by women both related to home and the farm. But in general practice it is assumed that all the jobs especially related to farming are the main jobs of men and women only support some, which is not actually true. Though women are able to take up jobs in almost all the areas as extension officials, computer professionals, teachers, doctors, engineers, police etc. most of our development programmes are aimed towards men and women are neglected both in terms of opportunities for study and jobs.

This typification has resulted in specifying the home related jobs for women which are not economically productive. It is important that we pull out of this typification and demand equal opportunities for growth. Looking to the paradigm it is clear indication that not much serious thought has been given to the realistic development.

The efforts put forth have resulted in improving the managerial ability of the farmers in relation to their technologies but have left a wide gap in terms of improving their overall standard of living and also the ability of women in the family. This situation has resulted in the non-utilization of half of the human resource for more productive activities. Since the overall objective of development is to bring in changes both in the economy and the levels of living, by utilizing all at the family, farm or at national level. Home Science extension education focuses on women as the clients and change agents. In a traditional culture, only women workers can approach the rural women, therefore, any development programme must not only bring about changes in the attitudes of the people but essentially among the change agents who are mostly local leaders and generally from the same culture.

The two aspects of Home Science extension are the well accepted aspects, called extension education and extension services. The governance of both aspects of extension education and extension services, is the management of Home Science extension. The management is the backbone of extension because it is like a conveyer mechanism which delivers the goods - that is, the professional services to the rural and urban communities. Without training and research programmes the extension services become irrelevant because the people's feedback is not utilized in making extension better through research and training. A continuous research and training results in continuous improvement of extension education as well as services.

The changing life styles and growing knowledge in science and technology, available for alieviating standards of living, have made it imperative for home science to increase its research and training in extension. Unless the extension education which consists of professional preparation, monitoring and evaluation, is conceived, regulated and modernized the extension services will not reach to the communities and specially to women in an optimal and usable form. This is only possible if it is founded on a strong research. The Research priorities are:

- Developing communication media for extension.
- Research in professional preparation of women for income generating activities.
- Research in promoting functional literacy among women of weaker section.

Rural women by and large have no access to information and training to improve their knowledge, skills etc., which are essential for improving the productivity and widening the occupational range of women. It is necessary to provide infrastructural support to promote the access of women to information sources and to avail of the training facilities. Training component is to be built into the Farm Women's training Krishi Vigyan Kendras, TRYSEM, allied sectors and for diversification of rural industries and services. Home Scientists can play a significant contribution in providing training to various categories of personnel.

Under the T&V pattern emphasis had been on identifying and concentrating on farmers. However in reality women are equal partners in the farms. It is very important that agricultural extension following T&V model should involve the rural women to be the contact farmers. We have seen that women in the rural areas are engaged in agriculture or allied related activities as their vocation. With growing science and technology and mechanization many people have been displaced from the traditional jobs. It is very important at this juncture that women are trained by extension educators to take up unconventional jobs to cope up with the changing world. The major objective of Home Science Extension is to develop the capacity of the women in problem solving along with it now the need of the hour is we incorporate and focus upon technology oriented activities which would yield economic returns.

The Home Science extension education will profit greatly by the encouragement of extension of the scientific researches mainly conducted in the research laboratories, never-the-less, it is beyond the scope of scientists to disseminate their achievements to the masses and even if they do so their main objectives (research) will be hampered. The means by which the extension teaching of Home Science researches can be effectively communicated through posters, slides and film shows. The mass media like radio, T.V. or folk media like puppet, bhavai or street play can be effective too for communicating development messages.

The medium of video tapes, films can be used very effectively for non formal teaching to women. The video films can be used as a persuasive medium to adopt different practices or methods is definitely needs to be put as a priority. The form of street play has been used by women activists to identify problems of unequal opportunities and biased treatment to women.

Home Science institutions can undertake the task of need assessment as well as identification of areas in which training to women would be useful. Home Science Colleges can also develop and test training packages and also prepare manuals for the trainers. They can also involve themselves in the task of evaluation of training programmes. Home Scientists through their extension programmes can act as intermediatories between the young farm women and government officials handling development programmes for performing all these different roles. The Education and Training being offered in home science institutions needs to be reviewed very critically. It is very crucial that we equip the youngsters to play this role.

Similarly the Agricultural Universities should also perform this role in a more aggressive and professional may. The Home Science institutions need to look into these major issues and take up the leadership role in training "Trainers" of girls and women for contributing to National Development Programmes. A well-balanced research and training programme is a pre-requisite for bringing development. The final evidence of an effective management of research and training in home science extension, would lead the alleviated standards of living of people and raise the socio-economic status of women and reduce inequalities.

REFERENCES

Anandlaksmy S., Status of Home Science- a summary of views of Home Science Teachers, Journal of Higher Education, 1984.

Apte Minakshi, "Rural Women and Development in Indian Journal of social Work Vol. 39 No. 4 Jan 1979.

Awasthy, Indira, Rural Women of India, B. R. Publishing Corporation Delhi 1982.

Dubey, V. K. and S. K. Bhanj, Uses of Video in rural development Interaction 2 (3), 82. 1984

Government of India, Agricultural Wages in India 1990-91, Ministry of Agriculture New Delhi 1992.

Indiradevi M. Women, Education, Employment Family Living Gian Publishing House Delhi 1987.

Khare, P. M. "Indian Women, Their Role in Relation to Planning" Social Welfare Vol. 7 No. 1 May 1980.

Lakoh, A. K. Extension agents job design job satisfaction and job performance model J. Ext. System 1, 90-93, 1988.

Mahajan M. P. A study of relative effectiveness of extension method. Indian J. Extension Education 5(1&2) p. 16. 1990.

Mazumdar V. Role of Rural Women in Development Allied Publishers Bombay 1978.

Nelson, N. Why has Development Neglected Rural Women? A Review of South Asian Literature, Oxford Pergamon Press 1979.

Swaminathan, M. S. Women and rural development, Mainstream (Annual Number) 113-118, 1988.

UGC Workshop "Thrust areas in Home Science Research" Lady Irwin College, New Delhi 1984.

7

Refocus Home Economics to Change the Status of Women

Concern for the family has been the historical core of Home Science - it has remained as its continuing focus. The definition of its "family focus" has shifted and no doubt will continue to change. This is a universal statement. The contents of Home Science are changing, the nomenclature of Home Science is changing but the concern for family has remained the same. In fact the family has had so many influences upon it that the contents of Home Science had to change visibly. The family in India has been the strongest social institution, perhaps, second to only religion. The Indian family has changed and has solidifying effects which have led to changes in home economics contents.

THE INDIAN FAMILY

A sketchy structural-functional picture of Indian family can serve as a prerequisite to our understanding of changing contents in home economics. The Indian family is sketched in a few sentences. First, historically Indian family was an extended, three-generational group which has its traces till today. Second, Indian family operated on authority of male members and on subordination, subservience and drudgery of female members, which also has been widely practiced till today. Third, Indian family glorifies motherhood but degrades womanhood, of which, the women are becoming increasingly aware. Fourth, the solidarity of Indian family is supreme, even at the cost of individual freedom and development, which is now being questioned. Last, Indian family is increasingly influenced by western values, which result in new structure and function of members of family. With consideration of such a background knowledge of Indian family, we can analyse the changing home economics contents in Indian context.

CHANGE REGARDING WOMEN AS FOCUS OF CONTENTS

The home economics contents in India have been family-based. The required change in their "family focus" orientation is because of the change in vocational and social needs of women. Home economics has remained a field of woman's education and therefore the new vocational and social needs of women have changed the contents. Home economics has reached the families through women. Indian home economists are now realizing that the "family focus" philosophy in India has somehow excluded women themselves. At least home economic has not made an appreciable dent in alleviating women's status, although the families are managed by women. The required change is that since woman as a wife and mother, is the most neglected member of the family, home economics must reach her. Two main matters in which women are neglected are : decision making particularly about her development, and enjoyment or realization of resources and facilities for woman's development.

In all possible home economics contents, the changes already accepted or are desired, are as follows:

The female child is unequally treated in providing education, supporting employment, choosing marriage partner, observing traditions and customs in all familial and societal matters, and singularly in its upbringing. The contents now accepted are for awareness generation of changing roles of women. There are women's studies on their unequal opportunities, exploitation and deliberate subordination. These form the basis of home economic contents.

The contents specifically are:

- Deprivations of Indian female child
- Evil of child marriage
- Unequality in education and employment of preparation of girls
- Sharing of house keeping by boys and girls
- Cooperative housekeeping
- Supportive housekeeping for working women
- Child-rearing fathers

The changing contents emphasize the emerging roles of Indian women; an employee, and woman as a person, besides a wife and a mother. Many believe that such new contents can be introduced in child development curricula but besides child development, education and extension and home management have scope for such curricula.

CHANGE REGARDING VOCATIONAL CONTENTS

The second change is the emphasis on vocational preparation of women. Indian home economics originally was using inclusive of the goal of professional preparation of women. Today home economics is considered a professional field, qualifying women for certain professions, carriers, jobs and services. The change is that courses are revised to include field experience, practicals and teachers and examiners are selected from professions for which home economics students are trained.

The extension services and education in home economics colleges, emphasize income generation by women. The escalating inflation rates, and the availability of many new commodities in the market at the same time, draw Indian women into gainful employment. Home economics contents become vocationalised. Some contents for small and intermediate jobs are:

- Food preservation
- Commercial tailoring
- Production of literature in home economics, puppetry and commercial production of puppets
- Batik and block printing
- Dietetics

- Community nutrition
- Nursery School Management

It can be seen that such vocationalized contents can only prepare girls for a very small scale self-employment, or a low-paying job. The only vocation and profession for which home economics contents are increasingly changing, is teaching. The largest number of Indian home economics graduates have become teachers of home economics because they are trained for teaching. This change came about soon after home economics appeared on the higher education scene. Because home science in India became popular, more college and school teachers were required, and teaching home economics became the most available job for home scientists. Baroda has trained so many college home economics teachers that there are hardly a few colleges where home economics graduates of Baroda are not found on the teaching faculty !

CONTENTS FOR MANAGEMENT INSTEAD OF HOUSEKEEPING

The traditional contents of home economics supported the housekeeping role of woman. Although the Indian housekeeping in rural regions has not changed noticeably, certain urban and suburban house styles have certainly changed. Many houses depend on readymade commodities such as, fast foods, bread, bun and biscuits, drink concentrates, pickles, spices, sweets, garments, cosmetics, furniture, mattresses, potted plants and interior decorations. There are services and facilities now available, such as, catering, dry cleaning and laundering, white-washing, painting, and polishing, gardening, car-driving, housekeeping and day-care of children.

Because the needy and affluent people can buy the readymade commodities, and hire the services, maintaining a house with or without a family, is quite a different undertaking, these days. The woman and man both manage the house rather than operate it themselves. They get things done by others, rather than doing themselves. Therefore, today's urban woman in India, needs to become an efficient manager to select and hire house-keeping services and facilities, rather than be herself a good cook and washer woman ! The home economic contents in view of emerging role of house manger are :

- Knowledge of local housekeeping services - availability, effectiveness, terms and conditions and charges (fees)
- Negotiation and Supervision abilities to employ servant, cook, gardener, car driver, baby sitter.
- Supervision and negotiation for services of hawkers of newspapers, magazines, milk, vegetables, fruit, etc.
- Account keeping for house services and purchases.
- Bank transactions and accounts
- Investment of money, land, house
- Work schedules of hired help and services.
- Selection of rented apartment and its maintenance
- Buying an apartment or house on installment or otherwise
- Coordinating schedules of self, husband, children, and invalid or old members of family.
- Coordinating time and resources for recreation, vacations and socializing of all family members.
- Space organization in the house for varied activities of the members of family.

CONTENTS FOR MANAGEMENT OF SINGLE (NUCLEAR) FAMILY

Many urban families in India have become single or nuclear families. The parents-in-law or families of brothers-in-law are not there anymore. The emergence of single family is the result of migration of sons and sometimes daughters to foreign countries, such as the USA and the Gulf-middle east countries, as well as to cities from villages. The older generation has either preferred to remain in their house rather than move into son's house in city or in the USA, or the son and his wife have not desired the cohabitation with them.

Under such circumstances, the single family has changed its life style. From the point of help extended by the older parents, the assistance in kitchen and baby sitting were the chief ones. The young or middle-aged family has to find hired help when both parents are employed. Hired help present problems of irregular service, more expenses, supervision, and adjustment in time allocation of other activities. Can home economics find appropriate hired help ? Advise in making timetables of activities of family members and hired persons ? Advise in shifting budget priorities ? The contents must change to fulfill such functions of the emerging single family.

On the emotional front, the older generation help to maintain cohesion, provided constant company, supervision of household, and sometimes acted as psychological bridge between young parents and children, or middle-aged parents and adolescent daughters and sons. In absence of such emotional support and collective decision making, the single family needs internal strength, courage and wisdom to survive by itself. Can home economics contents teach the future wives and single women, not to depend on older generation for emotional support and sharing of housekeeping ? Additionally, to arrange for independent stay of older generation ? Contents such as follows need to be developed :

- Child rearing in a single family
- Working woman in a single family
- Care of older people, staying independently
- Decision-making in single family
- Socialization in single family

As for the conflict and hinderance created by the presence of older people in an extended family, their absence is well accepted by the single family. But maintaining cordial relations with older parents who do not stay in the son's family, and availing them in time of need and crisis can be learnt in home economics.

CONTENTS FOR ANTI-DOWRY EDUCATION

The Indian family in cities as well as villages is harassed by the dehumanizing practice of compulsory and unreasonable dowry.

The evil of dowry deaths of young wives is even more barbarious. Indian marriage has turned into a contract wherein the girl's family gives to the boy and his family a huge amount of money, household gadgets, furniture, expensive bridal clothes and gold jewellery. The amount of dowry is decided by the boy's family. The marriage entirely depends on the ability of girl's family to abide by the dowry demands of boy's family. The boy and his family have such a coercive hold over the girl's parents that, huge dowry is normally extracted by the boy. If the boy is highly educated and is a doctor, engineer, IAS officer or chartered accountant, he and his family expect and also get dowry in five or six digits number. The girl's high education, good looks and good family does not much decrease the dowry amount, but the same factors on boy's side, increase the dowry amount ! The girl's parents are thus in a perpetual anxiety. They employ all means to collect the huge amounts in order to marry their daughter to a "deserving" boy. The unhappiness of having a daughter is widespread. The neglect of girl's education, health, recreation and employment are the results of unreasonable dowry demands to the parents of girls.

The greedy parents of boys, keep on demanding expensive gifts from the girl's parents or the girl herself if she is earning, even after marriage. If the girl cannot satisfy the demands of boy's family the girl is treacherously set to fire. Almost every day the newspapers have reports of such "dowry deaths" by burning. There is a law against dowry and killing women to extract dowry but hardly one percent parents of girls can reach, afford and get justice from the court of law. The evidence are suppressed, coercion is used, and even malpractice is used to silence the defendents. In order to rescue the girls from becoming dowry victims, besides law, social consciousness has to be revived. A strong collective opposition to dowry has to be developed. Can home economics impart anti-dowry education? It certainly can. Some suggested contents are as below:

Contribution by girls to family solidarity as a daughter, wife, mother.

Factors which make girl an independent person

- Education
- Employment
- Decision-making capacity
- Travel opportunities
- Equal opportunities in home and society

Factors which make a boy superior to a girl in marriage market

- Education higher than girl's
- Employment more paying than girl's
- Freedom to make decisions
- Rich parents
- Traditional views that boy is superior to girl

Why girl's parents give unreasonable dowry

- Fear of girl left unmarried
- Desire to get a son-in-law, of a much higher socio-economic status
- Traditional view that the boy must earn much more than a girl or than what girl is worth
- Family's strong insistence to buy a boy who has a high status, such as an American immigration
- Girl's greed to grab things from parents to show off to her in-laws

Ways of extracting dowry even after marriage

- Belittling the wife by taunting, comparing, scolding, criticizing her parents
- Beating, quarrelling, maltreating, ostracizing, extracting drudgery from the wife
- Demanding expensive gifts on birthdays, Diwali, wedding, from wife's parents
- Forcibly driving the wife away from her house or sending her away to her parents and refusing to let her return unless she brings a large amount of money or an expensive gadget.
- Threatening to burn her, to marry her husband to a second wife, to physically disfigure and mutilate the wife

Suggestions for not yielding to unreasonable, corruptive dowry demands

- Educate the girl to the best of her ability and parent's resources
- Let girl be employed in a best, possible job
- Let marriage be postponed till girl has a secure job
- Let self-arranged marriage culminate, whenever possible
- Let a girl be superior to boy in earning and education, so that decision-making in shared by her.
- Accept a less educated and less earning boy to avoid paying dowry. In such a case, teach girls to act as decision-makers, policy-makers, as heads of family and let husbands take subordinate roles.
- Let unemployed husbands do housekeeping while wives are employed.

Collective social actions against dowry

- Support education of girls
- Increase employment opportunities for girls
- Support residential arrangements for working girls, such as hostels for single working women
- Punish dowry givers and takers
- Form associations to support parents to negotiate dowry matters
- Report to police dowry demands, threats and deaths
- Introduce anti-dowry education in form of course, seminar, debates in colleges
- Support girls socially and morally, if they choose to remain single because they cannot meet dowry demands
- Educate people to limit the size of family by adopting family planning methods
- Let parents decide if they want a daughter
- Educate people about the equal importance of daughters in family life and economic production

GENERAL CONSIDERATIONS OF CHANGING CONTENTS IN HOME ECONOMICS

While changing the contents to meet new needs, several new specializations do not perceive themselves as part of home economics. For example, Foods and Nutrition specialization identifies itself with Biochemistry and Dietetics, rather than other departments of Foods and Nutrition within Home Economics Colleges. Each specialization within Home Economics must have a supplementary function, in order to contribute to the broad objectives of home economics. The excellence of each specialization can be increased but its place and role must be within home economics, in order to strengthen the specialization as well as the discipline of home science. As Haulthorne (1983) stated, cohesiveness and integration must be the curriculum, Faculty must perceive their specialization and their special competences as they contribute to the total program and not to their specialities alone. This does not lessen the importance of specialization.

As new specializations emerge, and as old specializations divide into several specialities, our aim of home economics must not be sacrified. An unnecessary fragmentation of home economics must be controlled because the cohesive and integrative nature of home science, strengths its multidisciplinary status. Our identification as home economist is our first concern.

Another consideration is that the changing contents must use and reflect current technology, science, and economic development in India. Although the standards of living in India are much below those in the developed countries, the change can reflect the available science, technology, and economic growth. Sparring a small group in India such changes may not be possible at national level because half of the Indian population is yet below the poverty line. To this group traditional contents are more suitable.

A third consideration is that the changing contents must reach to boys and men, and they have yet not, in a direct way. There are both positive and negative attitudes toward having boys in home economics classes, and having men or home economics teaching staff. The positive attitudes are based on assumptions that home economics contents are for both sexes; men are traditionally aggressive and they provide a stronger thrust to professionalism; home economics can achieve higher professional status if men are on teaching faculty. The negative attitudes are founded on views that home is traditionally kept by women so Home economics contents must be for women and girls alone; if men join home economics teaching staff, they will dominate, women will get only second and third echelon jobs, and; the competition will result in unemployment of women home economics graduates.

Its high time that home economics contents be taught to both sexes. Cooperative housekeeping is likely to be more accepted if both the boy and girl offered home economics curricula. The changing contents must take an asexual view or slant. All knowledge of housekeeping must be delinked from its female context. All home economics contents can be taught in a context of an individual and not of male or female. As for the presence of men on teaching faculty, it would mean that men will also join women in alleviating the status of home economics. A competition may make women more determined to progress professionally. If home and family are the concerns of woman as well as man, they both must be drawn into the profession.

CONCLUSION

The historical care of "family focus" in home economics contents has remained unchanged. But in India, the development of woman has been neglected. Home economics has not appreciably alleviated the status of woman. It is now the time to refocus home economics to change the status of women. The changing contents must concern woman-her opportunities and facilities must improve. Home economics must stress upon cooperative, supportive housekeeping and liberate women from overglorified motherhood and self damaging subservient wifehood.

Home economics contents must be increasingly vocational so that women gain economic freedom. Economic freedom is a prerequisite to development of self and family. Teaching has been a predominant profession of home economist but other professions need to emerge from the changing contents of home science. The contents must be for teaching management of home and family, rather than for encouraging the drudgery of women in self and absolute housekeeping. The available services, commodities and facilities must be known to the manager of the home and family.

As single families emerge in urban and suburban regions of India, the lack of help from and the absence of hindrance from the older members is a new factor in management of home and family. The decision-making and remote care of the older members are to be taught by changing contents. A greatest area of change in home economics contents in India, is the introduction of anti-dowry education. The suggested contents are : Recognition of girl's contribution to family, factors which make girl an independent person, reasons for demand and payment of unreasonable dowry, knowledge of unfair ways of extracting dowry even after marriage, suggestions for not yielding to demands for dowry, and collective social actions against dowry.

Three general considerations arise in changing the home economics contents. First, the cohesiveness and integrative character of home economics must be maintained. Fragmentation of home economics by delineating the identity of specializations from its whole, that is, home economics, must be checked. The second is the use of current science, technology and economic development in new contents. As India has 50% people under poverty line, income-generation becomes a prime area of changing contents. The third consideration is of changing contents to make them useful for girls as well as boys. In doing so, men will appear more on home economics enrolments, and on its teaching administrative staff. This may mean partial unemployment of female home economists, unless employment opportunities increase. The changing contents in home economics, in India are necessary and each region can change the contents while keeping the general considerations in view. The change in contents, broadly speaking must liberate woman from household drudgery, give her economic freedom and alleviate the status of home economics by increasing its employment potential and help women in changing India.

REFERENCES

Acharya Kuntala, "Women in national development" Social work Vol. 22, No. 6-7 Sept-Oct. 1979.

Chandra, A. and A. Shah. Non-formal Education for All, Sterling Publishers, Pvt. Ltd., New Delhi, 1987, pp. 180.

George, M. "Women's role in Social education under the community Projects" Indian Journal of Adult Education Vol. 15 No. 1 March 1984.

Government of India, "Census in India 1971, Series I, Indian II B (i) General Economic Tables, 1971.

Hawthorne, Betty E. Echoes of the past-voices of the Future, *American Journal of Home Economics,* Winter 1983 pp. 36-43.

Indiradevi M. Women-Education-Employment Family Living, Gian Publishing House, Delhi 1987.

Kishwar Madhu. The Search for Answers, Indian Women's Voice from Manushi-Zed Books London 1984.

Louti, M. Rural Women-Unequal partners in development Geneva ILO 1980.

Maurya, Sahabdeen, Women in India, Chugh Publications Allahabad 1988.

Mishra L. "Education of Women in India, McMillan Bombay 1966.

Mundra, S. N. and Pant, D. C. Transfer of Technology, Directorate of Extension Education, Sukhadia University, Udaipur, Rajasthan, India, 1987 pp. 48.

Nash J. Women in Development-Dependency and Exploitation, Development and Change The Hague 1977.

Sapru R. K. Women in Development, Ashish Publishing House, New Delhi 1989.

Thomas, L.E., M. L. Speers, and C. A. Jones, Will the Future of the Family Affect careers in Home Economics? American Journal of Home Economics, Summer, 1984 pp. 27-30.

University Grants Commission, Guidelines For Undergraduate Programmes in Home Sciences, New Delhi, India, August 1984 pp. 202.

8

Health a Fundamental Human Right

CONCEPT OF HEALTH

Health is a common theme in most cultures. In fact, all communities have their concepts of health, as part of their culture. Among definitions still used, probably the oldest is that health is the "absence of disease". Health continues to be a neglected entity despite lip service. At the individual level, it cannot be said that health occupies an important place; it is usually subjected to other needs defined as more important, e.g., wealth, power, prestige, knowledge, security. Health is often taken for granted, and its value is not fully understood until it is lost. However, during the past few decades, there has been a reawakening that health is a fundamental human right and a world-wide social goal; that it is essential to the satisfaction of basic human needs and to an improved quality of life; and, that it is to be attained by all people.

DEFINITIONS OF HEALTH

"Health" is one of those terms which most people find it difficult to define although they are confident of its meaning. Therefore, many definitions of health have been offered from time to time, including the following:

Webster: "The condition of being sound in body, mind or spirit, especially freedom from physical disease of pain".

Oxford English Dictionary: "Soundness of body or mind; that condition in which its functions are duly and efficiently discharged".

"A condition or quality of the human organism expressing the adequate functioning of the organism is given conditions, genetic and environmental".

Perkins: "A state of relative equilibrium of body form and function which results from its successful dynamic adjustment to forces tending to disturb it. It is not passive interplay between body substance and forces impinging upon it but an active response of body forces working toward readjustment".

WHO Definition

The widely accepted definition of health is that given by the World Health Organization (1948) in the preamble to its constitution, which is as follows:

"Health is a state of complete physical, mental and social wellbeing and not merely an absence of disease or infirmity".

In recent years, this statement has been amplified to include the ability to lead a "socially and economically productive life".

The WHO definition of health has been criticized as being too broad. Some argue that health cannot be defined as a "state" at all, but must be seen as a process of continuous adjustment to the changing demands of living and of the changing meanings we give to life. It is a dynamic concept. It helps people live well, work well and enjoy themselves. It refers to a situation that may exist in some individuals but not in everyone all the time; it is not usually observed in groups of human beings and in communities.

Operational Definition of Health

Studies of epidemiology of health have been hampered because of our inability to measure health and well-being directly. In this connection as "operational definition" has been devised by a WHO study group. In this definition, the concept of health can be seen as "a condition of quality of the human organism expressing the adequate functioning of the organism in given conditions, genetic or environmental".

DIMENISIONS OF HEALTH

Health is multidimensional. The WHO definition envisages three specific dimensions - the physical, the mental and the social. Many more may be cited, viz., spiritual emotional, vocational and political dimensions. As the knowledge base grows, the list may be expanding. Although these dimensions function and interact with one another, each has its own nature, and for descriptive purposes will be treated separately.

Physical Dimension

The physical dimension of health is probably the easiest to understand. The state of physical health implies the notion of "perfect functioning" of the body. It conceptualizes health biologically as a state in which every cell and every organ is functioning at optimum capacity and in perfect harmony with the rest of the body. However, the term "optimum" is not definable. The signs of physical health in an individual are: "a good complexion, a clean skin, bright eyes, lustrous hair with a body well clothed with firm flesh, not too fat, a sweet breadth, a good appetite, sound sleep, regular activity of bowels and bladder and smooth, easy, coordinated bodily movements. All the organs of the body are of an expectional size and function normally; all the special senses are intact; the resting pulses rate, blood pressure and exercise tolerance are all within the range of "normality" for the individual's age and sex.

Mental Dimension

Mental health has been defined as "a state of balance between the individual and the surrounding world, a state of harmony between oneself and others, coexistence between the realities of the self and that of other people and that of the environment. The mind and body were considered independent entities. Recently, however, researchers have discovered that psychological factors can induce all kinds of illness, not simply mental ones. They include conditions such as essential hypertension, peptic ulcer and bronchial asthma. Some major mental illnesses such as depression and schizophrenia have a biological component. Although mental health is an essential component of health, the scientific foundations of mental health are not yet clear. Therefore we do not have precise tools to assess the state of mental health unlike physical health.

Social Dimension

Social well-being implies harmony and integration within the individual, between each individual and other members of society and between individuals and the world in which they live. It has been defined as the, "quantity and quality of an individual's interpersonal ties and the extent of involvement with the community". The social dimension of health includes the levels of social skills one possesses, social functioning and the ability to see oneself as a member of a larger society. In general, social health takes into account that every individual is part of a family and of wider community and focuses on social and economic conditions and well-being of the "whole person" in the context of his social network. Social health is rooted in "positive material environment" (focusing on financial and residential matters), and "positive human environment" which is concerned with the social network of the individual.

Spiritual Dimension

Proponents of holistic health believe that the time has come to give serious consideration to the spiritual dimension and to the role this plays in health and disease. Spiritual health in this context refers to that part of the individual which reaches out and strives for meaning and purpose of life. It is the intangible "something" that transcends physiology and psychology. As a relatively new concept, it seems to defy concrete definition. It includes integrity, principles and ethics, the purpose in life, commitment to some higher being and belief in concepts that are not subject to "state of the art" explanation.

Emotional Dimension

Historically the mental and emotional dimensions have been seen as one element or as two-closely related elements. However, as more research becomes available a definite difference is emerging. Mental health can be seen as "knowing" or "cognition" while emotional health relates to "feeling".

Experts in psychology have been relatively successful in isolating these two separate dimensions. With this new data, the mental and emotional aspects of humanness may have to be viewed as two separate dimensions of human health.

Vocational Dimension

The vocational aspect of life is a new dimension. It is part of human existence. When work is fully adapted to human goals, capacities and limitations, work often plays a role promoting both physical and mental health. Physical work is usually associated with an improvement in physical capacity, while goal achievement and self-realization in work are a source of satisfaction and enhanced self-esteem.

POSITIVE HEALTH

The state of positive health implies the notion of "perfect functioning" of the body and mind. It conceptualizes health biologically, as a state in which every cell and every organ is functioning at optimum capacity and in perfect harmony with the rest of the body; psychologically, as a state in which the individual feels a sense of perfect well-being and of mastery over his environment, and socially, as a state in which the individual's capacities for participation in the social system are optimal.

Dubos said, "The concept of perfect positive health cannot become a reality because man will never be so perfectly adapted to his environment that his will not involve struggles, failures and sufferings". Positive health will, therefore, always remain a mirage, because everything in our life is subject to change. Health in this context has been described as a potentially - the ability of an individual to face the changing conditions of life. Recently, a broader concept of health has been emerging - that of improving the quality of life of which health is an essential component. This at once brings to focus that positive health depends not only on medical action, but on all the other economic, cultural and social factors operating in the community.

IMPORTANCE OF HEALTH

Health plays a vital role in our lives. As it is well said,
"When wealth is lost; nothing is lost"

"When health is lost, everything is lost"

So, in context to women's health it is a valuable asset for them. In most Indian household the women of the house eats last, after feeding the whole family. Though there are more illiterate women than men, we find women learn more quickly and respond more rapidly and promoting better health must be appreciated and arrangements should made so that the message of health educators reaches them.

Scenario health by 2000

Health for all the 2000 AD is not just a slogan a commitment made to the people of the world by World Health Organization and UNICEF. This declaration was made in 1978. India is also one of the nation to have sign to Alma Ata declaration. Thus the Indian government has publically undertaken the responsibility of providing health to each of its citizens. Health is therefore a fundamental right for all of us.

There are several forces in society which influence our health. The attainment and maintenance of health depends upon one's access to health goods and services. One cannot remain healthy if the environment around is unhealthy. There are many forces acting at our household workplace and societal level which determines our health. Apart from the individuals body differences and habits, the government policies, commercial interests, state of environment, quality of medical care, rural urban division are all the determines of health.

Environment is classified as "internal" and "external". The internal environment of man pertains to "each and every component part, every tissue, organ and organ-system and their harmonious functioning within the system. The external or macro-environment consists of those things to which man is exposed after conception. It is defined as "all that which is external to the individual human host". It can be divided into physical, biological and psychosocial components, any or all of which can affect the health of man and his susceptibility of illness.

It is an established fact that environment has a direct impact on the physical, mental and social well-being of those living in it. The environmental factors range from housing, water supply, psychosocial stress and family structure through social and economic support systems, to the organization of health and social welfare services in the community.

Functioning of the primary or community health center irrational prescription of medicines and costly medicines services. All they have greater rise to water/air/land/noise pollution related diseases, lack of control of communicable diseases. Again inadequate knowledge, informative education about safe and health practices has lead to the development of many new diseases and un-healthy condition to an epidemic proportion. However the advances in medical services are not able to provide a cure to main factor to control health danger. People are also illiterate, less awareness concerned about the various prevent, promotive and curative dimenation of healthy practices. Health therefore remains an insufficiently tackled social issue.

RIGHT TO HEALTH

Historically, the right to health was one of the last to be proclaimed in the Constitutions of most countries of the world. At the international level, the Universal Declaration of Human Rights established a breakthrough in 1948, by stating in Article 25: "Everyone has the right to a standard of living adequate for the health and wellbeing of himself and his family...." The Preamble to the WHO Constitutions also affirms that it is one of the fundamental rights of every human being to enjoy "the highest attainable standard of health". Inherent in the right to health is the right to health or medical care. Some countries have used the term "right to health protection" provide material security in cases of illness or accident, and free medical education, medicaments and other necessary materials and the right to be cared for by society in old age and invalidity. In an increasing number of societies, health is no longer accepted as a charity or the privilege of the few, but demanded as a right for all. However, when resources are limited (as in most developing countries), the governments cannot provide all the needed health services. Under these circumstances the aspirations of the people should be satisfied by giving them equal right to available health care services.

The concept of "right to health" has generated so many questions, viz. right to medical care, right to responsibility for health, right to a healthy environment, right to food, right to procreate (artificial insemination included), the right not to procreate (family planning, sterilization, legal abortion), rights of the deceased persons (determination of death, autospsies, organ removal) and the right to die) suicide, hunger strike, discontinuation of life support measures), etc. Many of these issues have been the subject of debate. It is left to the lawyers, ethicists and physicians to formulate a general outline of what is acceptable and what is unacceptable in human society.

Community health reflects the philosophy, religion, economic conditions, and form of government, educational system. science, aspirations, and folklore of any given period. The history of community health chronicles the advances and declines of societies and human conditions. Consider what has happened in your own community over the past few years, with population and industrial growth or decline, with economic improvements or setbacks. Consider the health - related headlines in your local newspapers; abortion, teenage pregnancy, drunk - driving laws, toxic waste dumps, fitness, the aging population, seat belt legislation, air pollution controls, computer invasions of medical and vital registration records. Such controversies reflect community responses to historical trends in health and attempt to shape the history of health and community development. Civilization depends on the quality and distribution of health in the general population. Health in turn depends on human advancement and community development in various spheres. Cast in a historical framework, community health is a result of life - styles as well as a barometer of conditions shaping life-styles. These observations describe community health, but they risk characterizing it as only a passive consequence of historical; circumstances. Community health also represents a dynamic human enterprise that shapes history. People devote their careers and organizations devote their missions to the promotion of community health.

What is Community Health Promotion ?

A leading figure in the history of public health, characterized public health practice as the science and art of preventing disease, prolonging life, and promoting health and well-being through organized community effort for the sanitation of the environment, the control of communicable infections, the organization of medical and nursing services for the early diagnosis and prevention of disease, the education of the individual in personal health, and the development of the social machinery to assure everyone a standard of living adequate for the maintenance or improvement of health.

By this definition, public health practice overlaps some aspects of medicine, nursing, school health, and personal health, and overlaps most aspects of environmental health, disease prevention, and health promotion. Public health tends to be associated with the work of official governmental health agencies, to the term community health promotion has come into increasing use to emphasize the moral local, collaborative efforts of various public and private sectors. The spheres of action in community health include aspects of public health practice; school health practice; the professional practices of medical, dental, nursing, and allied health personnel; and the personal health practices of individuals and families. Community health represents the areas in which these spheres overlap. Additional sphere of action overlap with these and contribute to community health, but usually as a by-product of their primary purposes. Such additional spheres include the worksite, in which employee health promotion, safety, and screening programs address adult health much as school health programs do for children. Likewise, the recreational system and the legal system contribute to community health in performing their primary functions. The coordination and integration of these spheres of action make up the practice of community health promotion.

Educational interventions may be directed at high-risk individuals, families, or groups, at decision makers, or at whole communities by the mass media, schools, industry, and other organizations. Social interventions may take the form of economic, political, legal and organizational changes, including the organization of health care services, designed to support actions conducive to health. Environmental supports include the structure and distribution of physical, chemical, and biological resources, facilities, and substances required for people to protect their health. The health behavior of a community includes the actions of the people whose health is in question and the actions of community decision makers, professionals, peers, teachers, employers, parents, and others who may influence health behaviors, resources, or services in the community.

Organized community effort defines community health. Some things the individual can do entirely alone, but many health benefits can be obtained only through collective action or united community effort. Community health promotion seeks to make the fruits of health science available to all citizens. Home Science of the future is at the crossroads and it needs to be conceptualized around the young families of today. The two most important priority areas in front of home scientists are programmes of income generation and of population control strategies. That means Home Science programs would have to be developed around two greatest problems, over population and poverty.

Over Population

Home economics colleges have started offering population education courses. Since a very small percentage of oriental students go to college, school and out of school programs will continue to be very much required. India, for instance has non-formal education programs but it needs to be strengthened. The ministry of health and different government programmes have been on going in the areas of family planning, birth control and family welfare services. These would be continued and strengthened. Home Scientists needs to start family planning and "small family norm" clinics for communities. Not only the education but the service component needs to be added in future Home Science programs. The government have started birth control programs but future Home Scientists would be to work harder either with government or independently to respond to this problem of over population. This is currently the most important problem in the developing countries. Due to population explosion people can not get the proper health facilities, housing water supply, sanitation and such facilities.

Poverty

The most striking and sad reality of our country is its poverty of material resources. One reason behind large-scale poverty is the unemployment due to unskilled status of the masses and the other reason is, of course, the poor health, restricted economy which has few jobs and lower salaries. Future home economics needs to develop income generating skills of its students. Vocational programs must take priority over fundamental research and theoretical classroom teaching. Traditionally home economics has generated teaching jobs and this needs to be continued. Creating new jobs and diverting home economics to make more women job conscious is the future need of home economics. There are vast possibilities of self employment for women in areas of food and clothing. The trend of small-scale catering, designing and constructing clothes and preparing interior decorations, becoming beauticians has already begun and future home scientists should strengthen this trend.

Similarly there are some more priority which need to be addressed. The changing life style of today's youth, calls for family living and family solidarizing for teen age parents, single parents and separated parents. The young ones of today's world face problems of AIDS, alcoholism, teenage parenthood and school dropout. Future Home Scientists programs here would need to direct themselves at solutions to these problems. Similarly the need of day care centres, not only for children but for all needy people. The day-care centres are probably for the victims of problems of teenagers, but the greater challenge would be the prevention of problems of teenagers.

Can home scientists give protection by an early safety education, make videos for such education and use them for non formal groups also ? Some prerequisites for success of future home scientists would be planned scanning of our needs, preparations and limitations or problems.

Needs

Empathy for people is the first need of the program. Because of vast cultural differences we need a tremendous amount of empathy to understand the values, customs and beliefs of people.

Preparation

Further, our preparation for future international programs would include our environmental scanning of cultural, economic and social aspects. No program can succeed without a prior analysis of socio-politico-economic status of people.

CONCEPT OF WELLBEING

The WHO definition of health introduces the concept of "well-being". The question then arises, what is meant by wellbeing ? In point of fact, there is no satisfactory definition of the term "wellbeing". Recently, psychologists have pointed out that the "wellbeing" of an individual or group of individuals have objective and subjective components. The objective components relate to such concerns as are generally known by the term "standard of living" or "level of living". The subjective component of well-being (as expressed by each individual) is referred to as "quality of life". Let us consider these concepts separately.

Standard of Living

The term "standard of living" refers to the usual scale of our expenditure, the goods we consume and the services we enjoy. It includes the level of education, employment status, food, dress, house, amusements and comforts of modern living. A similar definition, corresponding to the above, was proposed by WHO: "Income and occupation, standards of housing, sanitation and nutrition, the level of provision of health, educational, recreational and other services may all be used individually as measures of socio-economic status, and collectively as an index of the "standard of living". There are vast inequalities in the standards of living of the people in different countries of the world. The extent of these differences is usually measured through the comparison of per capita GNP on which the standard of living primarily depends.

Level of Living

The parallel term of standard of living used in United Nations documents is "level of living". It consists of nine components: health, food consumption, education, occupation and working conditions, housing, social security, clothing, recreation and leisure and human rights. These objective characteristics are believed to influence human wellbeing. It is considered that health is the most important component of the level of living because its impairment always means impairment of the level of living.

Quality of Life

A recent definition of quality of life is as follows: "a composite measure of physical, mental and social wellbeing as perceived by each individual or by group of individuals - that is to say, happiness, satisfaction and gratification as it is experienced in such life concerns as health, marriage, family work, financial situation, educational opportunities, self-esteem, creativity, belongingness, and trust in others". People are now demanding a better quality of life. Therefore, governments all over the world are increasingly concerned about improving the quality of life of their people by reducing morbidity and mortality, providing primary health care and enhancing physical, mental and social well-being.

Improvement in the quality of life of people depends to a great extent on the quality of physical environment. It is in recognition of this fact that the world conference of the International Women's Year" adopted a "World Plan of Action" in the year 1975 which included aspects related to housing amongst its recommendations. The plan suggested that settlement planning and policies should be formulated keeping in view the trend to recognize women's role in the development process and should prioritize investment in infrastructure there in according to the needs of woman. Subsequently, following the declaration of the year 1987 by the United Nations as the International year of shelter for the Homeless, the Ministry of Urban Development of the Government of India formulated a Draft National Housing Policy (March 1987) with a view to ensuring every family shelter by end of this century. Nowhere in this text, however, had the draft acknowledged that housing and women's needs required to be closely linked. Passing references to women was made only at page 12 para 13.4 of the draft where in it stated that special efforts would be made to improve women's skills and working conditions in the housing sector.

Socio-economic conditions

Socioeconomic conditions have long been known to influence human health. Health status is determined primarily by their level of socio-economic development, e.g., per capita GNP, education, nutrition, employment, housing, the political system of the country, etc. Those of major importance are:

(i) *Economic Status:* It is the economic progress that has been the major factor in reducing morbidity, increasing life expectancy and improving the quality of life. The economic status determines the purchasing power, standard of living, quality of life, family size and the pattern of disease and deviant behavior in the community.

(ii) *Education:* A second major factor influencing health status is education (especially female education). The world map of illiteracy closely coincides with the maps of poverty, malnutrition, ill-health, high infant and child mortality rates. Studies indicate that education, to some extent, compensates the effects of poverty on health, irrespective of the availability of health facilities.

(iii) *Occupation:* The very state of being employed in productive work promotes health, because the unemployed usually show higher incidence of ill health and death. For many, loss of work may mean loss of income, and status. It can cause psychological and social damage.

PROPER SANITATION

Sanitation means establishment of environmental condition favourable to health. Generally women living in rural areas have sanitation problems, which adversely affects the health of women. So proper sanitation condition should be made to keep themselves free from infections, diseases, and infirmity. Unhygienic conditions of sanitation leads to urine infections and other reproductive track diseases, so to avoid these conditions, we should maintain good sanitational environment.

Factors affecting women's health

Stage To	*Causes*	*Results*
Conception	Sex Determination Test	Death
Birth	Female Infanticide	Death or Morbidity
Infancy	Inadequate breast feeding, Food neglect	Death, Illness, Less resistance
Puberty	More restrictions, Less mobility, Inadequate food	Death, Anemia, Depression, Other health-hazards
Marriage	Early pregnancy, Repeated delivery, Abortions, Sex determination test	Death, Psychological problem, severe anemia, Impaired reproductive health
Motherhood	No control over sexuality	Death, Psychological prolem, Severe anemia

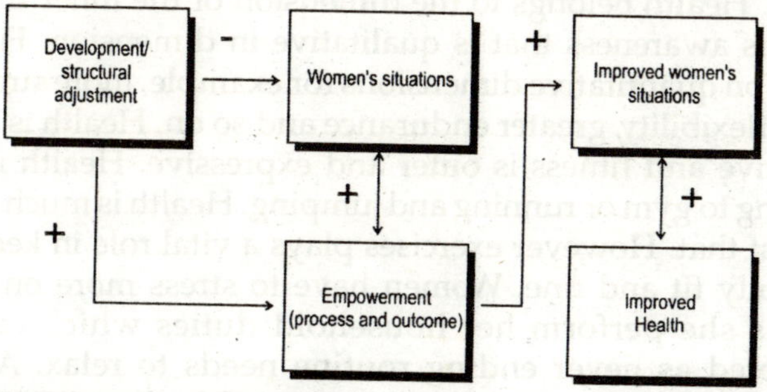

Women Empowerment and Health

Maintaining Good Health - HOW ?

Being strong is not falling ill and also if a strong person fall ill, he will get better, quicker than a weaker person would. The above statement is very much correct. We have to give a lot of attention towards our health. There are so many ways of remaining healthy some of them are -

1. Balance Diet
2. Exercises
3. Medical Check-ups

1. Balance Diet

Life can't be sustained without adequate nourishment. Man needs adequate food for growth, development and leads an active and healthy life. Nutritional conditions refers to the growth conditions which is directly related to the food eaten. The health condition and the nutrition condition are very closely related. In consideration to women as she performs the dual responsibilities of home as well as out side requires a balance diet to meet her body requirements. In the life phase of women since adolescence to old age requires diet containing nutritional value. As when she is pregnant, she has to eat more for the nourishment of her baby in her womb. Balance diet provides her all the nutrients, which she requires in her body. If she does not take balanced diet, she will suffer with lot of problem like anemia, which will affect her whole body. So it is important that she has to take balance diet regularly.

2. Exercises

Health V/S. Fitness : Health is personal, where as fitness is relative. Health belongs to the dimension of the inner fitness. Health is awareness that is qualitative in dimension. Fitness focuses on quantitative dimensions for example, more strength greater flexibility, greater endurance and so on. Health is inner meditative and fitness is outer and expressive. Health is not just going to gym or running and jumping. Health is much more than just that. However exercises plays a vital role in keeping your body fit and fine. Women have to stress more on their work as she perform her household duties which can be considered as never ending routine needs to relax. As we generally find that women work more and for long period but eats less and they have least excess to exercises, sports, healthy recreations and rests. All these factors affect her health. She needs different exercises at different stages of life cycle like - during pregnancy, lactation, old etc.

3. Medical Health Check-ups

Medical health check-ups are very important for healthy life. We should get medical check ups done, so as to avoid the problems related to health. During pregnancy she should do check ups on pre-natal and post-natal periods, so if any problem is detected, it can be cured easily. So from above it is clear that medical check ups play very important role in every bodies life specially in women's life.

PERSONAL HYGIENE

Personal hygiene is very important for our good health. If we do not consider hygiene in our life, it will definitely affect our health and as we all know that "if health is lost everything is lost" and because of poor health we are not able to give whole attention in our work which will lead to poor performance in all areas, so it affects many areas of individual life. And if we talk about women personal hygiene she should take lot of care of it because she has to perform other important functions in the home as well as outside also. She has many phases in her life through which she has to undergo like-puberty, marriage and motherhood. Puberty is the stage of changing emotionally, physically in all different shapes and form. At this stage only the menstrual cycle also starts, at that time she has to take care of her personal hygiene. Although menstrual cycle are normal part of every women life. Some people think that at that time women are "unclean", but it is not true. But then also she has to take care otherwise it gives rise to many other diseases like - RTD (reproductive tract diseases) which is caused by improper hygienic condition during menstrual period so she has to take care of it. Other problem that may arise due to this is STD (sexually transmitted diseases). AIDS is another problem which arises due to unhygienic conditions.

So, from the above, it is clear that personal hygiene plays important role in our life. So she has to take care of it and remain healthy and perform all her functions effectively.

ROLE OF MEDIA IN HEALTH EDUCATION

As we all know that Media is a powerful tool in the society and every, where in the world. Now, a days villagers also know about the all medias like television, radio, magazines, newspaper and people are influenced by the media.

Media is very important in dissemination of information regarding health. Through the media people know about How to become healthy? about personal health etc. which plays very important role in our daily life. Besides this through the media they know about the family planning and also the different schemes related to the health.

Magazines and newspapers are also very popular print media amongst the people. Through these media, they can ask queries or problems related to health. They can solve their problems through the media. For example - In the magazines and in the newspapers, we all read some questions related to the health and sex, which are asked by the readers and the answers given by the experts and they try to solve the problems of readers. The television is also very influential media. People give more importance and also spend more time in watching the television because in television they see the situation very lively and which are related to their own life. On the television they provide telephonic programmes where they hear the viewer's problems and also give information, which they want. Through the television they also give the programmes on the health schemes and the general health. They also arrange the talk show with the experts like doctors, social workers, Urban Community Development Officers (UCD). The teaching aids like charts and posters also play very important role in providing information and creating awareness regarding health. In the villages most of the people are illiterates, so one can understand better by seeing charts and posters. So, media play a vital role in educating the people for better health and hygiene and well-beings of life and family education.

The women have so far been the majority recipients of home science programs. The women in India are much less privileged and are in greater need of Home Science. The Home Science program need to concentrate on helping women to generate income, to simplify their housework, more importantly, to develop themselves and empower themselves. It is very shocking to report that female child is deprived of educational and social opportunities to develop into an independent individual, For instance, the motherhood is over glorified and women is expected to live for her husband and sons and not for herself. The future home science programs need to attract and support more women in developing themselves professionally and socially without abandoning their families.

The career women are attributed the guilt of neglecting the family, which is not reasonable. The future home scientists need to help men and women to accept new, more balanced and functional roles in context of family and career. The future home science programs can revive, support, or change the value systems of people so as to increase their survival potential in the 21st century. We have always talked about not imposing personal values on others. One may wonder ! In India, how can we change the values of young adults about accepting small family norm, or value of liberating women to pursue a career of their choice, or reforming men to accept sharing of child care and housework ? Similarly how can young ones be saved from reckless, unguided and over permissive life styles ? Can their values of sex and family life be changed ?

It is essential to understand that in accepting new values or reforming old values, some amount of manifest or latent imposition is essential. Once a value has been proved to be desirable, it can be inculcated into young minds : and if not, we have the hard decision to make about the imposition of value. The future home science programs will be more useful if we can communicate our reformed values and attitudes about individual, family and professional living to all people. The future home science program may become extinct or obsolete if they do not revise and reappraise themselves in the light of changing family, changing status of women, advancing science and technology. This means no educational program is an end in itself with long permanence. It must keep changing according to the social, economic and political environments.

CONCLUSION

Now, we have to value our health as our "valuable asset". It is in our hand to maintain our health as only a healthy person can lead a healthy and productive life. Health is our nature and illness is an attack on nature. Health, like life, is a process - a constant flux. It is not a state that can be permanently attained. It has to maintained by remaining alert about the internal and external environment. And ofcourse it is well said- "Health is beauty". As beauty is only a by-product of good health. Let's wake up and enter into the adventure and remember that Health is a fundamental Human Right.

REFERENCES

Agnihotri V. K. Reaching Health to the poor, Source Book on District Health Management VHAI Publication, 1998.

Bhanduria Mridula, Some Issues of Women's Health, Social Welfare, Vol. 46, No. 1 April 1999.

Channan, Karuna (ed) Socialism and Women Exploitation in gender identity, Orient Longman, New Delhi 1988.

Chatterjee Meera, Indian Women, Their Health and Economic Productivity, The World Bank Washington D.C.

CHETNA "Women's Health Mela, An Innovative Training Approach for women 5-7 April 1990, Ahmedabad Chetna.

Giriappa, S. Role of Women in Rural Development, Daya Publishing House Delhi 1988.

Kynch, J. and Sen A. Indian Women, well being and Survival Cambridge Journal of Economics 7, 363-80. 1983.

Rosenfield Ann, Handbook of Women's Health, Cambridge University Press 2001.

Sharma M., Science and Technology for the betterment of women, Kurukshetra 25(12), 4. 1977.

Shiva, M. Freedom from illness, Health Status of Women, Social Welfare Vol. 48(8) pp 28-30, 2002.

Swaminathan, M. S. Women and rural development, Mainstream (Annual Number) 113-118, 1988.

Tylor M. H. Training of Trainers. Kurukshetra, 9(6) 1980.

9

World of Advertisement and Women

Over the years, advertisements have developed and attained new dimensions. The computer long used for the common chores of accounting and billing has come into more sophisticated use providing breakthroughs. As information has increased, the computer is helping the management, advertising and marketing people understand the new world of product proliferation, market segmentation, population shift. Adequate care and modernization is required to keep in bounds the decency and morality. It calls for more responsible role of professional bodies. Some important points like creativity, imagination, foresight in seeing trends, the ability to reason analytically, sense of form are some of the qualities needed to make good advertisement. But truth remains that ADVERTISEMENT IS AN ART.

The concept and use of Advertising is as old as civilization itself. In the ruins of ancient Egypt explorers have found Papyrus posters offered rewards for the return of runaway slaves. In early Greek and Roman days signboards were placed above the doors and windows of business establishments to proclaim that merchants had certain wares for sale. After the invention of printing in the 15th century handbills, posters and then newspapers were used in increasing quantities to advertise products.

As newspapers and magazines circulation increased and new technological advances were made, at the turn of the century advertising developed new slogans, better copy writers and artists. The advent of Television showed a steady improvement in the techniques of advertising such as copy testing, the study of psychological campaign. During the decades advertising has widely used research methods such as readership studies and audience measurements.

In comparison with the "product era" in 1950's and "image era" of the 1960's, "Positioning" emerged as the primary characteristic of the 1970's. In the media oriented society many companies found it necessary to "Position" a product in the public mind - a position taking into consideration not only the product's own strength and weakness but their competitors as well. Since 1980's there is more emphasis on creative research, entailing repeated testing and weeks and even months of hard work became more important.

The face of advertising has also changed on the 1990's. The days of mass production have gone. The emphasis has been shifted to information based controlled production, distribution of goods and services. This change has brought enormous implications for economic, social and community structure, human psychology and cultures. Advertising being an integral part of socio-economic activity has to precisely adjust its operation involving selection of message, choice of media and examining target audience, glóbalization helped multinational capture markets around to world. Expansion of market is highly supported by advertisements flooding the satellite channels round the clock.

The subversive power wielded by commercial considerations needs special mention. Journals and newspapers depend heavily on advertising in order to reach out to the readers at a reasonable cost. As the print media is heavily propped up by the corporate world through advertising revenue, commercial considerations dominate.

A Harvard study for example indicates that the average adult is potentially exposed to 500 advertisements per day from Television, Radio, Newspapers and magazines. Add to that bill boards, direct mails, specialty items like book marks and ball point pens and packages in which products are displayed attractively, the amount of advertisement one is exposed to has increased immensely. A recent study showed that among 20,000 companies in India only nearly 800 odd advertise often enough to entitle them to contract rates. Except for a few mass produced consumer goods by multinational, we do not have a large number of products and services which are mass produced. The leading companies which offer consumer soft and consumer durable goods are mostly in the fields of textiles, tobacco, cosmetics and toiletries, medicines and home appliances.

Advertising can be defined as any paid form of non personal presentation and promotion of ideas, goods and services by an identified sponsor. According to E.S. Turner - "Advertising is the whip which hustles humanity upto the road to better mouse trap". If advertising merely sold products, it would cause less critical concern than it does but it also sells images, dreams, ideal ways of life.

Factors that affect the promotional mix

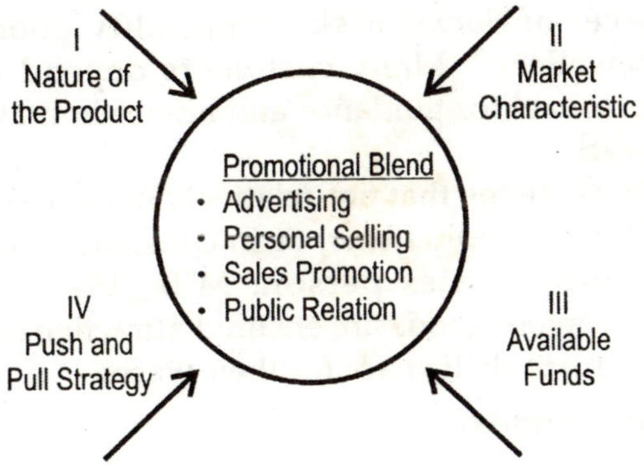

I Nature of the Product

Personal selling is most important in industrial goods and least important in consumer non durables.

Broadcast advertising is used heavily for consumer goods -promotion of particularly non durable goods.

Electronic and Print media is used for all the three categories. Expensive complex machinery, cars, new homes etc. which needs a lot of advertising in newspapers and hoardings.

II Market Characteristics

Widely scattered potential customers, highly informed buyers and a large number of brand loyal repeat purchasers generally requires a blend of more advertising and sales promotion. Advertising is used to locate potential customers by inviting the readers to "call collect" for more information or fill "the coupon" for a detailed brochure. Sales persons are sent to the potential customers as the calls or coupons are received.

(a) *Industrial goods*— Producers of industrial goods, with the exception of supply items, tend to rely more heavily on personal selling than advertising. Consumer goods are promoted primarily through advertising.

(b) *Convenience goods*— Cosmetics, pencils, soft drinks usually simple to understand and use. Attractive displays and brand familiarity advertising are often very effective.

(c) *Level of Social Risk*— Speciality goods such as "Jewellery". Many customers depend upon sales personnel for guidance and advice in making proper choice.

(d) *Cost*— Items that are relatively small part of a firms budget (supply items) or in consumer budget do not require a sales person. Milk, bread and other convenient goods are ensured attractive displays and adequate shelf space for their wares.

III Available Funds

Money or the lack of it. may easily be the most important factor in determining the promotional blend. A small undercapitalized manufacturer may rely heavily on free publicity of its product. A smaller well capitalized organization may not be able to afford the advertising rates of publications such as Readers Digest, Illustrated Weekly. The price of a single advertisement in these media could often support a sales person for a year.

IV Push and Pull Strategy

The use of aggressive personal selling and trade advertising by the manufacturer to convince wholesalers or retailers to carry its merchandise is known as pushing strategy. The whole sellers, in turn must often "push" the merchandise forward by persuading the retailers to handle the goods. The retailer than uses advertising, displays and other forms of promotion to convince the consumer to buy the "pushed products". At the other extreme is a pulling strategy to obtain product distribution. Rather than attempting to sell to the wholesaler, the manufacturer focuses its promotional efforts on the final consumer. As the consumer begins demanding the product, the retailer orders the merchandise from the manufacturers. Thus stimulating final consumer demand, pulls the products down through the channel of distribution.

This push and pull strategy are not limited to new products. If a mature product is not reaching its full potential, an aggressive pushing or pulling strategy may be undertaken.

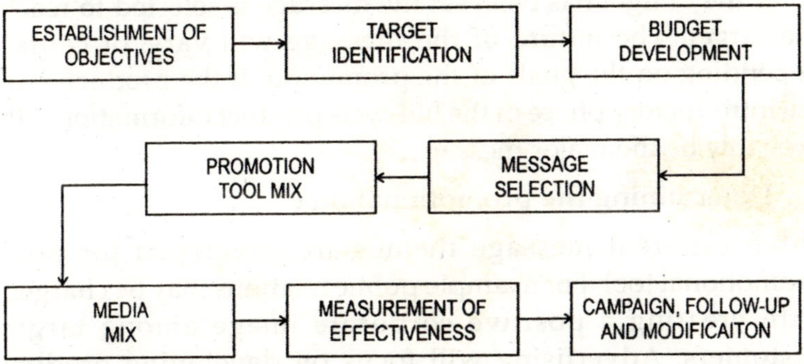

Each step follows in a logical sequence, resulting in a promotion campaign that is geared to specific objective. Several steps require the completion of an earlier task before they can be undertaken - for example the setting of objectives should come before budget development.

1. Setting Objectives

Setting of objectives is the starting point for any promotional campaign. Indeed it is impossible to plan a promotional programme unless the marketing manager knows what goals he or she is trying to achieve. Each tool, whether it is publicity advertising, sales promotion, should aid in placing the goods or services at a specific point on the positioning continuum for a specific target.

2. **Identifying the target audience**

Naturally the target audience should consist primarily of the individuals who are most likely to purchase the product within a relevant period.

3. **Developing a budget**

After a marketing manager has specified the promotional goals and identified the relevant market segments, a concrete relevant market promotional budget can be developed. This is no simple task nor is there any "cook book approach" that will lead to an optimal promotional budget.

4. **Choosing a message**

After the budget has been set the message is selected to reach the target. The nature of the message will vary, of course depending on the goals of the promotion. If the product is in the introductory phase of the life cycle product information will probably be the major message.

5. **Determining the promotional mix**

Often different message themes are developed for each promotional tool. For example public relations may be charged with creating a positive corporate image among target customers. Advertising will focus on developing product awareness to complement personal selling. The function of personal selling will be to interact with the customer by amplifying and explaining the advertising messages and designing for the right product or service to meet the specific needs of the customers. Sales promotion may come into the picture by communicating a "special discount" to prospective buyer if they purchase now. Thus public relation, advertising and sales promotion are all aimed towards increasing sales effectiveness.

6. Selecting the media mix

By what media it wants to send the message. Different types of media tend to appeal to different audiences. Also different specific media, such as country and western radio stations, will have different audiences than other specific media, such as audience who has the facility of Television viewing.

7. Measuring Effectiveness

It is incumbent on promotion managers to measure the effectiveness of their promotional campaigns, since the effectiveness of various tools is measured quite differently. Without some measurement of the outcome of promotional campaigns, there would be no way of determining whether objectives are being met.

8. Follow Up

After measuring the outcome of a promotional endeavour, it may be necessary to change the promotional plan. Change often occurs in the promotional blend, the media mix, the message, the total promotional budget, or the way the budget is allocated. Follow up must also ask the question - What do we know now that we did not know before we began the promotional campaign ? The firm should learn from its mistakes and ensure that policies are established so that the same mistakes can be avoided in future.

ADVERTISEMENT AND ECONOMIC FABRIC

When we think how large our country is, covering various kinds of terrains, population and living conditions - the degree of cohesion is remarkably high. People in the deserts of Rajasthan drive the same kinds of automobiles, eat the same kind of breakfast food and wear the same kind of shoes as their fellow men in chilly areas of Ladakh. They are able to do so because of two major factors in contemporary Indian life - Good transportation for moving the goods from the factory and a highly developed system of advertising and marketing. Advertisement is a part of our economic fabric as—

1. It informs readers.
2. It influences them.

3. It convinces them.
4. Companies which spend money to advertise their goods become larger and more profitable than their competitors who do not advertise. The advertising budget has become as essential in a company's financial operation as many designated for salaries, factory operating expenses and distribution of the products.
5. Reaches people inaccessible to sales people such as top business executives and professional people.
6. Enters new geographical market or attract new group of customers.

Consumers Point of View

7. The rival advertising of competing companies increases his range of choice.
8. Actually it saves time and money. Importance of advertising in everyday living is evident if we watch a housewife. She reads the grocery advertisement in her newspaper. She makes her weekend shopping list from these announcements. One market offers a special price on soap and other nearby market lists a bargain on sprouted pulse.

   She decides to shop first at the market offering the sprouted dal and may also visit the store featuring a special price on the soap. Without advertisements the housewife might have found these bargains by a prolonged search among the shelves that is if she had the time.
9. Advertising reduces production cost and price of the goods.
10. It improves the standard of living
11. It increases the national income
12. Helps in promoting new ideas and practices.

ROLE OF HOME SCIENTIST IN ADVERTISEMENTS

The preparation of any advertisement or campaign in which a home economist participates is a three cornered affair- a triangle made up of the copy department on one side, the art on the other and the home economist department on the third side. No one department works by itself.

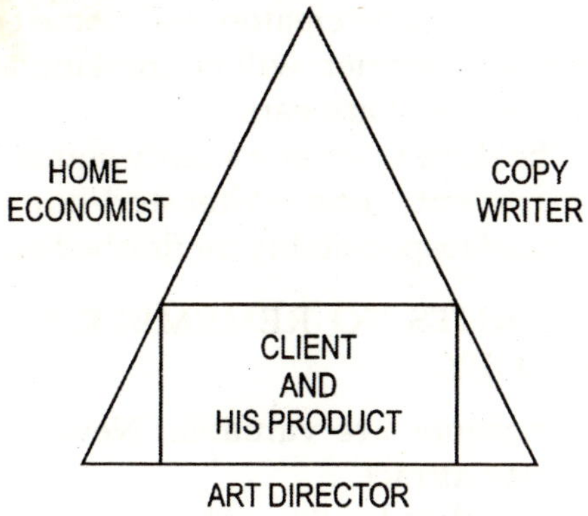

This situation like any other triangle in human relations can cause problems if not thoroughly understood and wisely handled. A complete understanding of each others responsibilities and how these fit together is necessary in order to avoid ruffled feelings and time and energy wasting friction.

e.g. 1 - It may be that one of the copy writers has a bright idea for a headline or a particular copy about which the agency heads feel should be worked up. In that case the home economist may be called in for her ideas before the art department is brought in.

e.g. 2 - It may be that the home economist herself suggests a new line of uses for the product in the house. She submits her ideas, accompanied by a message giving her reasoning. Any one of which could lead to a dramatic photograph and would be appealing and practical for home use. If the ideas are good then layout and copy departments are called in to discuss the matter and work up on the idea.

The Home Economist Offer

1. Judgement
2. Skill
3. Idea

The better use you make of all three, the more a copy is likely to appeal and influence a woman. The important thing is that the art department copy creators and home economist all think in the same way women will be thinking and doing at the time the advertisement appears.

Work should be done to keep it a fairly equilateral triangle with layout department, copy writer and home economist showing almost equal responsibility for finished advertisement.

IMPORTANT POINTS TO REMEMBER IN WRITING ADVERTISING COPY

1. New techniques are valuable. News about a new product may attract.
2. Advertising related to the problem of consumer is more effective than boasting. There is probably an element of boasting in almost any advertisement that is written to point out how a product will help, but generalized boasting about a product or the company that produce it usually has little effect.
3. Testimonials by celebrities are not automatically effective. Those that are believable attract consumers but consumer may get irritated by obviously spurious testimonials.
4. Over imaginative, tricky advertising is positive to both readers and viewers.
5. Keep learning more and more about how home making women work and their interests.
6. Keep learning more and more about how artists and layout persons and copy creators work and think.
7. Keep a growing file of ideas that you know and got from the home makers point of view and that have the makings of good selling copy and illustration.

QUALITIES NEEDED IN ADVERTISING

Creativity, Imagination, foresight in seeing trends, the ability to reason analytically, sense of form, broad general education in liberal art, communication, commerce or humanities or science or home science. Young persons with talents and ability to rise rapidly in advertising field.

ADVERTISING AND WOMEN

Before 1900, newspaper had been for men only becoming a force to reckon with in politics. Slowly new women's magazines and journals started coming up. Today women play an important role in every phase of advertising. Many women graduates get work immediately as copy writers for agencies and for department stores and other companies. A number of women sell space and time for the media, with most newspapers employing virtually all women for desk jobs in the classified advertising departments. A number of national advertising campaigns have been master minded by women functioning as account executives. The advertising directors of some of the largest department stores are female. More and more women are being made vice presidents of agencies and a number of very successful women now head firms of their own. Numerous career opportunities are also available in other advertising and related areas cited as follows with their annual estimates volumes of business.

Inspite of all this inadequate attention is paid in the media to issues of specific importance to women, to the activities of the women movement or to the social contribution made by independent and gifted women. In advertisements women are shown either as housewife whose interests are limited to domestic needs or else as the glamour world by making it more attractive and object of sex. Useful discussion and awareness sessions have little influence on decision makers. The achievement of full equality for women is a matter of justice and human rights, it is also necessary so that society progress. The world cannot afford to waste the great resources represented by the abilities and talents of women. This is the thought that should be constantly in the minds of those responsible for decision making in the field of communication.

Adequate care and modernisation in fact, a good deal of self discipline, have to be exercised by the advertisers so that they remain within the bounds of decency and morality. In India counselling of advertisers is done by the Advertising council of India which was founded in 1959. The council is an advisory and consultative body. It promotes the observance of an ethical code of conduct in advertising in the country.

The Indian government in 1986 introduced the indecent representation of women (Prohibition) Act, supposed to prohibit advertisements, publications and writing that are derogatory or denigrating women. There is lack of integrity on part of the media in following this act since we see media continuing to show half clad women selling products and to print vulgar illustrations and jokes about women.

A major objective for mass media should, therefore be to do programmes relating to women's status and image since the status of women is directly related to a country's national development. Clear guidelines on positive portrayal of women should be evolved. Policy makers should be sensitized to issues relating to women. A study of women's role in television and radio in five countries - India, Egypt, Nigeria, Canada and Ecuador, proves that women have a long way to go if they are to make any meaningful impact on society through the control of key management and policy making position.

The role of advertisement, at present is depressing. Media do cover women and they do more damage than help their development. Ad films, signboards, televisions, articles, magazines, newspaper all are guilty in this respect. The female body is used undiscriminately to promote sale of commercial, products in ad films, magazines and newspapers. This is true for male oriented products also. To make quick profit, the modern audio visual media have sought to erase the dividing line between modesty and indecency, thus lowering the image of women in the eyes of society. By showing all women as beautiful, shy, natural and instinctive mothers and dutiful wives, advertisements put before the masses images which are not existing in reality. Advertisements use beautiful women to sell products as diverse as soap, cooking oil, car, bedsheets, towels and even motor bikes. Such advertisements only objectify women.

Women are shown only in nurturing roles or in what may consider extensions of such roles. Poor women are ignored because they do not have purchasing power. For example certain brands of detergent imply that maid servants will stop grumbling and start smiling.

Most advertisements address women as housewives, excited by their new purchases. A family is projected as women's only source of happiness and identify and she must constantly use newer consumer product to fulfill herself as a wife and mother.

In short, advertisement encourages a consumer culture where in women are stereotyped as housewife whose only source of happiness is serving the family.

CONCLUSION

To conclude it can be said that advertising has come to stay and it has come of age. It has established its own credibility. But the professional bodies in the area of advertising and mass media have to realise their responsibilities for maintaining this credibility. It is time that professional bodies, advertising agencies and practitioners give serious thought to this problem especially as advertising has developed into an academic discipline with its introduction as a subject for specialisation in various universities. Introduction of guidelines with respect to advertising content and the values and attitudes it fosters, in accordance with national standards and practices. Such guidelines should be consistent with national development policies and efforts to preserve cultural identity. In this connection various mechanisms such as complaint boards on consumer review committees might be established to afford to public the possibility of reacting against advertisement which they feel are inappropriate.

Role of media women specially women journalists and film makers itself can be very significant in the promotion of development of women. They will have to come forward to support women by going deep into women's issues. Ultimately as more and more women became directors and writers and as women's perceptions themselves became clearer, there will be truer and less distorted images of women. Media will be effective instruments of change only if they can help liberate women from their traditional submissive roles. The time has come for women to identify the strengths within themselves and bring them out.

Indian society has to accept the need for a new dimension in women's role and that is their role as producers of and contributors to national income. This role is not at the expense of or to the exclusion of their traditional role. Welfare of women is a subject of great concern for the society and media has a major role to play in enhancing this aspect. The content of communication at any given time reflects the pattern of value are treated indicate to a great extent the prevailing attitude of that society towards its women.

REFERENCES

Alva, M. Borse S. and Pande M. "In Women and Development" Social Welfare Vol. XXXIII. No. 1 April 1986.

Bhasin Kamala and Khan Nighat Saed "Some Questions on Feminism and its Relevance in South Asia", Kali for Women, Panchshilla Park, New Delhi, 1986.

George N. Gordon, Communication and Media, Constructing a cross discipline, Hastings House Publishers, New York 1975.

India Urges Larger Role for Women, The Times of India June 3, 1994.

James Watson and Anne Hill, A Dictionary of Communication and Media Studies, Edward Arnold Ltd. 41, Bed Ford Square, 1995.

Lancelot Hogben, "From care painting to comic strip, A Kaleidoscope of Human Communication, Max Parrish and Company Ltd. London 1962.

Lewis Anthony Dexter, David Manning While, "People, Society and Mass Communication", The free press of Glencoe, London 1963.

Mass Media in India 1979 and 80, Ministry of I & B, Government of India Publication Division

Mc. Daniel Carl Jr., Marketing Second Edition, The University of Texas, Arlington Harper & Tow Publication, 1979

National Perspective Plans for Women (1988-2000) New Delhi.

R.K. Chatterjee, India, The land and people, Mass Communication, National Book Trust India, New Delhi 1973.

Richardson and Calhans, "How to write for Home Makers" The Iowa State University Press, Annes, Iowa 1962.

Sandra Ball Rokeach, Melvin L. De Fleur, Theories of Mass Communication, Longman New York and London, 1992.

Sinha Anjana Maitra. Women in a changing society, Ashish Publishing House, New Delhi, 1993.

Warren K. Agee, Philip H Ault, Edwin Emery, "Introduction to Mass Communications", Harper and Row Publisher, New York, 1995.

William L.L. Rivers, "The Mass Media Reporting, Writing, Editing, Harper and Row, 49 East 33 Street, New York. 1990.

10

Women Administrators: Myths and Realities

INTRODUCTION

In most societies of the world, women have been defined largely in terms of their functions as wives and mothers and by cultural image of their sexuality. Many people including women themselves think that they cannot think of performing any other role than wife and mother. Feminists tried to shatter this long held notion about women's place and the accepted belief of their nature and function. Even then, most women faced with the problem of dual role whenever they took up employment outside home. Despite the seeming progress, women still occupied inferior jobs and faced discrimination in entry to jobs as well as opportunities for advancement. Most Indian women do accept their traditional role of dependence on male relatives. But as possibility of economic independence through respectable employment becomes a reality for women, they do take advantage of the opportunity. The educated Indian women in contact with a broader culture than that or her home learns about new role potentialities and would like to adopt certain changes in the traditional roles. The present positively encourage women to take up administrative positions in different institutions.

On the whole, women administrators are well thought of in our society. Therefore, with this attitudinal change in climate around them the future is bright if women are determined to make their profession a success. However, for women to enter the professional and equality with men, appropriate professional training has to be extended and the same should be availed by them. In this context, it is important to create a suitable structure and climate for women to achieve professional competency and equality.

It is difficult to determine whether the women in administration today are similar to those who pioneered administration in the early part of the century. Aggregate descriptions of the women who have chosen to work in the male enclave of educational administration are abundant, although individual accounts are rare. Women in all levels of administration are older than men in similar positions, are less likely to be married, are more often members of minority and ethnic groups, more often come from more urban backgrounds, are politically more liberal, identify as non-protestant more often are more likely to have been a teacher for a longer period of time and earn less for doing the same job as a man.

Women have moved into administration later in their lives for a combination of reasons. It was felt that self-esteem increased and women discovers self-worth. This, coupled for women with children with fewer demands as mother, means that middle age often marks the birth of new or renewed career commitment and focus. It was found that the demands of the role of homemaker and mother were listed as a major difficulty for women attempt to move from teacher to administration for over 40% of the women took sole responsibility for housework, cooking and child care and addition to their jobs as teachers. These responsibilities lessened as their children grew up and women were able to add the additional tasks of school administration to their limited day.

Women taking up employment has helped in increasing their self esteem. In recent years it has been noticed there is a phenomenal change in the attitudes of working woman towards their status and role. According to he International Labour Review, in 1970, only 17% of the professional and technical workers were women. A mere 5% of the managerial and administrative workers were females. This percentage is too small in the light of the fact that the rate of graduate women in India is nearly double that of men. Since 1950, women started entering into executive jobs in the government. They have been entering professions which were only for men. According to the state of World's Women report 1985, which reviewed the achievements of the UN decade for women educational opportunities have given them the confidence and opportunity to venture outside their homes.

MEANING OF ADMINISTRATION

The word 'administration', as the Latin root 'minister' suggests, means service, i.e., work dedicated to the good of others. The main objective of administration should, therefore, be to secure for an individual or society or the nation such an environment as may lead to their fullest growth and development.

Administration determines in great measure whether an organization is going to progress, operate efficiently, achieve its objectives, and have a group of individuals, within its framework who are happy, cooperative, and productive. It has to do with directing, guiding and integrating the efforts of human beings so that specific aims may be accomplished. It refers particularly to a group of individuals, many times called executives, who have as their major responsibility this direction, guidance, integration, and achievement.

Administration is especially concerned with achievement-proof that the organization is producing those things for which it has been established. It demands capacity to coordinate many different and conflicting types of human personalities. Good administration should ensure that the associated efforts of individuals are productive. To accomplish this, administrator should possess those attributes which are conducive to bringing out the most creative and best efforts on the part of the members of the organization.

Administration also requires close supervisions of the facilities, materials, supplies, and equipment essential to the life of the organization. It implies a logical formulation of policies and the effective operation of the organization. In light of the above discussion, definition of administration can be as the following:

Administration is concerned with the functions and responsibilities essential to the achievement of established goals through associated effort. It is also concerned with that group of individuals sometimes called executives. These individuals are responsible for directing, guiding, coordinating, and inspiring the associated efforts of individual members, so that the purposes for which an organization has been established may be accomplished in the most effective and efficient manner possible.

ADMINISTRATION AS A TAXONOMY

Many efforts to define administration have ended in lists of classified activities which purport to describe what an administrator does. One of the earliest known lists which served as a pattern for subsequent taxonomies came from the French industrial scholar, Henri Fayol.

- To administer is to foresee (plan ahead), organize, order, coordinate and control;
- To foresee, that is to say, to look closely into the future and to draw up the program for action;
- To organize, that is to say, to incorporate the material and social organism of the undertaking (enterprise);
- To command or direct, i.e., make the personal function;
- Coordinate, i.e., tie together, unite, to bring into harmony all actions and all efforts;
- To control; i.e., to see to it that everything is done in accordance with established rules and given orders.

The word served for years as a handy device for recalling the elements of administration on the final examination, and stands for planning, organizing, staffing, directing, coordinating, reporting and budgeting.

One taxonomy led to slightly different concept of administration. That listing sought to define the job in terms of a person - the administrator. Some lists denote the desirable traits of an administrator; others merely the common traits of administrator. Attention was sometimes given to the behavioural characteristics of administrators; sometimes to only those observable characteristics of an administrator in a social setting.

ADMINISTRATOR AS MANAGEMENT

Earliest views of administration equated it with management. In explaining the meaning of management, the dictionaries use expressions such as command, govern, conduct, render and keep one submissive, bring about by contriving, judicious use of means to accomplish an end, and wield with address. Management originally meant conduct of business or household affairs.

These interpretations of administration explain. Why the management concept fell into disrepute. They are incompatible with a democratizing society, with respect for human beings, and with joint decision-making. The definitions imply a super-being with godly vision but with ungodly powers over serfs. They even suggest an activity less than moral - the attainment of objectives through manipulation. And yet elements of the managerial attitude are essential to administration. Certainly there must be governing authority vested in administration; there must be some directing of the affairs of others although the mellover terms "guiding and stimulating" are more acceptable today.

ADMINISTRATION AS ORGANIZATION

Administration has been defined as organization, the fitting of many pieces together into a workable pattern in order to accomplish a mission. Organization is the channel through which work flows toward completion. An organization is a unit with jurisdictional boundaries which circumscribe the total scope of operation. There is an arrangement of people in layers from top to bottom, each with carefully prescribed tasks, a flow of vertical control, and provisions for lateral communication and interrelation. The organizing mind is thought of as a mechanical organ, capable of seeing the numerous parts in individual entities and relating them toward a purpose, but probably incapable of devicing a new purpose. An "organizer" is popularly regarded as one who can put things together and can be counted on to get a job done. Today she is sometimes labeled a "systems man". In order to be an effective administrator under this interpretation, a person needs to learn the purposes of the entity and the processes involved in production. Armed with these knowledges, she is ready to begin.

ADMINISTRATION AS DECISION-MAKING

Another understanding of administrator envisions it as the singular activity of making decisions. It pictures the administrator as an omniscient figure seated at a mahogany desk to which all information is delivered. After due analysis of data, the truth emerges, commands issue forth, and the wheels roll. This is an unfair over-simplification. It has led to intensive study of how decisions are made, with the goal of determining how their accuracy can be improved.

Although the administrator unquestionably makes decisions, he devotes to them a comparatively small amount of his time today, unless one includes all of those trifling and frequent routine decisions: do I answer the phone or will the secretary? Do I choose the business man's special or a hamburger ? Were administration distinguished on these grounds, everyone would be an administrator. Even the extended problem-solving decisions do not consume the major portion of an administrator's day. The magic of electronics has reduced his allocation of time for this purpose. As further refinements are made, the major factor of making decisions may become merely that of collecting facts - a chore suitable for subordinates, researchers, and leg men - and then merely feeding data into the machine. The mentality of the executive will be needed only for the important and difficult decisions on facts to collect and for interpretation of machine-shuffled data. A second development is the trend toward involving more people in the action. Democratized administration relieves the administrators of nearly all steps in making decisions except the responsibility for seeing that they are made.

MEANING OF EDUCATIONAL ADMINISTRATION

Adapting this simple definition of general administrator to schools, one can say that educational administration is merely getting a job done in a school or school system. Using a dictionary implication one may say that educational administration is the performance of executive duties in an educational institution. But today the semanticist faces even more difficulty in clearly distinguishing school administration from that of other organizations. The most perplexing question of all is - Who is an administrator ? Because of the confusion of titles and functions, tabulators of the number of school administrators find it difficult to issue accurate reports.

That all full-time superintendents and principals could be classified as administrators would seem obvious, but more of their working day in teaching than executing, as they instruct others in the performance of duties. Hundreds of chief school administrators actually carry class-room teaching assignments. Still more complicating, every teaching has administrative tasks: record keeping, public relations, supervision and evaluation, maintenance of facilities. They manage, execute, make decisions, direct, organize, motivate, and lead. Thus any properly trained and motivated teacher who can perform these tasks well should make a good administrator, yet this syllogism is untrue. Likewise, there have even been some mediocre teachers who, when "moved up" to administrative posts have become excellent administrators. These observations suggest that there must be something in administration which distinguishes it from teaching.

One difference is in scope of operations. Both the teacher and the administrator will use similar processes and techniques in accomplishing their respective missions, but the administrator must apply his processes to a wider field - the entire building, system, or community. The effectiveness of similar techniques in the classroom may not carry over in the wider field. Another difference is in the type of person upon whom the techniques are applied. An able teacher who can organize, motivate, supervise, and lead a classroom of children may find that his skills dissipate when applied with adults.

Neither is it simple to distinguish educational administration from business administration, or governmental administration, or military administration. The quick conclusion that the purposes of the enterprise determine the methods of administration will not suffice. That a business exists solely for making a profit does not necessarily change the way its administrators behave. School administrators, too, should be concerned with economic operations; they, too, produce a profit, though its quality or degree may not be so easily measured. Business administrators deal with the same basic tools as do school administrators: people, ideas, things. They, too, organize, direct, motivate, supervise, plan, and make decisions. It is sometimes argued that administration is administration regardless of the organization and that if one masters the skills involved in the administrative process he can practice his skills successfully in many occupations.

It should be noted that while all types of administration have some common elements, each has a few individual characteristics of its own.

According to Lazarsfeld, all administrators should follow the following principles:-

1. The administrator must fulfil the goals of the organization
2. The administrator must make use of other people in fulfilling these goals, not as if they were machines but rather in such a way as to release their initiative and creativity.
3. The administrator must also face the humanitarian aspects of the job. He wants people who work for him to be happy. This is morale-the idea that under suitable conditions people will do better work than they will under unsuitable conditions.
4. The administrator must try to build into his organization provisions for innovations, for change and for development. In a changing world, people must adapt themselves to changing conditions.

The above principles are very well applicable to educational administration too. This can be illustrated with reference to any institution. The principal of the institute has to keep in the forefront not only the major objectives of the institution in his entire planning but has to strive towards their execution also. He cannot work single-handed in his enterprise, but has to seek the cooperation of his entire staff also. The process cannot be entirely mechanical. There should be enough scope for creative activity, if the institution has to advance on proper lines. A successful principal further develops a team spirit amongst his colleagues. This can be achieved in a proper atmosphere. Finally, the principal should have a dynamic personality. He should not stick fast to orthodox practices, but should introduce changes as changing circumstances may need and demand. As a leader, it is his duty to lead his entire team in that direction.

Educational administration has, however, a few individual characteristics of its own. It can be classed as public administration along with the administration of all other non-profit-making enterprises. But there is a large number of educational institutions, run by private bodies. Some of them are of the proprietory type and are conducted primarily for profit, but the majority of them receive stable grants and do not seek any profit. "Educational administration", as French and others hold, "therefore, along with the administration of social-service organizations of an educational, religious or philanthropic nature, quasi-public in character, may be considered as public administration."

Public administration is again that part of the science of administration which has to do with government, and thus concerns itself primarily with the executive branch, where the work of government is done, though there are obviously administrative problems also in connection with the legislative and judicial branches. Public administration is thus a division of political science, one of the social sciences.

Education administration is concerned with the management of things as well as with human relationships, i.e., the better working together of people. In fact, it is more concerned with human beings and less with inanimate things. It is, therefore, primarily a social enterprise.

Many women make clear choices that they don't wish to follow the same path as men, that they have reasons for choosing other routes. Because of these choices & because of sex discrimination in employment patterns in schools, women's career paths in education predominately exist at the teacher level. Growth & experience substitute for movement up the hierarchy. Women have attained positions of every type in the administrative hierarchy. The following is the list of the areas where women are working as administrators.

1. They are superintendents of big city schools
2. They are education commissioners.
3. Principal of elementary Schools
4. Some manage large systems with thousands of employees and budgets of millions.
5. Wherever there are public schools there are women holding position of leadership.

But despite of all these positions occupied by females, the majority of women are concentrated on the lower rungs of the ladder. If the women seeks a position on her own, rather than being tapped for it, and she doesn't get it, She'll try again only once or twice and then cease pursuing administration. Those who are tapped or who succeed in getting an administrative job in the first few tries generally move into one of two kinds of positions : the elementary principalship or a position as a subject matter specialist, particularly in reading language or fine arts.

ADMINISTRATIVE TRAITS

Scientists have been collecting data on the characteristics of both sexes for many years. The review of existing research reveals difference, some based on unfounded beliefs and some are psychological. It is being said that male administrators are more confident, decisive, competitive and aggressive than their female counterparts. The female administrators are honest, more efficient, sincere, confident and hard working.

There is no significant difference between male and female in the qualities required for an administrator.

1 Confidence

Women feel that they are more confident. In this competitive environment, it is essential that this trait should be cultivated more and more among women for their career development.

2 Aggressiveness

Men are considered more aggressive than women.

3 Decisiveness

Some Studies indicate that women are slow in decision making and this is mainly because they consider all relative aspects which delay decision making process.

4 Competitiveness

Men are rated more competitive than women. Women feel they are competitive, men do not think so about women.

5 Efficiency

Efficiency is an important characteristic. In this women are rated marginally better than men. The women considered themselves more efficient than men mainly because of the multiplicity of roles they have been trusted upon and efficiency with which they tackle then.

6 Sensitive to negative signal

Both men & women administrators scored equal on the characteristics of being sensitive to negative signal. Once they reach a particular position they cannot be very sensitive to every issue that come along.

7 Capacity for hard work

Any organisation with some growth potential and orientation need to have a great input in terms of hard labour. Both men and women are rated equally on this characteristic of hard work.

8 Honesty

Honesty is an important characteristic highlighted for women administrators.

9 Sincerity and creativity

Sincerity is another characteristic for which women scored more than men.

In most societies of the world, women have been defined largely in terms of their functions as wives and mothers and by cultural image of their sexuality. Most women faced problem of dual role whenever they took up employment outside home. In 1980's more than ever before, doors were opening for women. This environment was becoming positively encouraging for women to take up administrative positions in educational institutions.

On the whole, women administrators are well thought of in our society. Therefore, with this attitudinal climate around them the future is bright if women are determined to make their profession & success.

Following are few of the perceptions about women administrators:-

1 Women and Discrimination

Women feel that they are being discriminated. This discrimination is felt to a great extent in the male dominated institutions. In the organizations where there are predominantly more women or equal number of men and women, the discrimination is not felt to that extent.

2 Educational Administration a Respectable career

It is often felt that educational administration attracts able women because, it is a respectable career. People all over the world prescribed teaching as an ideal job for women. Therefore they are able to combine their familiar functions without sacrificing on the family responsibilities of creating conflicts in their role performance.

3 Educational Administration Combines well with families functions

Women prefer to take up educational jobs since it has some flexibility in terms of executive jobs which involve a lot of touring and heavy responsibilities. It is felt that this particular career can easily be combined with marriage and family.

4 Equal Pay for men & women Administrator

Generally it is felt that there is no discrimination in the pay scales for men & women administrators in education, women felt that there was some difference. Perhaps in some the privately owned institutions this type of discrimination is experienced.

5 Men working for women administrators

It has been the practice over the years that women work for men administrators. When the situation is reverse, there may be certain amount of resentment among men. More of the women perceived that men dislike working for women administrators which may not be correct.

6 Women working for Women

One would generally feel that women working for women in an ideal situation when both the subordinate and the boss understand each other and agree on a working formula for between coordination. It is felt that women enjoy working for women.

7 Women Lack Confidence

People in the past particularly resisted the idea of having women manager, since they felt that they lack confidence compared to men. But it is felt that most of the administrators disagree this statement.

8 Exceptionally good women succeed Administrators

It is said that generally women make a mark in their profession only if they are exceptionally good. Then only women and men give the necessary recognition to women managers.

9 Women want to make Contribution to society

Women of today want to make a contribution to the organisation by assuming powers of authority. They are confident of playing the dual role effectively. Women on the whole feel that they need to achieve some feelings of self fulfillment rather than be confined to only the domestic roles.

10 Work, a Necessity for Women

Both Men and Women feel that it has become a necessity fo women to work since the cost of living has risen to a great extent especially in urban areas.

11. Women and the Dual Role

Surprisingly more women feel that they cannot be thought of in only role of wife and mother. But women should work towards fulfilling this long cherished aspiration of professional advancement rather than a dependent attitude and the resultant role She assumes thereafter.

In spite of promising demographical statistics, equal opportunities for women to secure positions and advance in educational leadership are still hampered by some historical myths and contemporary barriers. As a necessary step to achieve success, We must find individual and gender-specific ways to progress.

Historical Myths as Barriers: Since groups of people have existed, women have been leaders. Even in prehistoric settings, when superior physical strength usually equated with leadership, women inadvertently led, controlled, and influenced others. Circumstance and mental abilities afforded women early opportunities to lead in societal progress, including agriculture, trading, domesticating animals, establishing communities, and early construction, were developed by prehistoric women (Valiant, 1978). Conflicts between the role of leader and expectations for female roles have occurred throughout history and in most cultures. In our own culture, we often find a view of women leaders weighed down by distorted images and stereotypes. Historical and contemporary myths full of icy virgins, fiery temptresses, and silent martyrs still encumber female leadership visions and possibilities in many ways. Women were allowed leadership roles in education as long as they accepted the responsibility with none of the authority. The higher paying leadership roles were, and often still are, reserved for men, with subtleties not in duties but in job titles that serve to differentiate pay.

Male Dominance of Key Leadership Positions: This presents a significant barrier for women moving into roles as educational leaders Traditionally, men have controlled the highest administrative jobs within school districts. Long-standing bureaucratic values have thwarted women's entering administration. Control was largely maintained by limiting change. The "system" fostered selection of .administrators who resembled their sponsors in attitude. Faced with negative environments for advancement, many competent women seek other more enlightened avenues for their careers. When opportunities in other professions exist, overt discrimination in education becomes the force driving scores of women away. We cannot afford this loss of talent.

Lack of Political Savvy: This has also prevented women from moving forward in administrative positions. With men dominating gatekeeping, deals are often made and agreements cut before many women know positions are available. Many times, competent women with stronger qualifications are not considered. Understandings have already been bargained during golf, on the fishing trip, on the basketball court, or at the club. Women are not usually privy to those venues or to decisions made outside the work setting. People in positions of power not only frequently decide finalists for other positions, but they also quite often determine their own successors. The "good ol' boy" network exists so strongly in many places that many men can tell you their number in line to the superintendency. They are just waiting their turn.

Lack of Career Positioning: Positioning is clearly discriminatory in job announcements requesting qualifications that women cannot meet because of closed ranks. For instance, a job application might require district or central office experience in a line position (traditionally male) rather than a staff position (traditionally female). One interviewee recalled a job announcement for a principalship requiring high school coaching experience. Coaching a background of high school teaching, and expertise in finance and negotiation have been nearly mandatory prerequisites for career paths of educational leaders to the highest levels. What usually happens is that selected "golden boys" or "young turks" are carefully positioned on the "right" district committees with the right people. They then are groomed to meet demands and specification that they will face further along in their career.

Often, women have been denied those experiences and, generally, have not assertively sought or recognized those routes. Lack of mentoring may have led to a lack of anticipatory career positioning for many women. The gap and limited scope of the right experiences necessary to gain a superintendency, for instance, have hurt women's chances. Glass ceilings have been easily installed and maintained.

Lack of Mentoring: Mentoring to increase women's political savvy and career positioning know-how has been lacking for a variety of reasons. In certain cases, potential male mentors did not consider that women would want to lead or were interested in leading. In some organizations, cross-gender mentoring was discouraged because the relationship held the potential for being misunderstand as something more than career support. Women in influential positions have also failed to mentor women for several reasons. Many pioneer female leaders lacked understandings of the power and processes of mentoring behavior.

Internal Barriers and Bias Against Women: Many studies have reported that "discrimination is as deceptively complex as it is pervasively subtle". Discrimination against women exists in every culture to varying degrees of intent, severity, cruelty, and damage. Historically and globally, classifying groups as inferior and weak has been comforting and satisfying to the self-image of others. However, as with any other discrimination, entire cultures suffer due to the loss of potential talents and contributions of the group being stifled.

Findings in a study of female higher education administrators in Florida ring true to women in other settings. Study participants identified barriers to their advancement as numerous subtle biases. For instance, they recalled examples of being ignored during important discussions, interrupted when attempting to make a point, and dismissed through references that indicate or assume that a male really was the one to complete a solid project or make a successful decision (Stokes, 1984).

Patterns of low expectation begin very early with the school experience of many girls. Studies by the American Association of University Women (AAUW, 1992) and compilations of research by Sadker, Sadker; and Klein (1991) highlight he gender bias existing in our schools at all levels. Female students are not just unevenly treated; they are harassed and abused by their male peers and by school personnel according to Shakeshaft and Cohan (1990). Early, consistent treatment conveying the message that females are less deserving and less worthy erodes self-esteem with lifelong effects. Internal barriers keep women from advancing in their educational careers. Barriers range from a personal lack of confidence to a fear of challenging the cultural expectations of their role. A study of Canadian school administrators by Brathwaite in 1986 attributed lack of female advancement through district ranks as stemming largely from their oversaturation with the cultural message of female inferiority within white male systems.

THE AREAS WERE TRAINING IS NEEDED

(A) KNOWLEDGE

Education
1. Economics
2. Problems
3. Trends and Innovation
4. Community Participation
5. National development

Educational Management
1. Principles of Management
2. Organization
3. Personnel Management
4. Leadership
5. Decision making
6. Public relations
7. Human relations

Educational Law
1. Education codes and Regulations

Educational Planning
1. All aspects

(B) SELF DEVELOPMENT

1. Ability to deal with the people
2. Clarity of objectives

3. Effective communication
4. Ability to accept criticism
5. Ability to listen
6. Judgement for situational appropriateness
7. Concern for self-respect
8. An aptitude for innovative thinking
9. Endeavour to derive satisfaction from job

(C) MANAGEMENT PROCESS

1. Identification of constraints and opportunities and planning towards long term development.
2. Decision making
3. Time management with special reference to time wasters and savers.
4. Financial managements
5. Training in co-operative and collaborative management
6. Develop ability to adopt more flexible management styles
7. Coping with problems and stress and be able to work in harmony regardless of gender

OTHER FACTORS

Besides training in self - development and management process, administrators need to be aware of the constraints from the environment and how the same could be converted to opportunities so that they could achieve the maximum possible development in line with their potentials.

1. There is felt need to have a shift from administrative procedures, rules and regulations mainly restrictive, inhibiting and over protective by nature to an -efficient management system where administrator can manage the resources– and talent with encouragement and trust. The present atmosphere of over centralization of policy and its implementation should give way to policy, only in broad terms and implementation left to the second line and junior level administration.

2. A large number of reports highlighted the subtle encouragement to women aspirants for positions of authority built in our system. There is apparently a - basic double standard latent in our educational system. A legitimate feminine perspective should exist as a healthy parallel to the dominant male role, and it must be integrated in the growth and progress of the country.
3. Women should be encouraged to participate in educational administration by way of offering suitable curriculum, providing opportunities for entry into the job's situat.cn and also opportunities for advancement These can he achieved only if we provide suitable working hours, management training for resource use especially time and energy, role adjustment providing incentives or facilities offering family support, appropriate socialization for girls to become career minded and providing residence close to place of work and providing the cultural and financial support.
4. In formulating policies for women's development and in particular active participation and association of women in higher education, there is a need for a shift in the recognition of women from being regarded as targets of welfare policies in the social sectors to their being regarded as critical groups for development. The country's development is not possible without the willing and conscious participation of one half of its population, namely, women. Through such participation women should be able to reduce if not overcome the resistance and barriers to equality and development. Another wind of change that is blowing is the new thrust that is being imparted in the development thinking which recognizes the impcrtance of economic independence, status, educational freedom and social freedom for women in society. The growth of organized articulation of

women's problems by social organization and revival of social debate on women's issues are so important that government should come out with strong legislative and institutional support.

For women, to be actively involved in administration, the major policy making activity should not be the prerogative of only one sex. It is in the national interest that the abilities of women need to be used as well as those of men. If the woman has the extra burden of caring for the family, some policy decision has to be made regarding the equivalent women positions to men positions in an organization. Because of the continued biological role women have to perform and the unwillingness of men to share household duties, some concessions in work load have to be given for women to do the assigned work effectively and meaningfully.

Most of the studies concerning administrators define the term with reference to the expected qualities or characteristics of the person holding such a position. The executive or manager should be innovative, alert, risk taking, progressive, tactful impressive and must possess leadership qualities. Traits like confidence, determination, dedication, hard work and boldness are necessary for career women.

REFERENCES

Agarwal K. C. "Female Executive in Government Systems" Social Change; Vol. 20 (2) June 1990.

Aparna Subramaniam, Work Patterns of the girl child, The Indian Journal of Social Work Jan. 52(1) 1991.

Kapoor Promilla, "Women in Administration in India" Vikas Publications Bombay 1990.

Kraisonswasdi Napasi "Women Executives, A Sociological Study in role effectiveness" Rawat Publications, Jaipur 1989.

Larson L. E. System and Subsystem perception of Marriage and Family, 1974.

Mahajan Amarjit, "Women's Two Roles, A study of Role conflict" Indian Journal of Social Work, Vol. 26 No. 4 Jan. 1966.

Parikh Indira J. and Shah Nayana, "Women Managers in transition, From Homes to Corporate officers" Indian Journal of Social Work VOl. L.V. No. 2 April 1994.

Rao V. N. and Parthasarathy R. "Stress and Strain" of Executive Implications for Mental Health Approach" Indian Journal of Occupational Health, Vol. 39(3) 1996.

11

Population Issues and Women

The National Health policy formulated by the Government of India in 1983 underlined the importance of health education in the country. It says: The recommended efforts on various fronts, would bear only marginal results unless nationwide health education programmes, backed by appropriate communication strategies, are launched to provide health information is easily understandable form to motivate the development of an attitude for healthy living. As the United Nations population division has revealed that every year, half a million young women die from causes related to pregnancy and child birth. Every year more than 14 million children die before reaching the age of five. Many of these deaths occur when births are more than four in total, or closer together than two years are to women who are younger than 18 or older than 35. Here education has a pivotal role to play in the reduction maternal mortality, infant mortality and in family planning, birth interval and utilization of maternal and child health care.

The gender ratio, the number of females per thousand males, was low in India to start with and continues to fall : as of the last count there were 927 women per thousand men. In South Asia, the discrimination against girls and women is wide spread. Bias against girls is evident when boys receive better care nutrition and access to health services, education and job skills advantages that carry over into adult life. A strong preference for sons, combined with social factors, contributes to the skewed gender ratio in the region.

The global attitude to population figures, especially of developing countries, has influenced many a nation's policy on fertility control. Women, on account of her generally low social, economic and political status has become the target of this control. Although the clamour to assert reproductive health rights rises to deafening volumes on all international for a, the poor women of the third world are not seen as deserving to claim them. The existing Indian social reality shows that the society is hierarchically stratified like layers of cake : about 15 million are rich enough to enjoy an abundance of the luxuries of a consumer society, followed by about 100 million comfortable well off, adequately clothed, fed and household. About 300 million struggling to remain above the poverty line, followed by 400 million below poverty line are unable to obtain even the minimum required for human survival.

In India the position of women is still worst and they are marginalized with in the marginalized society. Women are suppressed in socio-economic political and cultural spheres. Women have to struggle very hard to make a living. The demand of dowry, less employment opportunities, deprived of adequate health facilities, less preferences for education, sexual harassments and denial to get basic amenities are the everyday reality.

It is important that transformation of our social system so that not only are woman included, but existing patterns are changed. Intrinsic to this transformation is an understanding of how patriarchy has influenced our social structures. Patriarchy is actually is the 'rule of the fathers'. It pervades every form of life and is also reflected in our view of the organization of the cosmos. Most men and women are socialized into specific psychic development. We have been taught to feel in competent in exercising roles assigned to the other gender. The first stage of liberation therefore is an explosion of consciousness. To free oneself to think beyond gender stereotypes. Attitudes to women and their relationships with men are clearly an area where there is a struggle between the perspectives of most cultures. There is a need to express equality and mutuality of women and men at home and in society at large.

The cause of women's ill health are necessarily rooted in the economic and social realities of their existence. Abject poverty and the sheer burden of survival for her and her family resulting in over work, under nutrition and stress are the main causes of the majority of women becoming and remaining ill. Compounding the problem is the generally unjust social political and cultural order defined by patriarchal structures that denies her control over her own body and equality of treatment at all levels within the family, the community and society.

In the context of gender equality, the burden of gender roles and responsibilities is being thrust upon the women alone and the politics of gender is not being addressed. Gender equality is being seen an answer to all the problems of society. The historicity of subordinated gender roles and relations has been depoliticized. Women's perspectives are not sought on issues of trade, finance, the growth of military complexes at the cost of development, nuclear politics and so on. Unemployment and poverty lead to unhealthy conditions and hence to higher mortality. This reduced chance for the survival of infants leads to producing more children, low paid labour implies that more people who can work are needed so that the net income is a little more adequate for survival. Children are not a burden, they are a necessity in some social situations. All this is too complicated a logic for population controllers who have such simple solutions! It is not important for those who are confident of and aim at finding a single overall solution. All these implications of being poor unemployed and less privileged are ignored, and what is stressed and accepted ? That these conditions led to more sex and hence greater children! The underlying assumption is that people do not understand their situation and they will never do so either. Poverty, unemployment and ill health are only manifestations of a structure of sin and exploitations operating in our society. The poor and women are victimized and dehumanized due to their unquestioning passivity which arises from a state of repression. Their dignity is deprived and their self worth is degraded.

A recent report on South Asia states that : "India has 35 million people who have no access to 'basic health facilities'. 226 million lack access to safe drinking water, half of the adult population is illiterate, 70 percent lacks basic sanitation facilities and 40 percent of the population survives in absolute poverty".

POLICIES ON HEALTH

Over the years, there has been a considerable expansion of infrastructure of health services. Primary Health Centres (PHC) increased from 725 in 1951 to 21,009 in 1993. Similarly, hospital beds increased from 117.2 thousand in 1951 to 810.5 thousands in 1991. A three tier system comprising Community Health Centres (CHS), Primary Health Centres and sub-centres has been one of the Eighth plan. Since the introduction of economic reforms, the central plan outlay for progress of the Department of Health has been stepped up.

The envision a society, where development is people-centred, in which the principles of gender equity, social and economic justice, people's and especially women's participation in decision-making at all levels, cultural plurality and ecological balance and accorded more importance than mere economic growth.

The fundamentals of human security being:

- the right to food security
- the right to clean and adequate drinking water
- the right to work and employment
- the right to basic health and education

The origin of family as an institution is lost in antiquity and whatever its destiny. It is difficult to envision its complete desire. These words of William Kenkel, a family sociologist, assure us that family will always be there for us to belong to. It is this long lasting institutional attribute of family, which as triggered the attention of sociologists, educationists and theologians to systematically search and implement ways for preserving and enriching the family life. Human institutions invariably change over time, and in this point, the family is no exception. The change that Indian family has undergone is so tremendous and yet there exists traces of antiquity in contemporary family. The changing nature of the family, which is the result of the changes in the entire society surrounding the family. Many of the discussions about man-woman relationships have been very divisive in the Western World and are now beginning to have the same negative consequences in this country.

Men and women are to be so intimately united that as complementary members as husband and wife. Likewise, it is just as undeniable a fact that the wife is the one who can respond to the gift of the husband by conceiving and giving a child which he must receive from her. In other words, in the marital act the husband and wife unite as complementary members to form a higher body. In fact, the way in which husband and wife, with their complementary roles, form one body is a sign of the way in which God and his people form one body. The complexity of family life is also another reason which necessitates a formal education in family life. In recent years population growth has become one of the most crucial human problems. The number of people in the world is growing at a staggering rate. Today, every tick of the clock add 3.3 people to the population. The rhythm would increase to 6.4 by 2009 if the same rate continues. The picture is not very rosy to conceive. If the crisis has not yet arrived it is just 'round the corner'. Every seventh person in the world is an Indian today. In India there has been a phenomenal rise in the population in the last few decades.

Most of the countries of the world experienced rapid population growth after World War II but not as a result of an increase in the birth rate, as was the case in the United States and certain other western countries, but as a result of a commendable decline in the death rate which are continuing to come down as they should, while birth rates in the majority of the developing countries remain very high. It is now obvious to all people working in the field of population that the rising aspirations of the world's people can never be achieved unless population growth and economic development are brought into balance. Furthermore, this desired reduction in fertility will not be achieved by appealing only to the adult generation. The world's young people, who will become the magnitude of the population problem, if educated to recognise that a small family is not only proper but highly desirable and easily attainable.

The aim of education is to increase knowledge and ways of knowing, to develop understanding and awareness, and hopefully, to help us to achieve wisdom in the conduct of our lives, both as individuals and collectively These aims are shared by the new field that has come to be called population education.

POPULATION EDUCATION

Population education in a broad way can be defined as 'an educational programme which provides for a study of the population situation in the family, community, nation and the world, with the purpose of developing in the students a rational and responsible attitude and behaviour towards that situation'. Under this widespread umbrella many things can be included in population education but the selection of content, the emphasis and the methods of treatment will obviously vary from place to place, culture to culture and the stage of the development of a particular country. It is, therefore, necessary that there is no rigidity about the content or emphasis of population education. However, a few major areas are clearly identifiable which could form the core of population education. The specific objectives of helping the young, eventually to make more rational decisions concerning their own behaviour on population matters.

The goals of population education are to develop understanding the impacts of population characteristics and processes on national development both in the short and long run, as well as their impacts on the individual and his family. Thus, population education deals with society at both the macro and micro levels. As such, it serves a dual purpose. First, it serves to develop an informed citizen capable of understanding population characteristics and processes as they affect society, and capable of making responsible decisions with regard to public as it might affect, and be affected by these processes.

Secondly population education aims at developing informed individuals who will, as a result of the knowledge and understanding achieve through their education, make responsible decisions concerning their own reproductive behaviour. This is the beginning of wisdom which represents the moral and ethical purpose of population education. Population education seeks to bring about a realization of the individual, family, social and environmental effects of the explosive increase in human population, the rapid shifts in concentration and distribution of people, the implications of changing age and other demographic patterns and the conceivable options that may be open to mankind to cope with the consequent problems. While it is not confined exclusively to a particular age group, it is focused primarily on students who will become the principal child-bearers within one or two decades.

It is obvious from these rather evolved statements that it is not easy to reduce the content and objectives of such a broad area of learning into a concise definition. Population education is a relatively new concept and it seems more logical to explain it, in terms of objectives rather than by a single definition. One of the best such enumerations was compiled by Bhatia in 1969. His six primary objectives of population education are :

- Basic understanding of population dynamics including the growth rate and structure of population in the country in the context of world population.
- Appreciation of the significance of the population characteristics for the present and future quality of life including economic development and the attainment of a high level of health, education, housing, diet and other amenities of life.
- Realization that the size of the family can be easily planned for the benefit of individual families and that Large families are not necessary in the present day.
- Understanding of the health risks involved for the mother and the child.

- Appreciation of the small family as a setting in which a high quality of life for each person is more likely to be attained.
- Understanding of the Governments' Family Planning Programme in relation to the country's need.

NEED FOR POPULATION EDUCATION

- Rapid population growth is a threat to economic development, specially with respect to the per capita economic growth. The greater the population, the less there is to distribute to the people. In India the growth of economics is just being 'eaten up by even more rapid growth of population. The main reason why the Indian economy continues to be an economy of shortages is that the country's excessive population growth. This means that the population increases rapidly as a result of death control but the increase in the production of food and other necessities does not keep pace.
- The second crucial problem which the country is facing is that of providing adequate food for more and more people. While the achievements of the green revolution have been spectacular for the welfare of the millions of Indians, it is still modest in terms of actual needs.
- Rapid population growth in the last half century has also affected the structure of our population, for a growing population is usually a 'Young population'. Almost half of the population of the country today is less than 16 years of age whereas the median for most advanced countries is 30 to 35 years. A young population requires a particular kind of expenditure to support it, a proportionately large outlay is required for supporting the social services needed for it, like education, health and other facilities etc.

Due to the realization that this is where the problem is most immediate, existing population programmes tend to be aimed at those already in the reproductive group. In this regard it would be worth-while to remember Sloan Wayland's very emphatic remarks. "As countries around the world have been working to bring the population increase into a balance with the general effort at economic and social development one important lesson has been learnt. The lesson is that the dramatic success experienced in reducing death rates in a short period of time cannot be duplicated in action to decrease the birth rate." The whole business of family planning and reduction of birth rates is not "once for all" affair, nor is it concerned with only the population currently capable of bearing children. Perhaps more vital problem is that of young people who will constitute the adult population of the world in the next three decades. Over 45% of our population is under 15 years of age and this group will strongly influence the demographic in the cultivation of a desire amongst the youngsters to adopt family planning as a way of life. If the future population behaviour resembles that of their parents, today's population problem will be regarded by comparison, only as a minor one. If on the other hand, these young people become cognizant of the factors of their population situation and recognize that it warrants more decisions on an ever more rational basis which is of vital importance for developing responsible parenthood. Perhaps the quintessence of "Responsible Parenthood" is their capacity and the desire to take rational decisions in regard to one's own family size. In other words, responsible parenthood and responsible fertility behaviour are very close.

These can be achieved only when we catch them young and through proper education develop right attitudes amongst the vast population which has yet to enter fertility age-group and thus strengthen and enlarge the area of commitment towards checking population here that population education becomes relevant as a motivational instrument which will prompt the younger generation with a desire to adopt small family norm. This desire should grow out of both the concern for 'over population and quality of life. Thus, population education is not only concerned with population awareness but also with developing attitudes and values so that quality and quantity are taken care of.

ROLE OF HOME SCIENTISTS IN IMPARTING POPULATION EDUCATION

To a great extent, what makes us healthy, or unhealthy, is how we are able to live our daily lives - what we eat, how we exercise, how much rest we get, how much stress we live with, how safe or hazardous our work-places are, some of these things are under our control as individuals. Many, however, are not; we can influence them only by working with others to bring changes (Narasimhan, 1993). Information that is made available to those who want it, in the form of pamphlets. Audio-visual materials is also made available, for the dissemination of unbiased information so that women may "make their own decision as individuals". Such information is essential, because they rarely have access to unbiased and complete information on drugs and procedures imported from the West as "the latest" in medicine or treatment".

1. Academician

As we say, if a man is educated, he is educated individually but if a woman is educated, it means that the whole family is educated. The Home Scientist can give population education, teach them about family planning devices / methods and explain their advantages, importance and uses.

As an academician, she can teach the students about population growth, birth rate, death rate, migration, reasons and consequences of the population growth. Like this, she can give the education to the students as a part of the curriculum and she can also take up research and action project related to family planning. She can also teach all these things to her family and also to her neighbours. She can impart education to her child at the time of his/her marriage and let them know about different safe methods of family planning.

2. Communicator

As a communicator the Home Scientists can also impart population education. In the rural areas as well as in the urban communities, the home scientists can arrange talks, discussions for family planning. They can teach about methods, devices of family planning to the people, number of children one should have in the family, spacing between the two children etc. The population education can be effectively given by using teaching aids like charts, posters, flashcards flannel boards, video films, etc.

3. Non Formal Educator

Home scientists can play a very important role by:

(a) Continuing to develop and refine the objectives, scope and content of population education at various levels.

(b) Helping in stimulation and orientation of various concerned agencies is another major task that Home Scientists can undertake - starting on one hand with Ministries of Education and Educational Administrators and including all types of educators and teachers. It is most important to present them with the relevant facts and convince them of the importance of population education as a part of their teaching experience.

(c) The third area of work for Home Scientists lie in the sphere of conducting pilot programmes in schools, colleges, in teaching-training activities among out-of-school groups.

(d) Home Scientists can take studies and research and can provide invaluable help by carrying out attitudinal, cultural and other studies to help evolve the content and methodology so essential for a new and unprecedented programme dealing with human relations and humanity.

(e) Teachers can also arrange role plays, street plays, bhavai, puppet shows and folk media for giving concerned information to the people.

CONCLUSION

Population education is a new area and no model exists which could be adopted to suit the conditions prevailing in our country. We have to tread a new ground keeping in view our cultural background and present needs and future aspirations. The essence of the program should be to give the learner an insight into the totality of issues connected with population including the nature, causes, determinants, consequences of population growth, both at the micro and macro levels, the nature and dynamics of the reproductive process and finally the possibilities of planning family size and population growth.

Hopefully, the acquisition of such an insight may develop an understanding and attitude that contribute positively to rational decision making, both at an individual level and as a member of society when occasion for such decision-making arises. To quote Stephen Viederman "The aims of education are to increase awareness and hopefully to help us achieve wisdom in the conduct of our lives, both as an individual and collectively. These aims are shared by the new field to be called Population Awareness Education - population education as a result of the knowledge and understanding achieved through their education and make responsible decisions concerning their own reproductive behavior.

Research and Programme Evaluation should be included as a part of the development of a national programme from the very beginning. Knowledge of the nature of population learning and the development stages of population learning are obviously of the greatest importance to teachers and curricula developers. Thus, population education is no more nor less sensitive than anything else that we may teach in schools. It differs from much else that we teach in the sense that it may be more relevant to the students' own life, both now and in the future.

A UNDP report said that about 500 women who die daily from AIDS are between the ages of 15 and 25. The report said that the most of the third World where AIDS is predominantly a heterosexuality transmitted disease, there are as many women infected as men and sometimes more. The UN report cited physiological social and behavioural causes for the high rate of HIV infection among young women. "Society needs to break the silence surrounding the infection of young women", the study said, adding that more is known about the genital tract of female monkeys than of young women.

According to the report one factor that puts young women at greater risk for HIV infection may be the immaturity of their genital tract. From the onset of menstruation until their early 20s, the vagina is lined by a thin, tissue membrane that provides a less efficient barrier to viral attack than the thicker membrane of older pre-menopausal women.

In the field of reproductive health, not enough attention is paid to research and the production and distribution of safe contraception for women and men. The market for contraceptives is booming and, therefore the corporate world also maneuvers birth control policies of many states callously to ensure their profits, regardless of the implications the contraceptives hold for women's health.

Ignorance, illiteracy, poverty, lack of communication and transport add to the problems of inadequate availability of appropriate maternal care at desired places. Women need to be educated about their own health and men need much greater awareness about the health problems women face. All these factors create obstacles in the way of availability as well as utility of scientific maternal care. A vast network of health service units in hospitals and clinics provide maternal and child health care and family welfare services. An intrinsic part of the total family welfare programme is the extensive government machinery providing information, education and communication services to mobilize public opinion. Information, education and communication are fundamental to the persuasion and mobilization of couples to avail of health and family welfare facilities as well as for removal of fears and misconceptions. In all these activities, engagement of women can get fruitful results. Since the inception of the Family Welfare Programme, the strategy of the government of India has been to involve large number of women in the implementation of the programme. The strategy of involving women voluntary organization on a large scale to promote family welfare services as a people's movement can provide unique results in the field.

REFERENCES

Anthony, A. 1974. et. al. Population Growth and Development, Indian Social Institute, New Delhi.

Chalam, K. S. Promoting Family Planning through Non Formal Education, Indian Journal of Adult Education, Vol. 42. No. 1-2. Jan.-Feb. 1981. pp. 25-28.

Jersild, A. T. 1974, The Psychology of Adolescents, McGraw Hill Book Company, New York, pp. 278.

Kothari, Prakash, Sex Education mist, Times of India (Delhi) 5th Feb. 1991, p. 4.

Kakar, V. N. Communication in Family Planning, India's Experience, Published by the National Institute of Health and Family Welfare, New Delhi.

Mehta, T. S. 1972. et. al. Population Education Selected Reading, Population Education Cell, National Council of Education Research and Training, New Delhi.

Moses, S. and C. Praveena, A study on Sex Education, Its need and attitude of adolescent, Journal of Family Welfare, 30 Vol. Dec. 1983, p. 34.

Nair, G. R. Towards Zero Population, Communication Revolution in Family Planning, Social Welfare XXXIV, No. 9. Dec. 1987, pp. 32.34.

National Baseline Survey of Population Education in India, National Council of Educational Research and Training, New Delhi. 1980.

Pandya, K. 1990-91, Development of a question bank of sex education unit of science syllabus of IXth Std. at the Rural Secondary Schools of Baroda, M.Sc. (Home) dissertation, Faculty of Home Science, M.S.U. Baroda.

Sen, A. K. Population growth and nutrition problems, A case study for population education, Indian Journal of Adult Education, Vol. 43 No. 3 march 1982 pp. 10-13.

12

Environment Education a Tool to Protect Mother Earth

Discussion and disputes on environment mainly centre around the man made world and its environment as created by human agency. This man-made environment is the outcome of his cultural evolution, which has far outstripped his biological evolution, defying often the force of natural selection. Industrial revolution necessary for improving human existence making life comfortable and of general interest, green revolution to do with poverty, transport for comfort. But during this process of development the same man forgot to realize that he has but this one planet in which to live, and that he must learn to work for this environment and not against it. This main aspect which was till now ignored engaged the attention of the whole world. The knowledge of how to maintain, protect and improve the human environment through appropriate environment education programme is therefore, vital to bring about environment consciousness of all people.

Man and environment are inextricable linked and what effects politicians, teachers, and students. No longer is environment education the sole concern of scholars of biological sciences. The knowledge and study of environmental problems is probably a subject of general education, it is only appropriate that people in the social sciences, and humanities now find it as relevant as their colleagues in the natural sciences. Sciences should not be separated from arts. Establishing relationship between world of objective reality is the function of art. The great artist is one who has successfully integrated vast areas of human experiences. Art serves to integrate when a man is intensely involved in his craft, he is at one with it and thus he is at one with nature and with himself.

The cost of correcting past and present mistakes are already staggering, not only this, the technologies which have produced them are now deeply embedded in the economics, social and political structures of developed nations. It is this aspect that the developing countries like India have a edge over the rich countries if we are willing to have a population policy and to reach just our goals on the so called standard of living we can restore and preserve the biological quality of our environment.

ENVIRONMENTAL EDUCATION IN THE INDIAN CONTEXT

India is a land of diversity and geographically from the Himalayas to Kanyakumari there are wide variations of topography. The mountains, the hills, the rivers, the plateaus and the plains offer a colourful variety. The question hence is, should education given to the children from these varied environment be uniform or should the educational planners and curriculum-makers, attempt to provide education best suited to the environments and the needs of the environment?

The variations in the environment include the following aspects :

(a) The urban and the rural,
(b) The industrial and the agricultural,
(c) The hills and the plains,
(d) The tribal and non-tribals, and
(e) The slum dwellers and the sophisticated.

The culture of any people is determined mostly by the environment in which they are brought up. Living conditions, needs, interests, attitudes, vocations, socio-physical education conditions, the economic situations and the cultural background of people vary based on the physical environment in which they live and grow.

Education at different levels should take cognizance of these factors and if they are ignored, it will not be a meaningful education. We require need based, life-oriented, environment oriented education. For a nation like ours which offers a wide variety of environments and hence a variety of culture and living styles, advocating a uniform pattern of education for all will fail to bring about the desired effect of education. Physical infrastructural facilities such as the building, administration aspects such as working hours of the institution, working days, vacation, the curriculum, the teaching methods and the teacher employment will all be influenced by the environment in which the educational institution is located. Education would then become realistic and pragmatic. Considering individual students capacity, mental ability and other such internal variables which are important in the context of education, environment is not the determining factor. Students will be of various mental levels, in all the environments. Environment may help to determine the achievement of students. A congenial local environment, where exposure to real education is provided by the elder will be a motivating factor for the pupils. Apathy and an attitude of disinterest deter the learners from doing their best in the context of education.

Today with the spread of mass media of communication such as the television, the computer and the other much needed equipment, the distinction, due to advantages or disadvantages of the availability or non-availability of the media as the case may be, between the rural and the urban environments is slowly fading away. Till such time, it is obvious that the learner placed in a city school has more exposure to knowledge in any area and especially science and technology, compared to the village school child. In competitive examinations, the city bred learner stands a better chance compared to his rural counterpart in the village. In the village, the learner enjoys excellent physical facilities such as extensive playground and pure air and unpolluted water, the crowded city student usually misses these great things of nature. Pupils placed in the midst of nature as in Courtallam or Kodaikkanal, are good at subjects like Botany, since they are surrounded by the plant kingdom, whereas the city child is more exposed to other sciences, since facilities in the environment are better for these subjects. Education programmes and courses should be planned and implemented, taking into consideration, the very vital role played by the environment in the life of learner.

SCOPE OF FORMAL ENVIRONMENTAL EDUCATION

The content of environmental education has four, integrating and interrelated components -

1. *Awareness:* It includes making the individual conscious about physical, biological, social and cultural aspects of environment. The environment is linked with the life support system which in itself has six components : air, land, water, flora, fauna and sunlight. These components have dynamic relationship. Man is the most important organism and has great responsibility.
2. *Real-life Situation:* These link environment to life. These conditions are location -specific. Thus, problems and priorities of each area are different.
3. *Conservation:* It means utilization of natural resources not only by the present but also by the future generations. It does not include the process of exploitation.
4. *Sustainable Development:* It aims at the wise utilization of resources for development. All resources are finite and there is also a limit to the growth of living system. Thus, efforts should be made to utilize the resources wisely and intelligently.

STAGE-WISE COURSE CONTENT

The course content of environmental education has been classified stage-wise, in the following four stages :

1. *Primary Education Stage:* Here the emphasis should be mostly (75 percent) on building up awareness, followed by real-life situation (20 percent) and conservation (5 percent). Thus, attempt should be made to sensitise the child about environment. The content to be used are surroundings from home to school to outdoor situations. Teaching strategy includes audiovisual and field visits.

At the school level NCERT has been playing vital role in designing syllabi, textbooks, help books, guide books, charts, kits, teaching materials and aids both for students and teachers.

2. *Lower Secondary Education Stage:* From the lower secondary stage onwards, the quantum of awareness must decrease while there should be increased knowledge of real-life situations, conservation and sustainable development. At lower secondary level, the objective must be real life experience, awareness and problem identification. The contents to be used are those used at Primary School level supplemented with general science. Teaching, practicals and field visits are to be done.
3. *Higher Secondary Education Stage:* At this stage the emphasis is laid on conservation, assimilation of knowledge, problem identification and action skills. The content used may be science-based and action-oriented work. There should be proper teaching, practicals and field work.
4. *College Education Stage:* At this level, the picture would be almost reverse of the Primary level. Maximum emphasis would be laid on knowledge regarding sustainable development based on experience with conservation followed in a descending order, by real-life situations and awareness. The content must be college-university based on Science and Technology. Teaching, practicals and action oriented field work should be done.
5. *University Education Stage:* Environmental Education at this level is being looked after the University Grants Commission. There is a high powered Committee to suggest areas of environmental education at postgraduate level. There are about 10 universities teaching courses in environmental areas. Besides these, there are also research institutes and professional institutions as Indian Institute of Technology, Engineering Colleges, Schools of Planning and

Architecture, which offer courses in environmental engineering. The University education has three major components : teaching, research and extension. At postgraduate level, four major areas are recognized.

(a) Environmental Engineering: It includes the subjects like architecture, civil engineering, town and country planning, including human settlement, slum improvement, landscape architecture, industrial design, regional science and urban ecosystem studies.

(b) Conservation and Management: It includes fields like land use, forestry, agriculture, energy, waste management, wildlife management, national parks, biosphere reserves, biological diversity, water management, mining management, non-polluting renewable energy development etc.

(c) Environmental Health: It deals with public health and hygiene, sanitary and chemical engineering, occupational health, toxicology, nutrition and drug use etc.

(d) Social Ecology: It includes subjects like human ecology, sociology, social planning, cost-benefit, community organization and services, psychology and counselling, environmental ethics and related areas of humanities.

Some institutes, centres assisted by the Department of Environment, provide formal education/training in environmental areas. For instance, Centre for Environment Education (CEE), Ahmedabad, Indian Institute of Forest Management, Bhopal and Indira Gandhi National Forest Academy, Dehradun.

NON-FORMAL ENVIRONMENTAL EDUCATION

The environment education has been designed both formally and non-formally. The environmental education is lifelong process for the welfare of mankind and the development of the society. It is designed for every age group, participating in social, economic, cultural development of the community. Groups or clubs arrange exhibitions, public lectures, meetings and environmental campaigns. The following constitute main content of non-formal environmental education.

1. *Adult Education:* It may influence adult members for better ways of life, through local language, information packs, posters, slides, audio, audiovisuals, etc.
2. *Rural Youth and Non-student Youth:* Organizing these into group the programmes of education may be taken up by involving their community leaders, women and youth in an important content of our forest wealth for tribals and forest dwellers.
3. *Children Activities:* These may include essay competitions of different age groups. With the help of United School Organization of India, the Department of Environment organizes such activities. On the spot painting, modelling and poster design contests are conducted for children by the National Museum of Natural History (NMNH). Short-term courses are also given by NMNH every year.
4. *Eco-development Camps:* These help in sound rural development involving youth. A set of guidelines has been preparea by Department of Environment in 1984. Its main objectives are to create awareness in student and non-student youth about basic ecological principles; to identify root cause of ecological/environmental problems; and to develop a spirit of national integration and emotional integration.
5. *Non-Governmental organization s (NGOs):* There are over 200 NGOs, involved in environmental education and awareness, including conservation, pollution control, afforestation and social forestry, floristic and faunal studies, rural development, wildlife conservation and waste utilization and eco-development.
6. *Public Representatives:* To discuss environmental problems facing the country India has Environmental Forums for MPs and MLAs. They may build up sound public opinion and stimulate public interest.

7. *Training Senior Executives/Administrators:* Regular courses should be arranged for various institutes imparting such training. General environmental management, industry-specific environmental management etc. should be included in M.B.A. courses.
8. *Foundation Courses:* The courses for the probationers selected for the I.A.S., I.F.S., I.P.S., and cadets and three wings of Armed Forces must be suplemented with foundation courses on environment relevant to their area of work.
9. *Research and Development Programmes:* In man and Biosphere and basic and applied environmental problems such programmes are supported by Department of Environment.
10. *Centres of Excellence:* Department of Environment has established two Centres of Excellence in India which generate knowledge and methodology and training in areas of Tropical Ecology (Bangalore) and Environmental Education (Ahmedabad).
11. *Development of Trained Manpower:* There must be training programmes for the trainers, professionals, technical personnel and legal experts.
12. *Development of Educational Material and Teaching Aids:* Audio, audiovisual materials, materials for media (TV, radio, films, newspapers, etc.), mobile exhibitions etc. must be designed by competent manpower. Centre for Environment Education, Ahmedabad in one such centre.
13. *World Environment Day:* All Governments in the States and U.Ts., academic institutions, universities, colleges, schools and voluntary organizations should organize suitable activities on June 5, The World Environment Day. The Department of Environment should support this financially.
14. *National Environment Awareness Campaign/National Environment Month:* Commencing from 1986, Department of Environment conducts NEAC and NEM. Every year from November 19 to December 18

is observed as NEM. Each year has a major environmental theme.

15. *Ministry of Environment:* There is separate Ministry of Environment in India.

Table 1
Impact of development activities on environment

Development activities	*Impact on Environment*
Forest clearing and land settlement	Extinction of rare species of flora and fauna, create breeding grounds for mosquito.
Shifting cultivation in upland agriculture	Soil erosion in upland areas. Soil fertility decline. If shorter cultivation cycle, flooding of low land areas.
Agro-industries e.g. Sugar and tapioca	Air pollution due to burning of bio gas as fuel in mills, large amount of highly polluting organic with surface water pollution.
Use of pesticides	Organisms develop resistance & new control methods needed. Leads to complex and widespread environment problems. Biological magnification, poisoning.
Timber Extraction	Degrades land, destroys surface soil, reduces production potential of future forest.
Urbanization and industrialization	Concentration of population, making huge dent on rural environment, air and water pollution.
Water resources projects	Human settlement and resettlement, spread of e.g. extensive irrigation, waterborne irrigation disease schist to somiasasis as in Egypt after Aswan construction, reduction of fisheries, salutation, physical changes, e.g. temperature, humidity.

Source: Lohani, Bindu, N. 1984. Environment Quality Management, Delhi.

Women are primarily responsible for the health, nutrition, hygiene level and comfort of their families. In this context women's access to natural resources like water is of extreme importance When women are facilitated, their homes and their hearths radiate with health and well being. When they are deprived dirt, disease and hunger are their lot.

Thus their involvement and interaction with their environment is intimate and immediate. Yet they have arguable access to the food they help grow, to the water they need to cleanse their families and maintain good health, to the fuel which they must gather to keep their homes fires burning and finally to the forest produce which they gather and sell to make a living. It is also sadly true that women have to walk long distance in search of these basic resources for less and less of them with the degradation. In the forests they are at the mercy of the forest guards, contracts and officials.

In the Third World countries, the lives of women and this is particularly so in the rural areas, are intimately tied around the households. And to manage the households, the women are inextricably dependent on their primary resources : land, forest and water. These resources are a gift that Nature has lodged in the immediate environment and eco-systems surrounding the human settlements. Over centuries of experience and observation, the women have developed a knowledge and talent for conserving and nurturing these resources. They have learnt to manage them both respectfully and sustainability.

Three levels have been identified to underline the relationship between women and the physical environment. First environmental problems should be gender-sensitive because any deterioration in the physical environment results in a heavier burden on women in the performance of their multiple domestic roles Secondly, women's lives interest with changing environments in the context of poverty and lack of loss of their traditional rights in the forests. And thirdly, the women's role as environmental problem solvers through their group strategies calls for their empowerment. These measures will materially help the process of reorientation of development from pure economic growth to one of ecological advancement which has no doubt, an urgent need. Politicians, policy makers and bureaucrats need to understand the link between women, environment and development. Many times we have seen either women alone are addressed or environment alone. The true has come now to realize the symbiosis between the two.

Women's work often interfaces with their physical environment. They are not only nurtures and nourishers of their families, children and dependents but are also economic producers, though often in an intangible manner. Their work in food production, agriculture and farm work, in forests - whether in afforestation or in gathering forest produce, is an area that is most often taken for granted as part of wider activities in the community. It is now being increasingly conceded that environmentally sustainable development will be best strengthened by empowering women and their grassroot organizations. The emphasis has to be placed on the participatory process which allows women to increase their control over their own lives. Many recent attempts at development have only served to women the position both of women as well as of the natural resources.

In order to both conserve the environment and promote the advancement of women, it has become necessary to give the issues of ecology and development an intellectual analysis from the view point of women. We need to harness rural resources and Technology for empowering women.

1. Need for Technology

1.1 Improves earning capacity «- increases output better publicity

1.2 Widens women's employment opportunities

1.3 Lessens drudgery of daily life

1.4 Encourages participation in general development of society

1.5 Mechanisation needed not only in agriculture but also in household tasks

1.6 Mechanisation contributes to professional mobility.

2. Implications of Technology for Rural Women

2.1 Positive implications

(a) Improvement in working conditions

(b) Dissemination of Information

(c) Work simplification.

2.2 Negative implications

(a) Displacement of women workers from employment

(b) Poverty in women headed households

(c) Poverty in poorest of poor families-widows, divorcees, handicapped, old women

(d) Decline in women's economic activities, thus, lowering their economic status
(e) Push back to manual drudgery-physical, nutritional, agricultural, occupational, social.

3. Reasons for Negative Implications

3.1 Biased traditions, customs and values
3.2 Stereotyped sex roles
3.3 Rigidity in implementation of sex roles
3.4 Overglorifying women's role of motherhood
3.5 Distrust of women's ability on part of employers

4. Appropriate Technology

4.1 Wind Mill
(a) Traditionally human or animal power
(b) Using diesel and electric pumps
(c) Several modern technologies utilised
(d) Use no costly energy
(e) Intermediate Technology
(f) Contribute to more efficient water lifting for irrigation and drinking purposes.

4.2 Biogas Plants
(a) An alternative to scarce energy sources
(b) Product of fermentation of animal and/or human excreta and water
(c) The gas suitable for cooking, lighting and running engines
(d) Byproduct - Slurry - high quality fertiliser
(e) Reduces energy requirement
(f) Intermediate technology

4.3 Solar Cookers
(a) An alternative intermediate technology to reduce use of scarce energy
(b) Mechanisation is extremely simple not more than a black box covered with flat glass plate.

4.4 Power Crushers
(a) Small scale oil crushers
(b) Use electric power

(c) Replaced labour intensive oil crushing equipment using animal power
(d) Oil crushed for cooking purposes

4.5 Potters Equipment
(a) Traditionally earthenware pots
(b) Produced by specialised castes of potters
(c) On potters wheels
(d) Shaila Potters wheel (Power wheel - KVIC)
(e) An improved fuel saving design.

4.6 Hand Pumps
(a) To improve water supply
(b) Water lifting from open wells by means of bucket and rope
(c) More convenient and hygenic
(d) Electric pumps also used
(e) Hand pumps more dominant technology
(f) Shortage of electricity
(g) Repair and maintenance of electric pumps.

5. Points to ponder

5.1 Application of technological innovations in areas of women's work in developing countries.

5.2 Assessment of impact of new technologies on the quality of life of women.

5.3 Analysis of problems which women confront in utilizing technological innovations.

5.4 Evolving strategies and mechanisms to overcome these problems and maximise positive impact of technology on women.

5.5 Communicating and disseminating technological information and skills to women in formal and non-formal ways.

5.6 Evolving and implementing necessary legislations to promote and protect women in these jobs where technologies are used.

5.7 Creating political will to encourage use of technologies in women-dominated jobs.

ROLES OF THE HOME SCIENTIST

1. She should correlate the topics of environmental issues while teaching her own subject matter.
2. She should help individuals in providing awareness of and sensitivity to the total environment and its allied problems.
3. She should create an awareness regarding renewable and non-renewable resources or environment.
4. She should help her pupils to acquire basic understanding of the total environment, it associated problems and humanity's critically responsible presence and role in it.
5. She should use play-way techniques to make them understand the significance of food chains and food web on ecological balance.
6. She should help her students to acquire social values, strong feelings of concern for the environment and the motivation for active participation in its protection and improvement.
7. She should conduct activities like drama and Role Plays on environmental conservation.
8. She should help individuals to acquire the skills for solving environmental problems.
9. She should organize field trips to zoos, national parks, polluted cities, polluted rivers, birds sanctuary, etc.
10. She should help her pupils to evaluate environmental measures and education programmes in terms of ecological, social and aesthetic factors.
11. She should organize seminars and workshops on environmental issues like soil erosion or population explosion, etc.
12. She should help students to develop a sense of responsibility and urgency regarding environmental problems to ensure appropriate action to solve these problems.
13. She should arrange lectures on topics of environmental concerns.

14. She should teach the interdependence of living things as the relationship between the needs of society and the interaction with the environment.
15. She should discuss environmental issues alongwith simple teaching activities through which people understand the significance of environmental resources.
16. She should motivate and train to acquire and spread knowledge and skills that will help society solve interrelated environmental problems and prevent their occurrence.

REFERENCES

Adam, D. Planning between cultural paradigms, Traditional knowledge and Transition to ecological sustainability, Dissertation Abstract International, Vol. 60(7). Jan. 2000.

B. N. Neelima, Communication for Environmental Education, JRF, Deptt. of Journalism, Sri Padmavathi Mahila University, Tirupathi.

B. R. Kukreti. Environmental education-A Blue Print, University News, August 16, 1993.

Bharat B. Dhar, Environmental education in ındia, University News, 38(6), February 2000.

Bhatia, A. Women's Development and NGO's, Rawat Publications, Jaipur and New Delhi. 2000.

Francois, N. Cultivating the human environmental for the adoption and use of information technology, Dissertation Abstract International Vol. 60(7), Jan. 2000.

G. R. Chhatwal, Encyclopaedia of Environmental Education, Anmol Publications Pvt. Ltd. New Delhi. 1998.

Iyer S. Blue Print for Environmental action, Social Welfare 40(8) June 1996.

Jain, R. Sustainable Development, Policy and Practices 1st ed. New Age International Publishers, Australia 1997.

K. B. Powar, Environmental issues and University, University News, November 22, 1993.

Onkar N. Srivastava, Environment and Sustainable Development, University News, January 13, 1992.

Prakash, J. Srivastava, S. K. Environmental problems, policies and strategies, Mohit Publications, New Delhi 1999.

Rs. 60 crore for environmental studies. University News, November 12, 1990.

Sharma, S. Managing Environment : A Critique of "The Tragedy of Commons", Journal of Human Ecology, Vol. 12(1) 2001.

Subramanyam, V. and K. R. Rama Moham Tribal Ecology and Food Scarcity. Journal of Human Ecology, Vol. 12(5) pp. 351-356. 2001.

Vishwanandha K. R. Environmental Impact on the Economic Life of Yeruka Tribe, Journal of Human Ecology Vol. 12(4) pp. 267-270. 2000.

Yogendra K. Sharma, History of Problems of Education (Volume-2), Kanishka Publication, 2001.

13

Handling Globalization by promotion of Consumer Education

Introduction

Balanced development can only occur if we do not outright oppose the globalization yet find out ways to make people the stake holders in the change process. Thus it can be safely concluded that the globalization which is in a way result of new technology and communication. The globalization has given such a face lift that was not even dreamt before.

Globalization is a term which first appeared in the late 1980s in articles by Japanese economists in the Harvard Business review. According to the sociologist Donald Robertson, who is credited with popularizing the term globalization describes the tempering effects of local conditions on global pressures. Globalization is a perspective, be it in the context of institutions or organizations or services conceptually in terms of fashion or philosophy, as opposed to localization at the other end of the continuum is globalization. A culture of real virtuality, constructed around an increasingly interactive audio-visual universe has permeated mental representation and communication, integrating the diversity of culture in an electronic hypertext.

We have experienced in the last decade of the twentieth century the process of globalization. This has resulted into a sea change in the way different societies are interacting because of opening up of boundaries across the nations. This breaking of the political/geographical borders began to be termed 'globalization'. However what do we mean exactly by globalization? Is it the unconsidered consequence of the free flow of capital or the result of a deliberate political process ? In theory globalization means free flow of goods, ideas, individuals, capital and information. The impact of globalization is only just beginning to be felt. The globalization that affect the future of Indian economy and Indian families as a particular are of two kinds. First and foremost there is a strong demand for more materials, by every one they may be living in village, kasba, town or big Metros. Second due to change in the banking system and use of technology as a delivery tool to deliver goods anytime, anywhere just to promote marketing. The development of ATM machines, electronic cash registrars have become more and more part of everyday life.

The social and cultural invasion is the result of globalized world. We find international brands easily in the market and in the popular T.V. serials. The impact of globalization is so drastic that it is fundamentally transforming our environment, the way we may look, work of the market and the society itself. The new century being referred to as a "knowledge century" is, a century of innovation, enterprise, eco-entrepreneurship and genetic enhancement. Information technologies have given a new meaning to the concept of the world being a global village. At the same time, there are unacceptable levels of poverty, deprivation, environmental degradation and social and gender discrimination. "The rich-poor economic and technological divide is not only causing inequity at the level of the present generation, but is also enhancing inter-generational inequity".

CONSUMER

A consumer is a user of goods. Any person who uses goods for one or another purpose is a consumer eg. food, clothing, housing, books, transportation etc. Besides being a user of a commodity, a consumer is also a spender of money for satisfying wants.

The Importance of Consumer Education

Consumer education implies to educate the consumer and make her aware about her roles her rights and responsibilities. Consumer education helps the consumer to become conscious of considering the most urgently needed, highly useful and essential commodities suitable to her budget and also helps in developing decision making ability. Consumer education explains the role of the consumer in public policy and government regulations affecting the existing market system.

Today, more than ever before the consumers are faced with series of fundamental questions:

- How they can keep up with the rising cost of living ?
- How can they manage their personal resources are constantly becoming more and more scarce ?
- How they can distinguish between wise and unwise buying decisions ?

In order to deal effectively with these questions, today's consumers must be clearly informed consumers. Consumer education makes a person able to understand:

- What are the consumers problems ?
- How to purchase wisely ?
- How to evaluate sales and advertising ?
- How to guard against unwise buying practices and dishonest selling practices ?

Characteristics of the present day buyers

1. They are unorganized.
2. They are untrained as consumers.
3. They operate largely as individuals.
4. Many are unable to judge quality and price relationship.
5. Consumers lack reliable, measurable standards by which to judge products and services despite the sincere and useful effects of consumer organizations to help consumers improve their standard of buying.

Consumer Rights

15 March - World Consumers right Day

Consumers have many rights:

1. Right to safety
2. Right to be informed, correct, clear, adequate information about label and manual.
3. Right to choose - (No monopoly)
4. Right to be heard - Consumer to be heard
5. Right to seek redressal - If consumer are victims of some malpractices than they have a right to seek redressal i.e. they should get compensation for inferior goods and services. Under this right consumer can also seek help of court.

Consumers Responsibilities

Along with the rights consumers have also responsibilities.

1. Regarding the right to choose the consumer have the responsibility to.
   - Understand their personal motivation for buying certain products and services.
   - Recognize persuasive selling techniques.
   - Compare products for both price and quality.
   - Avoid buying-buying habit.
   - Choose carefully from whom they buy.
2. Regarding the right to safety consumers have the responsibility to.
   - Use products with reasonable, care and report defects. Carefully read products, labels and use products.
   - Question sellers about the safety attributes of products.
   - Inform Retailers manufacture industries and Government agencies when a product does not perform safely.
3. Regarding the right to information consumer have the responsibilities to.
   - Use available information.
   - Read advertisement and promotional materials carefully. Seek out accurate information about products and services.

4. Regarding the right to be heard consumers have the responsibility to.
   - Become informed and speak up about issues that affect all types of consumers.
   - Seek remedies to consumer problems.
5. Regarding the right to redress consumers has the responsibility to.
   - Know where and how to go seeking redress.
   - Seek satisfaction directly from the seller before using other form of redress.
   - Speak up when safety problems occur and when the quality of products or services are inferior.
   - Well appropriate use the legal (law) system.
   - Legal system such as state, country or city office of consumer affects.
6. Regarding the right to environmental health consumers have the responsibilities to.
   - Be informed about environment issues.
   - Learn the environmental effects of alternative products.
   - Compare products for their effects for the environment.
   - Make responsible and environmentally sound consumption choices.
   - Support sellers who practice positive environmental policies.
   - Support sellers to stop the use of consumer product that are harmful to the environment and to enhance availability of goods which are friendly to the environment.

The gap between the have and the have nots - those individuals and people that participate in the new economy they prosper and progress and those who do not lag behind. This is a problems of unequal support system like education, road, bank and communication.

All over the world the revolution in communication technology has influenced our lives. Globalization is the result of this phenomena. It has changed the quality of product and even the value system of man kind. There are several reasons of this change earlier the consumer had to go to the market to buy the products but it is not necessary any more he can just put up on the net, and collect the information or the product of his choice. As the world has come closer is just the most clichéd sentence we hear everyday. Communication ease has completely revolutionized the commercial arena with shop being in your house.

Shopping around the world today seems to be accessible, affordable and attainable with credit cards and bank loans; all aimed at attracting consumer. The other major impact of globalization is technologies are fuelling globalization, opening new markets and giving rise to new factors such as economic competition, empowerment and culture diffusion. The easy access to city and information due to globalized market to the rural woman has its impact on their overall life styles. Here it is important to mention that globalization to be successful it requires great foresight and systematic planning. Otherwise it may not yield good results. At the International scenario it may have worked but to make it work at grass root level a lot of initiatives and imagination is required.

The new concept calls for effective networking with the formal and non formal systems as well as innovation because the knowledge that one gathers during formal education system also gets out dated and needs to be updated. In view of this modern mode of communication can play a vital role in imparting consumer education. We know information is power. The arts and science of using information to one's advantage is one of the keys to widen influence and capture any society. Different government and NGOs, could generate necessary awareness among the masses. This can build important informed citizen to face the globalized world with confidence and ease. Following are some important strategies for promotion of consumer Education.

1. Public Education

The education represents formal, non formal and informal approaches to learning for developing the knowledge base, aiming to help in

- understanding the consumer laws, rights and responsibilities.
- forming independent opinion.
- knowing relevant methodologies.

This is a long term procedure it is important that proper curriculum should be planned and implemented so that the globalization impact is well taken. As education is a key to development. For any development to be self sustaining it is very important that values, attitudes knowledge and skill also change. To bring this change education plays a very important role.

Today the Educational and social demands have changed tremendously. We know that education helps in meeting the learning needs, societal expectations. However today's need is much more challenging as it needs to prepare the ground for accepting globalization and education can help as a catalyst for progress of the society by extending modernization.

2. Training Programmes

Training involves a set of learning activities oriented to objectives of improving knowledge; skills and attitude of individuals to carry out specific tasks based on appropriate techniques. Thus it may include the short term training programmes and exchange of knowledge through seminars, conferences, workshops, and group meetings. Training can help in moulding the mind of the next and current generation. The globalization has permeated into the society as well as in the business environment. This development of Globalization has lead to several changes in the behavior pattern of consumer and it is now important to have required competencies to cope up with the changing world. The competencies like make wise decision, critical thinking, communicating effectively. Well planned and designed consumer education can help cope with these situation to change.

The training and consumer education programmes aim at generating awareness/updating knowledge and skills of people at various levels. These programmes will not be very efficient and effective unless those who participate in these activities take very active interest in the related activities. Arrangements should be made to involve the persons who are active, failing which the spirit of the programmes will not gather momentum. Entering the new world which has globalization as the pattern of life. It is important that it may have many disputes between groups of people having different values and beliefs and which may create problems in our rapidly changing societies. It is strongly felt need to give training and education so that problem does not arise.

3. Extension Programmes

Community or village based out reach worker can be trained to provide consumer education. For this purpose of public information, radio, television and printed media with well designed and projected messages can be of great help. The process of training and education for living and working requires a continuous improvement and knowledge transfer between the various stake holders, like researchers, community leaders and volunteers. Training and education programmes in the area of consumer education are multidisciplinary and should have the following :

- Education and training programme must be an integral part of development planning.
- Oriented towards the most vulnerable sections of the society.
- Institutionalized as on going process.
- Based upon the outcome of training need analysis.

4. Research

The institute of higher learning which are involved in conducting research in traditional sciences and social sciences should include the area of Consumer Education and Globalization. The research findings may form the basis of formulating policy and may also open certain commercial ventures.

Research programme are strongly influenced, if not completely determined by the choice of the path to development. Sustainable development is a concept heavily dependent upon science and technology, but which dictates that it be not assumed that there exists a "technological solution" for every problem. It is important to have alternative path to sustainable development.

5. Technical Adivses

Senior faculty members of reputed universities / colleges can be consulted by various government, non-government public and private organizations for their expertise in the areas of consumer education as well as phenomena of globalization. We need a concentrated effort to use this vast human resource potential for conducting research and socio-economic analysis and globalization.

6. Knowledge Transfer

Course work in the subject Consumer Education can shape the minds of young people and also can accelerate their enthusiasm for working in this field. There is a major change in the government policy towards development. Since learning is essentially life long, an integrated, multisectoral approach would perhaps be most beneficial. While countries have been making efforts to bring about multisectorial coordination and integrate the functional literacy programmes with other developmental concerns, there is still a great opportunity to make consumer education a part of the agenda of other developmental agencies.

7. Literate Environment

It is important to develop a literate environment to help sustain the literacy and numeracy skills gained. This becomes particularly challenging in rural areas in multi-lingual societies Partnership with governmental and non-governmental bodies, to develop reading materials related to consumer education and make them widely available may be the most feasible approach. The environment-building activities would involve massive use of media of different kinds, ranging from folk media to electronic media including radio, T.V., press etc.

8. NGOs as an interface

Voluntary organizations can significantly contribute to strengthening the capacity of neighbourhood groups and local communities more effectively through awareness campaigns participatory capacity building training programmes, media campaigns etc. It is important to choose approach on the basis of contextual characteristics. Successful interventions have always tried to incorporate people's choices as they have evolved their coping strategies to several challenges facing their routine existence in adverse circumstances and globalization can be one of them.

9. Strengthening the capacity building initiatives

It is essential that the communities recognize that more effective approach will be preparedness; patience and feeling of brotherhood can reduce the damage to property and loss of lives when disturbance in the value system takes place. The capacity building efforts can be through sensitization, awareness campaigns, training programmes, printing and distribution of brochures and posters in regional languages etc. Print media and electronic media can be used to disseminate these messages. It is found to be effective if street theatre and Folk art forms are used in the awareness campaigns for promotion of consumer education.

10. Capacity Building in the Communities

It is necessary that the feeling of dependency which the people have on government and the sense of helplessness and expectations of external support to meet local needs should be replaced by a strong sense of confidence, self-dignity and self respect among local communities. This is possible only by conscious efforts of activities for real development, the "beneficiaries" must be replaced by empowered stake holders who are able to assert their self respect and dignity rather than being treated like objects destined to stay in misery, starvation, illiteracy and abject poverty. The collective will of the women can radically transform the society and can march ahead keeping pace with the globalized world. The coming together of union's from different countries and regions for exchanging experiences, learning new ways of overcoming the difficulties and facing challenges would go a longway in getting a better deal for women. This networking definitely would bring a new hopes for collective advocacy and struggles for a better future.

11. Home Scientist can play an Important role in promotion of consumer education

Home is the first school that any child goes to. The learning's acquired by the children about the science of Home are therefore, the most fundamental in the entire education of the children. Home science in India is recognized is fundamental education because of three major reasons :

1. There is a cultural, philosophical and religious value placed on "home" in India, which makes all knowledge and services to home worthy of teaching and research. Home Science fulfills a role which is fundamental to Indian philosophy and culture, by its virtue of specialized knowledge about improving the home and family living.
2. The industrialization in India has affected the structure and function of homes. The aspirations of people about their standards of living, jobs, and education, have been so much elevated that the traditional home and family living have been rendered less contributory to the development of individuals.
3. The social consciousness of Indian people is the highest in the current decade. The people have felt the need to make their own efforts to improve heir health, education, clothing and shelter. Home Science gives knowledge to achieve better health; buy or make better garments and fabrics; and build or improve the house and its equipment and furnishings. The modern need of education is in addition, fulfilled by making home science a vocational education.

The broad objective of home science as stated by Thyagarajan (1977) as follows: To impart general education in preparing pupils for a satisfying personal living, developing a wholesome personality, acquiring happy human relationships, and enriching one's life. At the same time it is also necessary to find the vocation for which one is most suited and getting the preparation for it.

Home Science is an interdisciplinary field of studies has linkage with other subsystems in the family as well as at national perspective, it is important to interact with all these systems for pooling the resources. Because of the tremendous change in the political, social and economical scenario it is need of the hour to educate the prospective consumer as well as prospective employees also.

The home scientist can help in consumer producer interactions and can help as catalyst. We have already established our role for family welfare, other roles should not be under estimated but it should be tapped. Home Scientists have very successfully contributed in the various government programmes. In the same lines, it is high time that linkages should be established between developed and developing worlds to ensure an exchange of better understanding of different value system and culture, knowledge of technology will ultimately help in better quality life.

Today this society is no longer only the immediate village, town or nation, but the world as global political, economic, social and cultural trends are bringing sea changes in all the countries of the world and India is no special ? No society remains static. A section of our Society is already moving towards a so called "Western" culture as global changes and leading to a homogenized world society.

Home Science has a unique problem to be tackled. There is a change in the urban section, which is very fast while another large section which co-exist in the rural society which is tradition bound culture of oppression and exploitation. Both women as well as traditional families need intervention to cope up with this change.

Today the environment in which the families are attempting to meet their needs for food, clothing and shelter are constantly changing. So we need to constantly analyse the development opportunities and research possibilities relevant to the local situations.

In order to reflect the social and economic realities of current needs we must consider the following points. Life style issues and emphasis on training home based business for self employment, community based participation to develop skills to help poor households.

- Skills in formulation of public and family policy measures, which can help the policy makers.
- Consumer affairs, consumer advocacy and consumer protection issues.
- Economic development of families in this era of globalization.

With the world rapidly becoming a global village, the role of teacher becomes a more responsible one. They should reorganize and rearrange the curriculum to build the future generation more capable of utilizing the global network for the benefit of mankind.

RECOMMENDATIONS

- Appropriate strategies should be evolved for improving interaction between journalists and consumer forum.
- Success stories of consumer forum need to be published through involving eminent personalities.
- Reports on consumer education, should be made news worthy by highlighting their relevance to society.
- Research on consumer needs to be strengthened.
- On consumer day, special supplements should be sponsored by advertisers in leading news papers.
- Out reach of folk media needs to be expanded through the involvement of Panchayati Raj Institutions and NGOs in the development and utilization of media.
- Notwithstanding all the attractions of the media, nothing can substitute the vital interpersonal contact of the teacher and taught (here the volunteer and learners) who are close to each other.
- Objectives of consumer education have to be carried to the people in the shortest possible time. This is a public relations functions.
- The massive training programme of consumer education personnel is to be reinforced by communication media.

- Interaction between media and civil society is an on going dynamic process and this new waves of technology "especially digitalization and compression can be new binders on media and civil society.
- Students can play an important role in environment building like slogan writing, nukkar nataks etc. As they can provide an important service in creating awareness about consumer rights and responsibilities.
- The centers should have a good network with other organizations working in the promotion of consumer Education in the country and abroad.

SUGGESTED CURRICULUM INPUTS

1. Non formal educational packages for all to develop work skills, social awareness and information about consumer education.
2. Formation and management credit and marketing cooperative.
3. Communication technology especially to develop programmes on consumer Education.
4. Media skills related to the many focal areas of the curriculum for use in media for promotion of consumer Education.

CONCLUSION

The fact of today is that there is less access to development resources and there lacks economic independence for women. Poverty, unequal pay, illiteracy, training poor participation in decision making has hit women very hard. Despite the fact that women work with land, cattle, looms, fish textiles etc. they have very limited access to market space, work space, training and market which would improve their economic future.

In India the female economic activity and participation is low as 30% as against 5% for men. Gender related discrimination in employment practices against women effect adversely. The problems faced by rural women are both structural and functional. Most women workers are unaware of their rights and implementation of legislations. The whole process of globalization, liberalization and privatization leading to SAP (Structural Adjustment Programme) and WTO (World Trade Organization) conditionalities is further pushing the women to the margins.

The broader understanding of the forces that shape women's lives is necessary to develop strategies that counter globalization's adverse impacts. Since there is gender oppression, it should be kept in mind that investing in women's capabilities and empowering them to achieve their choices and opportunities is the surest way to contribute to social, economic and overall cultural development. It is important that we must ensure an equal chance of access to knowledge, fulfillment and opportunity for both men and women equally.

The gap between the rich and the poor is increasing day by day, with disastrous consequences to achieving the U.N. goal of reducing poverty by half by 2015. Achieving FAO's World Food Summit goal of reducing the number of children, women and men going to bed hungry by half by 2015 from the present number of over 800 million may also not be achieved, since hunger today is essentially poverty induced.

It is important to know how change takes when local and global interface takes place. It ıs very important to understand how people in Asia need not be marginalized but can live with the market and yet have property rights of indigenous knowledge and have benefit from globalization.

Balanced development can only occur if we do not outright oppose the globalization yet find out ways to make people the stake holders in the change process and simultaneously gain from commercial exploitation of their resources. From the advent of globalization in 1991 it has affected the performance of all the major sectors of economy agrarian, industrial, banking, and monetary, state, enterprises, trade and environment.

It is very important to understand globalization as a multi-dimensional process rather than as a project with a predetermined objective. Thus it can be safely concluded that the globalization which is in a way result of new technology and communication which has tremendously shaken up the Indian psyche it has enlarged the horizon on one hand and on another it has diluted the concentration of quality. The globalization has given such a facelift that was not even dreamt of before. So it becomes very essential to concentrate and handle globalization by promotion of consumer education.

REFERENCES

APPEAL, Monitoring and Evaluation of Literacy and continuing Education Programmes, Practitioners Manual, UNESCO-Bangkok 1998.

C. Subramaniam, "Entering a New Age", The Hindu, May 10th 1999.

Chowld N.L. "INSAT, New Hopes, New Challenges", The Times of India, New Delhi 6th April 1982.

Clarke Arthur C. "New Communication Technologies and the Developing World" Media Asia, Vol. No. 1 Singapore 1981.

Das, Selvie P. Home Science for Better Child Development, In the proceedings of Eleventh Bienniel Conference of the Home Science Association of India, Pragati Art Printers, Hydrabad, 1973.

Delors, Jacques (1996) Report to the International Commission on education for the 21st century, Paris UNESCO Publication.

Francis Soundararaj "Our Colleges should Respond to Global Trends" The Indian Express Sept. 21, 2000.

"Globalization and Culture", The Competition Master, Nov. 1999, p. 294.

Hemaprabha, G. Home Science in Secondary Education, In the proceedings of the Twelfth Biennial Conference of the Home Science Association of India, Bagyam Printers, Coimbatore, 1974.

Kittrell, Flemmie P. The Mission and Future of Home Science Today, Lecture given at the Faculty of Home Science, Baroda, India, December 8, 1977.

M. S. Swaminathan, at the World Conference on Science, converned by UNESCO and The International Council for Science (ICSU), in the Budapest, July 1999.

Maddison John, "Radio and Television in Literary" Reports and Papers on Mass Communication No. 62 UNESCO, Paris 1990.

Mrinal Pande, "Neo rich of the 21st century", The Hindu Folio, Aug. 2000, p. 18.

Swami Agnivesh, Rev. Valson Thampu, "Is Resistance Dead ?" The Hindu March 21, 1999.

Taylor Richard (2004) "The Market, Rules OK ?" Adults Learning Vol. 15. No. 8 April 2004.

Thyagarajan, Nirmala. Home Science in Secondary Education and Higher Secondary Education. In Perspectives in Home Science Silver Jubilee celebrations Commemorative Volume of the Home Science Association of India, Vani Printers, Coimbatore, 1977.

Tuckelt, Alan (2003) "Global citizenship social power" Adults Learning Vol. 15 No. 1 Sept. 2003.

UNDP (1995) Human development report 199. New York oxford University Press.

UNDP, Human Development Report 1999.

14

Health and Nutrition Education for Women

India lives in villages. This adage which emphasis the agrarian character of the Indian economy and to which such pointed attention was drawn by Mahatma Gandhi, continues to be true to this day inspite of the industrial development that has taken place in the last four decades since independence. The industrialization has not made any substantial difference to the proportion of the population that lives in the villages, though the exodus from villages in recent years has created problems and added to the urban slums.

HISTORICAL BACKGROUND

The first effort in this direction came when the community development programme was launched by the Government of India on 2nd Oct., 1952. By way of 55 project, with each block as a unit covering about 300 villages having population of 2 lakh 500 square Miles of area.

- Poverty Alleviation
- Integrated Rural development programme
- Schedule caste
- Schedule tribe
- Women's health : fifty years of independence
- Reproductive health

Health is fundamental to the national progress in any sphere. In terms of resources for economic development, nothing can be considered of higher importance than the health of people both male and female which is a measure of their energy and capacity as well as of the potential man hours for productive work in relation to the total number of persons maintained by the nation. For the efficiency of industry and of agriculture, the health of the worker is an essential consideration. It has been stated by the Planning Commission.

Health is viewed differently by different people all over the world. The World Health Organization defined health as - "a state of complete physical, mental and social well-being and not merely an absence of disease or infirmity".

Thus, there can be no two opinions that health in basic to national progress and in terms of resources for economic development nothing could be of greater significance than the health of women. Poor are the deprived classes but women among the poor are still the more deprived lot in a poor family women is the member who receives the least share of all resources - be it food, education or health.

When we talk of development experts and policy maker all over the world agree to the fact that quality of life of the citizens of a country is the major criteria to measure development and non just Gross National Product (GNP) Net National Product (NNP) and other such financial criteria.

Reproductive health is a major health concern all over the world and in developing countries in particular. Lack of nourishment and health facilities resulting from poverty leads to low standards of reproductive which severely affects not only the women but also the children they product and this the society accumulates unhealthy malnourished population. Therefore the status of reproductive health among women and the infrastructure to take care of reproductive health are major indicators of general health infrastructure available to the citizens and the development of human index in country.

DEFINITIONS OF HEALTH

Health is one of the terms which most people find it difficult to define although they are confident of its meaning. Some definitions of health are :-

(a) "The condition of being sound in body mind or spirit especially freedom from physical disease or pain (Webster)".

(b) "Soundness of body or mind, that condition in which its function are duly and efficiently discharged" (Oxford English Dictionary).

(c) WHO Defination : "The widely accepted Defination of health is give by the WHO (1948) in the preamble of its constitution.

THE CONCEPT OF NUTRITION

Nutrition may be defined as the science of food and its relationship to health. It is concerned primarily with the part played by nutrients in body growth. The work' "Nutrient" or "Food Factor is used for special dietery constituents such as vitamins and minerals". Dietics is the practiced application of the principles of nutrition. It includes the planning of meals for the well and the sick. Good nutrition means maintaining a nutritional status that enables us to grow well and enjoy good health. Nutrition has been expressed as a right in international human rights instruments since 1924.

Within the well recognized risk group viz. The children, the girl child particularly in the Asian countries has been recognized to be at a relatively high risk of suffering ill health and mortality compared with the male children. A major need of the developing countries is to raise the standard of living of the people especially in rural living of the people especially in rural areas. Raising standard of living in the developing countries calls for disseminations for information on farming, home making, industrial techniques, health among other things.

The required amount of information and learning is so much, the magnitude of desired social change is so big and the time needed to reach the standard is short, that only by making effective use of the great information multipliers, the developing nations can hope to achieve in a few years what the developed countries took centuries to achieve.

Health Education is an essential component of any programme to improve the health of a community, and it has a major role in promoting

(a) good health practices - for example sanitation, clean drinking water, good hygiene, breast feeding, infant feeding and oral rehydration.

(b) The use of preventive services - for example immunization, antenatal and child health clinics.

(c) The correct use of medications and the pursuit of rehabilitation regimens - for example, in Tuberculosis and leprosy respectively.

(d) The recognition of early symptoms of disease and promoting early referral.

(e) Community support, for primary health care and government control measures.

AIMS AND OBJECTIVES OF HEALTH EDUCATION

The main aim of health education is to help women to achieve health by their own actions and efforts. Health education begins therefore with the interest of women in improving their conditions of living, and aims at developing a sense of responsibility for their own health betterment as individuals and as members of family and community.

The general objectives of health education are-

1. To make health a valued community asset

The value place in health by women depends mainly on social and cultural factors such as the needs, problems, social organizations, the standard of general education and the economic resources of the women.

To enhance the importance of health in one's culture, education encourages women to come together to find ways of tackling problems of their community. The immediate problem concerning the community may not directly be related to health. This active participation and being responsible for their own health is enhanced by insisting the women to find solution to the problems of immediate interest.

2. To help individuals to become competent in and carry on those health activities for themselves as individuals or in small groups, in order to realize fully the state of health

Health is not a commodity which can be bought by individuals for their improvement. Individuals have to accept the scientific knowledge and health practices and act accordingly. Therefore health education, aims at encourage the individual family and community to take responsibility for their own health.

3. To promote the development and proper use of health services

The usefulness of any health service depends on the services provided by the health agency. It depends upon the confidence of people's utilization of the services provided by the health agency. It depends upon the confidence of people in the health personnel and the attitudes which health workers have towards the women. By educating women one can avoid the economic loss incurred by wrong or inadequate use of service.

4 Participation of Community Representatives

Involvement of all members of community in health and family planning programme may not be always feasible and effective for several reasons, of course, in a small community with limited population complete involvement of all the people can be considered. In addition, through small group meetings and campaigns support from entire community can be derived. While involving the community for support, care should be taken and group dynamics be studied properly as involving the local group leader may help in deciding who can be useful and effective in promotion of Health Programmes. For effective community participation we must involve the following people like teachers, community leader, Sarpanch, Dais, NGOs, Mahila Mandals. All these can help in increasing the utilization of existing facilities, leading to cost effectiveness of the programme and to reach the goal for health for all.

Different strategies can be adapted for integrating health and nutrition education in Home Science. Through formal as well as non formal education the awareness of Health and Nutrition Education can be imparted. These components are incorporated in teaching, research as well as in extension activities to the non formal learners. The Health Education can be effectively integrated in formal classroom teaching as well. Home Science teachings contain considerable health education. The specialization of extension, child development, food and nutrition and home management teach health considerations for either students or the target groups of children, adolescents, women.

TEACHING FOR HEALTH EDUCATION

First priority, can be given to students' health, as they are the health ambassador and of students is positively affected by our teaching. Home Science students are to be taught about health by following correct dietary practices, within their budget. It is not only the food intake but the provision of needed food at colleges and hostels. The problems could be of not having nutritious food and clean drinking water and good food canteen in the college. Unless the health of Home Science students is exemplary, the integration of health education would be only an idea on paper.

INTEGRATING HEALTH AND NUTRITION EDUCATION WITH RESEARCH

The Home Science Education can very well integrate health and nutrition education with research. Different type of research, action projects on health and nutrition, hygiene and teaching nutrition by using various methods such as film strips, video films and handouts and through folk media. These research studies are several and documented in the form of Research Reports. These research studies along with action research in Home Science are done to know the health needs of students and other target groups, in the college as well as outside the college. If action cannot be taken on the basis of action research, by home science college, the reports and requests can be forwarded to different agencies in the University, NGOs, Government Sectors, who can be helpful.

The hostels, colleges, can be approached to collect researchable health problems on which master's and doctoral research will be carried out by home science students. Research reports can be very useful in giving direction in determining how to integrate health and nutrition education for women. Home Science teachers must use the available research findings to update their teaching. If M.Sc. and Ph.D. students are encouraged to conduct research on health and nutrition, an available source of such research will be created.

HEALTH AND NUTRITION EDUCATION FOR NON FORMAL LEARNERS

The third way of integrating health education in home science is to have all possible experiences for the teachers and students to use their knowledge of health education in non formal situations. The home science colleges carry on extension activities in villages and towns and cities. All possible types of health education can be given through our extension activities. But the colleges have very limited resources, so collaborating with voluntary agencies may be necessary. If possible, taking up funded projects on health education, is also a way of integrating health education in home science.

SUGGESTED AREAS OF HEALTH EDUCATION

1. Population control and reproductive health are the most urgent areas of health education. Teaching, research and extension must be all geared for better health of women.
2. Hygiene and sanitation in cooking, eating in all household tasks, is also an important areas.
3. Child care practices and problems of parents in all socio economic classes need to be taught, researched and extended to nonformal learners.
4. On all the five technological missions, research and extension can be done. The missions on water supply and food production, are directly related to Home Science.

The following module can be followed by the teachers as well as extension workers for imparting Health Education. This illustration explains in detail, one component "Anemia". This can act as a guideline for planning other Health Education projects for women.

MODULE FOR IMPARTING HEALTH AND NUTRITION EDUCATION

1. Discipline	:	Home Science
2. Subject	:	Non Formal Education
3. Chapter/Unit	:	Adolescent Health
4. Teaching points	:	Anemia in Adolescent girls
5. Theme	:	To reduce iron deficiency anemia in Adolescent girls
6. Content overview	:	1. Prevalence 2. Causes 3. Classification 4. Consequences 5. Strategies to combat anemia

Anemia is common in Adolescent Girls because of non-availability of healthy foods. Generally food serving is done by females as males eat first and by the time vegetaoles or salads are over but, because of patriarchy system Mother as well as daughters do not mind this pattern of eating because it is the way they have been socialized since their childhood.

Recent World Health Organization (WHO) statistics indicate a worldwide anemia prevalence of about 30 percent with higher rates in developing countries. According to National Institute of Nutrition (1991) anemia is most common in all the groups of adolescents girls to the tune of 20-25 percent irrespective of the social class.

UNDER NUTRITION IN PREGNANCY

Severe restrictions of food consumption during pregnancy has affected the outcome of pregnancy whereas the results of moderate restrictions are equivocal., For example, Antonov (1942) reported that due to severe and prolonged food shortage during the siege of Leningrad, birth-weight were reduced strikingly and premature births as well as neonatal mortality were increased.

Beaton (1961) has suggested that metabolic adaptations occur in pregnancy on the basis of his clinical and sub-clinical examinations of pregnant and non-pregnant women subsisting on diets poor in food energy, protein and minerals.

Bose and Bagchi (1962) have proposed that catabolic processes are reduced during pregnancy. The nutritional status assessed clinically in pregnant and non-pregnant women was remarkably similar in spite of the felt that the pregnant women were taking a more restricted diet than the non-pregnant women. At different stage of pregnancy the concentrations of haemoglobin, serum proteins, serum iron and ascorbic acid were measured. The result of these biochemical analysis indicated that although the pregnant women were under greater metabolic stress, their biochemical indices were similar and in some cases better than that found in the non-pregnant subject. A significant reduction in catabolism, made possible by hormonal changes, seemed to be the only satisfactory explanation. Bagchi and Bose (1962) concluded also that the nutritional status of pregnant women was no significantly different in two economic groups, one belonging to a low socio-economic stratum and the other to a higher economic status. It might also be presumed that if the restriction of the nutrient intake was very severe adaptive mechanisms might fail leading to adverse effects of malnutrition.

The available data on the food intake of pregnant and lactating women in India were summarized by Rajlakshmi and Ramakrishnan (1965). Pasricha (1958) found that, contrary to expectations, the dietary intake during pregnancy was more unsatisfactory than it was before the onset of pregnancy due to ignorance and perhaps also due to the reduction in earning capacity of the pregnant women.

- Under-nutrition during lactation
- Dietary requirement of pregnant and lactating women with respect to protein, thiamine and riboflavin.

Anemia is a major global, public health problem, affecting about one-fourth of the world's population and its health consequences affects all the age groups to varying degree, with pregnant women the most susceptible (Benoist, 2001).

Although human adults require only about 1 mg of absorbable iron per day, the problem of iron deficiency anemia is widespread (Seshadri, 2001) estimated prevalence of iron deficiency anemia is 3.6 billion in the world (UNICEF / WHO, 1999). Anemia is defined as hemoglobin concentration below normative cut-off values that are based on age, sex, physiological state and altitude (WHO / UNICEF, 1998). Iron deficiency anemia is a serve stage of iron deficiency which occurs when iron stores are exhausted and the supply of iron to the tissues is compromised (INACG / WHO / UNICEF 1998). It is known to impair psychomotor development, affect physical activity, work capacity, lower resistance to infections and adversely affect birth outcomes and infant and maternal survival (Benoist, 2001).

Due to poverty, inadequate diet, diseases, pregnancy and lactation and poor access to health services, the prevalence is higher in developing countries as compared to developed nations.

Various factors contribute to the widespread prevalence of iron deficiency anemia (IDA) (Gilliespie, 1998).

- Insufficient quantity of dietary iron intake in relation to need.
- Poor bioavailability of iron consumed related to a low consumption of iron absorption enhances and a high consumption of iron absorption inhibitors.
- Increased requirement at certain stages in the life cycle notably during pregnancy and during rapid early childhood and adolescent growth.
- Blood loss due to both menstruation and child birth among women amplified by repeated and closely spaced pregnancies, infections and infestations.

In view of the known etiology and consequences of IDA the strategies advocated for prevention and treatment of iron deficiency anemia are (INACG / WHO / UNICEF, 1998)

- Dietary modification to increase iron intake and improve the bioavailability of dietary iron.
- Food fortification with iron
- Supplementation with medicinal iron
- Prevention and treatment of parasitic and other infections

Relationship between Maternal and Foetal Nutrition

Inadequate food and poor nutrient utilization

↓

Maternal Malnutrition

↓

Reduced blood volume

↓

Decreased blood and Nutrient supply to the foetus

↓

Reduced nutrient transfer

↓

Retarded foetal growth

OBJECTIVES

1. To make the students aware about the prevalence of Anemia among Adolescent Age Group, in girls and boys.
2. To sensitize the students about the various causes of anemia amongst Adolescents and severe repercussions amongst girls.
3. To sensitize the students at a younger age to incorporate green leafy vegetables to combat anemia.
4. Educate the adolescents
   (a) that girls should be given more of Iron, and rich foods - so that they can contribute to healthy living for themselves
   (b) to the future bearing of children.
5. Sensitize the male adolescents
   (a) to help to bring change in the current scenario where girl subjects are neglected in the family

(b) Explain them the friends which are changing so that they realize that they also have to contribute towards their female counterparts.

PREVALENCE OF ANEMIA

The percent of anemia in India for Adult Women ranged from a low of 24% to a high of 97% which is higher than the percent prevalence of Anemia. Iron, an essential element present in the porphyrin complexes of hemoglobin, myoglobin and a variety of home containing, enzymes, plays a vital role in oxygen transport and other metabolic processes. Iron is carefully conserved and reutilized in the body. Therefore, the physiological requirement per day is small, ranging from 1 to 1.5 mg per day for adults, despite the relatively small requirements for iron, which is far smaller than the amount present in the daily diet, nutritional iron deficiency is present throughout the world, affecting five hundred million to one billion individuals representing 15-20% of the world's population (WHO, 1991).

Inefficient absorption of iron from diets predominantly based on plant foods is considered to be an important limiting factor in fulfilling iron needs of people subsisting on such diets (Narasinga Rao, 1981). Therefore, iron deficiency results not solely due to a low intake of dietary iron but also due to a low bioavailability of iron. In India, the iron intake of a large majority of the population its derived almost exclusively from non-home iron, inhibitors, of iron absorption in the Indian diets far out number of enhancers, thus resulting in very low reported values of absorption of 2.5% or even lower (Narasinga Rao, et al; 1983).

Approaches to Combat Iron Deficiency or Strategies to Combat Anemia among females:

Both, the understanding of the epidemiology of iron deficiency anemia and technical means of preventing and controlling it have expanded greatly in the recent years. The three basic approaches to solving iron deficiency anemia are:

1. Improving the availability of dietary iron
2. Supplementation with medicinal iron
3. Fortification of staple foods with iron

Gender as a Determinant of Health

Structure of society and hierarchical position of gender are closely reflected through the state of their health. Gender issue is therefore quite significant while talking of health. Women, Adolescent girl are the most vulnerable group exposed to adversities of life. On the other hand they significantly contribute to the health of the family.

Teacher has to be very conscious of the fact that the issue of health of men and women is not mere a physiological problem but due to different biological make up and socio cultural valuation girls health is differently perceived in comparison to boys health. It is at this juncture where teacher must put her input and make students understand how we need to be sensitive towards the gender issues related to health. Because of their Reproductive Role they are exposed to more infections and diseases resulting in morbidity and death. It is important for both boys and girls to understand the biological make up, their function how and why it is important to be healthy individuals.

Vicious cycle of a Anemia and Malnourished Women

If this concept is understood by both boys and girls during adolescent age they themselves will be serious when they will be Adults. The girl will take care of her own body as and when she will be mother similarly the boy will be more responsible husband of tomorrow.

They would know malnutrition, including anemia as a serious health problem, specially in women who have too many pregnancies too closely spaced. This implies how many pregnancy/child birth will be decided by both the parents and not mere burden of female only. This would be only possible if as a young adult boy he was taught about Anemia that too with gender sensitivity.

Father will be aware of the women's nutritional status as he knows that it influence her chance of having a normal delivery and child with adequate birth weight. Anemia is common in Adolescent girls because of non-availability of healthy foods. Generally food serving is done by females as males eat first and by the time females eat many times vegetables or salads are over but, because of patriarchy system mother as well as daughters do not mind this pattern of eating because it is the way they have been socialized since their childhood.

Recent World Health Organization (WHO) statistics indicate a worldwide anemia prevalence of about 30 percent with higher rates in developing countries. According to National Institute of Nutrition (1991) anemia is most common in all the groups of adolescent girls to be tune of 20-25 percent irrespective of social class.

Gender Socialization and its Agents

(A) Family
(B) Peer Groups
(C) Literature
(D) Media

These agents reinforces socialization patterns of an individuals. Teacher can play very important role by planning. Learning experiences such as:

(A) Family

(a) Assigning students to record and maintain diary of food intake
(b) Notes on Meal Planning
(c) Observation schedule
 - Who eats first ? In the family
 - Who eats last ? etc. etc.

(B) Peer Groups

Taking measurements and examining each others for clinical signs of anemia. Reporting and sharing if it is same for boys and girls ? It is more for girls ? If yes ? What should be done? It is women and girls are facing more ideologically rooted restrictions on their eating habits and behaviors.

(C) Literature

Review of Reports and Research studies. Reporting of Trend studies related to Anemia and Adolescent girls and boys. Teachers can take up projects and discuss with students and make them sensitive about how women health has been neglected. What efforts need to be done to combat this evil ? This can only be done if both Men and Women try it together.

Publishing successful Action Projects in different Journals. Inhouse literature in the form of leaflets, folders and magazines can go a long way. In disseminating information regarding any field tried project where both boys and girls took active part in promotion of health messages. This kind of literature when documented and read by others they can act as catalyst in promotion of gender sensitive messages related to Anemia or Malnutrition among Adolescent girls and boys.

(D) Media

Media helps in awareness building.
Non projected Aids

(1) Puppets-

Puppet plays can be written and performed by both boys and girls depicting situations how anemia is caused? or consequences of Anemia. Puppets have great educational value with children as well as with people from slums and rural areas.

(2) Drama-

Drama, Role play and street plays depicting situations where people in the audience starts visualizing themselves with the actors. This can be very effective media for creating sensitization among Adult girls and boys. After the play teacher can have evaluation session where situation can be evaluated.

(3) Folk Songs/Garbas

The educational messages can be successfully translated with music into songs as they are very catchy people are attracted to listen and learn from them.

TEACHING METHODS

1. Lecture by experts - Doctor, Dieticians, Nutritionist
2. Discussion
   a. Panel Discussion
   b. Brainstorming on Topics like
      i. Anemia
      ii. Causes
      iii. Ill effect

   Such topics can be given to the students and ask them to present in the class.
3. Situation analysis - where students can go to communities and study the "Anthropometric" details. They can present the comparative data of Boys and Girls.
4. This presentation can be followed by discussion highlight the differences on the basis of "gender".
5. Media
   (a) Slides : can be made under the course "Media Production" these can be used for teaching this unit of "Anemia".
   (b) Video film : Video films can be made on "Balanced Food" and which are rich in Iron and Vit. C. These films can be good teaching materials as they can b used several times.

ACTIVITIES

- Students encouraged to develop messages on Iron, Vit. C.
- Posters on Women - Children who are Anemic
- Slogans with messages on Adolescent health.
- Survey in nearby areas to record health problems which are gender related.
- Students can check each other for signs of anemia (Pale tongue, pale eyes, pale nails) using the Anemia detection card.

Group leader can record and document the readings and Highlight the differences between girls and boys.

Observation with check list are females discriminated in Indian Homes in dietary practices.

Teachers can be an effective instrument in promotion of good health as she can be a nutritional counseller.

FILE WORK : PROJECT WORK

Photographs, bar graphs and pie graph showing Nutrient value of foods consumed. As a teacher while giving feed back teacher can bring out highlights in case she finds difference in the food consumed by boys and girls after the presentation of report.

Teachers can sensitize the Adolescent girls and boys about anemia which is more during Adolescent and that too among girls.

EVALUATION CRITERIA

- Written Test
- Oral Presentation in the class
- File submission

WHAT ELSE YOU CAN DO AS A TEACHER

- Get involved in issues that concerns women and girl child and their health.
- Help boost public awareness about women's health and problems.
- Form a network, create awareness - share best practices, reports and studies.
- Listen to and involve women and girls in issues and programmes that concerns women's health. Both at Formal Education that is in the classroom teaching. As well as at Non Formal Adult Education outside the four walls of classrooms.

Health and Nutrition education aims at enabling women and men both to gain control over the determinants of health and health behavior and the condition that affect their health status. Advances in human ecology has taught us that ill health is not only the result of interaction of man and woman with the biological environment but also the physical, social, religious and educational environment.

Decisions and actions by various sectors of society do influence the health and living conditions of not only people belonging to that sector but that of the society and the generation as a whole. Health education has therefore to play a key role in influencing all health related sectors to see that their policies and actions are in congruence with the national health objectives. It has to play a key role of an advocacy so that people are motivated and play effective role in educating and adapting sound health practices.

REFERENCE/READINGS

Anita P.P. (1986), Clinical Nutrition, Oxford University Press, Bombay,

B. Srilakshmi (2002), Dietetics, New Age international (P) Ltd. Hyderabad.

Beggs D.L. (1990), Measurement and Evaluation in Home Economics, Hongthton Miffin Boston.

Borzak Lenore, (1988), Field Study, Sage Publication, New Delhi.

Chaubey B.K. (1990), A Handbook of extension education Jyoti Prakashan, Agra.

Dhama O.P. (1980), Education and Communication for Development, Oxford and IBH Publication, Delhi.

Mishra S.N. (1997), Poverty Alleviation Programmes and Gram Panchayats, Himalaya Publication, Delhi.

Patel Srisha (1985), Ecology, Anthropology and Nutrition, Sage Publications, New Delhi.

Rajalaxmi R. (1974) Applied Nutrition Books (Pvt. Ltd.) Prasin Bangalore.

Swaminathan, M. (1974), Essential of Food and Nutrition Vol. I and II Ganesh and Company, Madras-17.·

Toylor C. (1978), How to design a programme evaluation in Home Economics, Boston.

Verma K.K. (1992), Health Care and Family Welfare Alternative Strategies, Gyan Publication, New Delhi.

Waghmare S.K. (1995), Exploring the Extension Excellence, Multi Technique Publication, Mumbai.

15

Entrepreneurship New Venture Creation for Women

The common old belief that women dedicate their lives solely to look after their homes and in bringing up children is either set aside altogether or partially and now women are going in for self employment and entrepreneurship. Women entrepreneurs are overturning the stereotyped image as being passive and subservient to their men folk. Instead of taking preparatory and supportive roles, women are venturing to independent creative roles.

Women represent over half of the world's population. They also make a substantial contribution to national development. Hence they should be given access to necessary inputs required for enhancing their productive ability and for their equal share in the benefits of development. In order to achieve this, in recent years the percentage of women beneficiaries in development programmes is increasing. Thus in self-employing areas the need for training of women is necessary.

Indian people know that "when you educate a woman, you educate a whole family" and they are fully aware of the fact that her learning will go into the bloodstream of the generations that will follow her. She can bring grace and dignity to the place where she lives, she can build a new nation and can mould a rather new era in the history of mankind. Her role and effectiveness has been fully realized and accepted.

Women can now choose from many new careers. They have a vast choice before them, they can enter any field, which previously was the exclusive domain of men. They can hold the highest position which men have been holding. Women can even become industrialists, entrepreneurs, exporters, beauticians, craft-persons, electronics technologists and so on for which they would need proper training.

Women can be successful at entrepreneurship or self-employment. Women get a higher economic status through self-employment. This is the basic requirement for raising their status. They are regarded as "inactive labour" or "secondary workers" or "dependents". Only women themselves can change this situation. Self employment will give them money, power and status, both in the family and society. For those women, who would like to remain at home and earn, having self employment at home premises will serve the purpose. This self employment promotes the idea of a flexible work time, helping women to work in the hours that suits them, giving women a chance to do something other than the household work, which can make the lives of many women pleasant and satisfying.

Women constitute half of the population, contribute more than half of the duties and responsibilities of the family but are hardly empowered to participate in decision making. They are not given any rights, they are supposed to do domestic work and to look after children.

In India, the term entrepreneur seems to have a much restricted meaning. It covers only a limited sphere of enterprising and endeavor i.e. establishing and running of factories and industrial enterprises alone. It has also been viewed as a phenomenon, occurring around, individual and benefiting only an individual. It is only recently that it is being appreciated a one that could be utilized successfully to benefit larger groups.

For the past three or four decades, employment of women is becoming an important issue at national level in India. This trend has made it more essential that women who have the potential to develop certain skills, get the right kind of training to join the work of employment with all the confidence and faith. So with the help of training only, women's earning power can be developed. Training programmes provide training in selected vocations to the women with skills which would enable them to earn through self employment.

Definition of entrepreneur is one who innovates, raises money, assembles inputs, chooses manager and sets the commercial organization going with his ability to identify and is able to fulfill such economic opportunities. Similarly other definition of entrepreneur is one who always searches for change, responds to it, exploits as an opportunity. Entrepreneurs innovate, Innovation is a specific instrument of entrepreneurship. Entrepreneurship is the purposeful activity of an individual or a group of associated individuals, undertaken to initiate, maintain profit by production or distribution of economic goods and services. Entrepreneurship is the dynamic process of creating incremental wealth. This wealth is created by individual known as entrepreneur, who assumes the major risk in terms of equity, time and career commitment of providing value for some product or service.

EVOLUTION OF THE CONCEPT OF ENTREPRENEUR

The word 'entrepreneur' has derived from French language it originally meant to designate on organizer of musical or other entertainments. Oxford English Dictionary also defines entrepreneur in similar way as "the director or a manager of a public musical institution, one who 'gets up' entertainment, especially musical performance". It was only in the beginning of the 18th century the word was used to refer to economic aspects. In this way, the evolution of the concept of entrepreneur is considered.

Over more than four centuries. Entrepreneurship was a common topic in economic essays for much of the 18th and 19th centuries. During that time French, British economists quote about entrepreneurs as the "change agents" of progressive economics.

An entrepreneur is a person with a dream, originality and daring, who acts as the boss, who decides as to how the commercial organization shall run, who coordinates all the activities and other factors of production, who anticipates future trends of demand and supply and prices of products. According to Higgins, 'By entrepreneurship we mean, the function of seeking investment and production opportunity, organizing an enterprise to undertake a new production process raising capital, hiring labour, arranging the supply of raw materials, finding site, introducing a new technique and products, discovering new sources of raw materials and selecting top managers for day to day operations of the commercial organization.

An entrepreneur of every business enterprise invents and introduces new ideas, new products, new processes or revolutionary machinery and who, in general, carries out new activities in his business organization. Due to these reasons in modern times, the role of an entrepreneur is recognized as an important factor of production of every business organization. Economists have identified entrepreneurship as the essential element in generating investment opportunities in an economy.

Entrepreneurship comprises of all these productive functions that are not thought to be rewarded by wages, rent or interest. It is not associated with routine human efforts, it does not involve the use of indestructible natural resources and it does not imply the provision of capital funds.

STATUS OF WOMEN ENTREPRENEURS IN INDIA

Nature has made a division of labour of the responsibilities of man and woman for betterment of process of evolution. In this division of labour, the women have been endowed upon with gift of motherhood and upbringing of the future generation. The women, the mother, has been the symbol of continuity of culture, tradition and religion, being the binding force of the family system. Quality of the indicated how well or how badly women performed her duties. Gradually women withdrew to the four walls of the home to take care of the children, while men worked outside forging for food.

With the advancement of science and technology, an increasing number of women wanted to participate in economic activities of the nation. Thus, we find the emergence of women entrepreneurs.

CATEGORIZATION OF WOMEN ENTREPRENEURS

1. Entrepreneurs in Large and Medium Sectors
2. Entrepreneur in the small sector
3. Entrepreneurs in cities and slums

FOR SOLVING THE PROBLEMS THAT WOMEN FACE TO BECOME AN ENTREPRENEUR

1. Separate cells for women should be established so that women entrepreneurs have easy access to credit.
    - Women co-operative banks should be established.
    - Those women who have been successful can help other women with advice and giving facilities to see that the percentage of failure in the scheme is kept down to the minimum.
    - To develop a greater degree of mutual confidence between bankers and women entrepreneurs, separate institutions should set up for women.
    - Larger financial institutions should have separate cell for women.
2. Multiplicity of laws and regulations and their different connotation in different state of India limit the market especially for non-traditional products.
3. With the technological advancement India has to face many problems like:
    - Developing countries have merely sold technologies to India.
    - Some imported technologies are not suitable for India. India needs some technologies which can help small and medium industries to increase the production using the labour intensive method which will be beneficial.
4. Easy access to infrastructure is also important. Women entrepreneurs have to face many hurdles in obtaining power and licenses wherever necessary, to set up an industry.
5. In spite of the progress that women entrepreneurs have made, there is still a lack of awareness among women entrepreneurs especially in development countries. It

is obtaining knowledge essential for identifying projects as also for credit, for marketing and training.

6. There is need for co-operation amongst women entrepreneurs with limited resources to group together to set up an industry.
7. Another problem women entrepreneurs face is due to mental reservations and attitudes of policymakers, planners and administrators.
8. Most of the women entrepreneur are handicapped and cannot continue with their business or trade activity for want of guidance on consumer demand, market mechanism, designing and resources for producing capital and raw materials apart from managerial and training support.

CHARACTERISTICS OF ENTREPRENEURS

- *Hard working* : This quality of willingness to work hard distinguishes a successful entrepreneur from rest. The women folk fits very well in this quality as they have been brought up and socialized to work hard, where as men can relax, have recreation and take out time for entertainment contrary to this women are tuned to work hard, the idea behind this is this quality of "hard work" amongst women can be harnessed and can help them to be successful entrepreneur.
- *Desire for High Achievement* : The entrepreneurs have strong desire to achieve high goals in business. The high goals in business. The high achievement motivate and strengthened them to set up and run a successful business. This characteristic or quality is not found very often among women. Here inputs are required in the form of education and training so that the women can think fresh and be more optimistic with self confidence. This is not impossible as several studies have proved that education and training have power to change.
- *Independence* : One of the common characteristics of successful entrepreneurs has been that they do not like to be guided by others and follow their own routine.

This quality to be inculcated among women is a tough job as in India we have patriarchy that is because of male dominated society women are not allowed to be independent in their action. Because of social, cultural, economical and educational reasons women are dependent for all small or big decisions to their fathers, husband or sons. If as a social scientists we want to empower women and make them independent which requires strategic planning and combating at all fronts. Than only women will be independent and can be successful entrepreneurs.

- *Good Organizer:* Different resources are required for production and it is the ability of the entrepreneurs that brings together all resources required for starting up an enterprise and then to produce goods. Basically women are good organizers be it money, food, time, relationship you name any front women are ahead than men in this quality. It is God gift that they are more emotional and good organizers so it won't be difficult for them if they are trained to be entrepreneurs. It comes to them naturally to handle many things at a time and this quality of multitask ability is an advantage with women. East West Center Home Cell has identified some more traits in entrepreneurial persons from extensive review of research studies like confident, independent, optimism, leadership, innovative, resourceful, flexible, responsible to suggestion, profit oriented, hardworking, foresight, risk taking ability and likes challenges.

Organizations in the Service of Women Entrepreneurs

1. Entrepreneurship Development Institute (EDI)
2. National Small Industries Corporation Limited (NSIC)
3. Government Stores Purchase Programme
4. Prototype Development and Training Centre (PDTC)
5. Small Industries Development Organization (SIDO)
6. State Industrial Development Corporation (SIDC)
7. Delhi State Industrial Corporation (SIDC)
8. Industrial Consultancy
9. State Financial Corporation

10. National Alliance of Young Entrepreneurs (NAYE)
11. Voluntary Organizations

NEED FOR INCOME GENERATING ACTIVITIES

Illiterate women are mostly in the low income and do not have much attraction for literary education alone, therefore, it is necessary that income generating activities (handicrafts) are planned for the workshop. Income generating activities will not only help in motivating, but also in sustaining their interest in continuing with the 'Women's Empowerment Programme'.

This is one way which women can contribute to the family income. These activities will enable women to give a better income to the family. These activities will thereby:

- Improve women's social status
- Make them economically independent
- Can make them fight against the ill treatment rendered towards them by the family and society.

Some important characteristics of an Enterprise as:

1. It consist of people working together primarily for the purpose of production, sales, purchases, etc.
2. It consumes other valuable resources to produce output, that is, raw materials, workers time and energy, shop space, utilities, fuel, etc.
3. An enterprise is a continuing entity. It is not an adhoc effort to produce a single product or output, but rather a recurring and continuing effort to produce a stream of products or services.
4. Every enterprise carries out some sort of final net profit or less calculation.

The following products can be selected by women to start the income products can be many but to name some simple and sure to click :

1. Chalk making
2. Agarbatti
3. Paper Bag
4. Candles
5. Soap and Detergents

These particular products can be selected by considering the following criteria and justify the selection of products.

- *General utility of the product:* The product selected are used by majority of the people in society like Agarbatti, Soaps and Detergents, Candles, chalks and paper bags.
- *Daily consumption of the product:* Agarbatti, Soaps, Detergens and Candles required daily by the people, It has the everyday demand and consumption therefore it will have market demand for the sale.
- *Require less technical skills compared to other products:* The expected target groups may not have highly technical skills. If they required to learn to make these product they need to learn technical skills and knowledge. These products require less skills compared to other products.
- *Need low investment of time, energy and money in the production:* In comparison with other products the time, energy and money required to manufacture these products are less and it will be possible in the beneficiaries to invest these resources.
- Availability of raw material is another significant point which would make production easier and without many obstacles. The target group would be able to manage to avail the raw material.

Looking at all the above points it is expected that the women will be interested to manufacture and marketing these products to generate the income for themselves. Thus, interest of the women should be given a prime importance as criteria for justifying these products. The very objective of National Development is to raise the standard of living of all the citizens of the country from different strata and to bring the social and economic equality among them.

Therefore all families need to develop themselves in all different walks of life. The economic and educational aspects are the important pillars of the development. The economic development could be possible only if the human elements regardless male and female are participating in economic activities. In Indian situation well generally are involved in economic activities. Now with all technology development and increasing monetary crises the women are expected to indulged in the economic activities.

Studies and literature in the past have indicated that women have the strength and capacity to participate in economic activities what they need is the little guidance and assistance to start and initiate the work.

Methodology for conducting project on entrepreneurship for women

Major Steps

A. Preparation
B. Training
C. Actual Production
D. Marketing
E. Repayment of loan

A. Preparation

1. Selection of content of training
2. Training of Field workers
3. Identification of Beneficiaries
4. Identification of Experts
5. Co-ordination with other agencies

B. Training

1. Deciding with the communities the time table for training.
2. Actual conducting the training programme for "Self Employment" of girls and women in making different hand made articles.
3. Practicing the product making of Quality.
4. Proposal making and submitting to DIC for availing loan from Bank.

C. Actual Production of various articles

Practicing till the group is able to make quality products at the given place with estimation of cost under the supervision of the project officer.

D. Marketing

Different strategies will be used for marketing the products

- Demonstration/Publicity
- Home to home sale
- Contacting few shops
- Exhibition and sale at institution and community

E. Repayment of Loan

- Every month calculation of the sale
- Profit distribution among the women/girls
- Repayment of money to the sources from where the fund was availed to start manufacturing.

The various organizations/institutions are working for women empowerment through self employment and entrepreneurship. The strategies used under this project on self employment will help other organizations as well as institutions to follow and conduct the self employment projects. These economic activities in the weaker-section will motivate the women other than those who are participating.

Since society is now looking forward the women's empowerment, the efforts are required on the part of Educational, Government and voluntary organizations and institutions to focus the development of women through making them engaged and allowing them participating in self employment and entrepreneurial activities. According to employment survey it was found that...

There are less job opportunities for men and women both self employment is becoming work and more appropriate for families of survivals. Since women have dual role of looking after families it may certainly be difficult for women to work as an employee with time bound conditions under the public or private employees, self employment and entrepreneurship provides women better opportunities to work at her own leisure timings and give them mental satisfaction for working.

The design of the project can be as follows

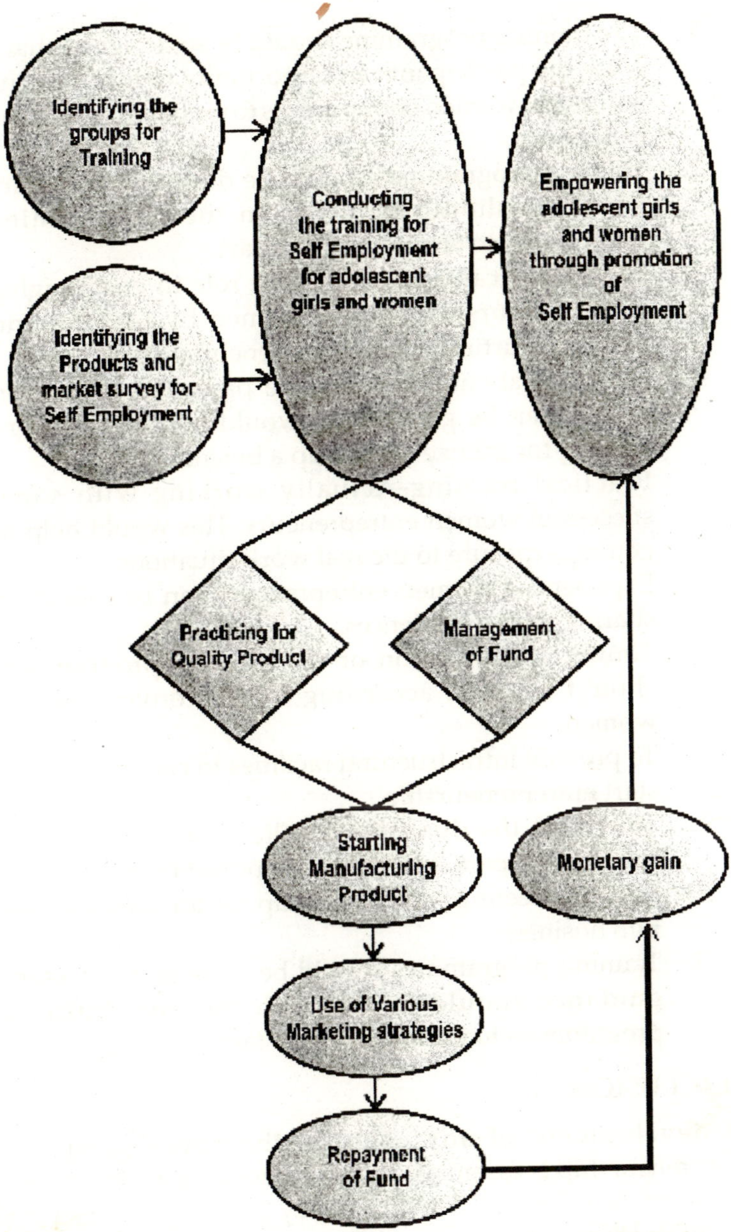

SUGGESTIONS

1. The training programme should be so designed that it gives the participants an opportunity to interact with successful women entrepnreurs to exchange views and experience.
2. Training programmes should be done and necessary guidance should be given in the post training programme to ensure a better start.
3. The family can play important role in encouraging entrepreneurship among women by tapping and properly nurturing the entrepreneurial spirit.
4. Guidance about prospects of a particular product in market can be given. This would help in decision-making for trainee to take up a business.
5. Practical training-Actually working with some successful women entrepreneurs. This would help in getting exposure to the real work situations.
6. Experienced women entrepreneurs can be called for sharing their experiences.
7. Timing and duration of the training programmes should be done according to the convenience of women.
8. To provide infrastructural facilities to rural women to start entrepreneurship.
9. To reduce the dual role conflicts, mainly husband should take part in domestic responsibilities.
10. Regular meetings and follow-up for trainees who are into business.
11. Training programmes should be done and necessary guidance should be given in the post training programmes to ensure a better start.

CONCLUSION

For development of any country, the development of entrepreneurship is essential. The entrepreneurs are the prime movers of the economic activities. They are the pioneer in the field of economic development. The country which is rich in entrepreneurship, can attain the economic success and ensured the economic augmentation. The entrepreneurs constantly strive to innovate new things to serve the country The economic success of entrepreneurs of any country spreads over the boundary of the country and influence the global economy The entrepreneurs organize the economic venture for producing goods and services at lower cost with the objective of maximization of profits and thereby contributing the economic development. In the era of globalization the development of entrepreneurship is the key factor for ushering economic prosperity and well-being of any country. Thus, entrepreneurship has become one of the four mainstream economic factors : land, labour, capital and entrepreneurship.

More women entrepreneurs training education, guidance and support from husband, parents, relatives, friends and others in their entrepreneurship is required. Husband plays a major role in career of married women. To be successful entrepreneurs, women should be confident, intelligent, alert and good decision makers. Also by motivating women to set up enterprise wide gap between the genders can be narrowed down.

The backwardness of the Indian economy is reflected in its unbalanced occupational structure and place of women in amongst poorest of poor. In reality we find large scale unemployed and underemployed population both in rural as well as in urban areas leading to major economic and social problems.

The Indian economy has stressed positive change since mid 1990. Because of new government policies the Indian economy is largely isolated from the global economy. To get concrete results from the new policy and looking at the market scenario in the country the need of the hour is self employment and entrepreneurship. It is high time that we focus our efforts and promote entrepreneurship systematic intervention need to be developed and analytical capability of women be enhanced so that they could undertake enterprise successfully.

BIBLIOGRAPHY

Bhupatani, D.D. and Singh, H. Women Entrepreneurship Development Training and its Effectiveness Delhi, NIESBUD, 1990.

Chetana Balbalbagh, Women and Development Discovery Publishing House, 1991.

G.R. Basotia and K.K. Sharma, Handbook of Entrepreneurship development, Mangaldeep Publication, Jaipur (1999)

J. S. Saini, B.R. Gurjar, Entrepreneurship and Education, Rawat Publications 1999.

Jose Paul and Ajit Kumar, Entrepreneurship, Development Himalaya Publishing House, 1999.

Kalyani Kulshreshta, Successful entrepreneurship Kanishka Publication, New Delhi 1999.

Lalita Rani, Women Entrepreneurs, APH Publishing Corporation, New Delhi, 1996.

Planning Commission, Government of India Ninth Five Year Plan, 1997-2000, Vol. II, P. 123.

Prasad K. Planning at the Grass Roots, Sterling Publishers Pvt. Ltd., New Delhi, 1988.

R. K. Mittal "Entrepreneurial management" Rawat Publication Jaipur, 1999.

Rathore, R.S. and Chabra, R. Promotion of Women Entrepreneurship Training Strategies, National Bank New Review Bombay, 1991.

S. S. Khanka "Entrepreneurial development, C. Chand and Company Ram Nagar New Delhi.

S. S. Khanka and S. Chand Entrepreneurial Development, New Delhi, 1995.

Tllis, N and Jessi, B Towards self reliance and Income generation for women, Selena Castocateran Publishing, Hyderabad, 1979.

Vasant Desai, Entrepreneurial Development, Himalaya Publishign House, 2000

16

Women and Development: A complex interrelationship

Planning for the socially, educationally and economically disadvantaged groups in India has been accelerated during the last few decades. The women, however have been the focus of our planners attention only since last decades. with the celebration of the International Women's Year in 1975 and the subsequent UN declaration of Women's Decade.

A timely action is necessary at different levels by several agencies to educate and change the Indian women, encouraging them to keep pace with the women of the developed countries of the world. Women are marginalized, oppressed and neglected group, even though their contributions to social economic, family and agricultural productivity within a country are enormous. As proposed by Kabeer (1994) will not only increase the number of the individuals involved in a social transformational action but they will also provide contexts in which empowerment is more actively and energetically pursued.

The Beijing Declaration was made on 15th Sept. 1995 in the Fourth World Conference on Women. Progress has been made on gender equality, human rights of women have gained recognition and violence against women is now an illegal act in almost every country. Progress however, is uneven and far from sustained. Women continue to represent the majority of the world's poor. There has been no breakthrough in women's participation in decision making process. They have no voice to improve their situation.

The Message of UN Secretary General of International Women's Day 8 March, 2003 states that women represent a new way of doing development business. India being the Welfare State, the Government has to play a pivotal role in planning and carrying out actions for the development of the less privileged sections of the society, of whom women form a large part, and for the improvement of their quality of life.

On examining the policies and programmes of Government one would find that the approach has shifted from a welfare to a development and to an empowerment approach. The development approach starting from Equity approach to anti poverty approach to Efficiency approach and finally Empowerment approach.

The unavoidable effects of modernization, westernization, urbanization and industrialization have been instrumental in bringing change. The gap between city and village in most areas has decreased. At the same time village population is suffering from poverty, lack of resources and large masses are compelled to live under impoverished conditions. The worst hit of them is the woman because of so many interrelated reasons. Proper attention has not been given to her needs and requirements. These problems have been recognized by our leaders as well as planners and attempts have been made to change the situation. The most important reason for this is that development of women's personality is neglected and girls are not treated as equal to boys in society. Although a change in people's attitude towards women is witnessed in the present decade and status of women is also improving but this change has occurred in urban areas and only among educated people of our country.

Role of Women and Development has not been understood properly. The political overtakes, however makes the puzzle too important, though many do not want to analyze and understand it. It is thought that if advances are to be made in reducing world poverty, women must have access to appropriate education and training from basic literacy training to technical training. World Bank reminds us that when women farmers were allowed access to a primary school education, farming yield increased by 24%. Educated women are also more able to make informed decision on crop and technology selection, capital allocation and credit schemes, health and nutrition issues.

Development is a multi-faceted phenomenon, which must not be imposed by must rather involve active participation of all and sundry for it to be effective, meaningful and sustainable. Most development programmes do not only use a pyramidal structural approach but they are more importantly elitist in nature. In other words the bureaucrats in the corridors of power, often "think" and "plan" for rather than work with the general masses, majority of whom are women who live in rural neglected areas and are stereotypically viewed as being ultra conservative, naïve and apathetic to change.

The real development can only be assessed by the criterion of active participation of people at all levels of national development, including essentially women, who are the neglected group. Failure to acknowledge women's contribution in development puts brakes on the progress of the nation. Empowering women to participate actively in national development will start rrom their initial involvement in analyzing their own problems, proposing solutions and consequently taking collective action.

Nothing can be more conceivable for the home scientists than to think about the connection between home science and women's upliftment. It may be through development projects or through any other approach, but women's upliftment is the major objective of home science. Not only the upliftment of women but the improvement of the quality of life of the entire family that is the aim of home science. But in India, somehow Home Science have been identified with only women and home science institutions have unisex, which has many disadvantages. If we analyse the two concepts; home science and developmental projects, we will find that all the developmental projects undoubtedly are aiming at raising the socio-economic status of people, which is actually improving quality of life.

Some how majority of the developmental programmes seem deliberately blind to the beneficiaries, or the beneficiaries are unreachable because of their profound attitudinal backwardness and sense of hopelessness. In either of these two situations, the aim of uplifting the women who are low in socio-economic matters, is not achieved. What should be the role of home science ? The role is two fold. The home scientists need to intervene in the policy making of developmental projects. Any political reason, or sheer ignorance of planning and executing the projects, should be removed from the administrative machinery. This of course is much harder to do than say, but home scientists must register their intervention in the policy making and executing tasks to ensure that the developmental inputs do reach to the intended targets i.e. women. The Home Scientists can help to a large extent in removing the mind blocks amongst the women. They can use different extension methods like demonstration, workshops and experts talk and initiate change and help women to be more open to adopt change and be productive. They can be motivated to adopt and use technology and thus remove attitudinal backwardness. Repeated contacts with functioning of home science institutions and with all community bound programmes can change the attitudes and values of women.

Similarly the voluntary organizations need to be integrated with the different development projects. As it is well proved fact that networking with NGOs is a must if we want desired results. NGOs have strongly motivated individuals who liaise between illiterate and powerless and with the government agencies.

Another important role which Home Scientist can play is to collect and make available relevant data about rural beneficiaries mainly women and methods, approaches and procedures of working for and with them. Educational institutions like Home Science Faculties and colleges have many expertise in extension methods and materials, communication techniques, and evaluation and monitoring and welfare projects. These capabilities should be used in collaborating with voluntary organizations. No developmental programmes can be sustained without systematic diffusion and evaluation of developmental inputs. And it is this task which is of educational nature that home scientists can perform well.

Review of literature has shown that Indian poverty is due to an economic system in which vast masses are alienated from property structure and women are most hard hit and they are alleniated from property structure and mode of production and from fruits of production. Thus, how to safeguard the economic interests of the poor women is the baffling question that policy makers have to answer. Home Scientists needs to make efforts to create awareness and make women organized into small help groups this will help them in fighting poverty and give them visibility. These efforts will also contribute in upliftment of social status of women. Employment creates in women new attitudes which gives new status provided by employment.

The Home Scientists can help in creating more employment for women. The employed women especially in the rural areas and in the weaker sections of urban communities will then be freed from their traditional sub-ordinates roles. These women will be more empowered and will be ready for change as they would be receptive to new ideas, attitudes and values which will lead to upliftment. Capability to be employed is in itself an upliftment and it leads to further progress.

The Role of home science in upliftment of women is to make more women employable and secondly to strengthen and protect the occupational right and privileges of employed women. Many times we find women because they are unskilled and take up jobs which are low paid and are first to go when automation is introduced. So home science needs to introduce or collaborate with other entrepreneurs to develop sellable skills to women. In rural areas for instance, for all kinds of handicrafts jobs, women should be given assistance in forms of finance, materials, marketing, and training.

The role of home science in developmental projects and in enhancing the resulting uplift is thus, both manifest and latent. The manifest roles are those of executing the developmental projects either independently or in unison. With selected voluntary agencies, which have truly identified the bonafide beneficiaries. The latent roles are that of participation in policy making and monitoring of developmental projects. These latent functions will mean cultivating the employment potential of women, in order to liberate them from attitudinal backwardness. In brief, the role of home science is to explode the myth of female inferiority and to divert the economy to let the developmental benefits flow increasingly to women. When because of globalization we are facing changed situation all around us be it any sphere of our life and living conditions, it becomes imperative that we as home scientists too should consider these changes and shape them and direct them towards a more meaningful social metamorphosis. Because of globalization we find change in our environment, communication, dressing as well as the thinking of the individual. In short we find social development in one of the many aspects of the total phenomenon of change but it is the most fundamental for the home scientists. The home scientists has to look at it from three angles. Should home scientists be the agents of change for the social development ? For it is a challenge to them to either direct the social change to a better purpose, or to let them sweep the country towards an economic and social chaos. Second, how can home scientists maximize the benefits of the change ? And third, how can the home scientists minimize the evils or the undesirable effects the social changes ?

Materially speaking the evidence of social development is the elevated social and economic status of people, but what about the status of women ? attitudes of people towards girl child ? crime against women ? The role of home science in enhancing the social status of women and uplifting the people is only too obvious. The three dimensions of social status, namely, education, occupation and income need to be enhanced through the efforts of home scientists. The Government has launched the functional literacy programmes and non-formal education programmes as the first step in elevating the educational level of people. The role that home science can play is to support all non-formal education and literacy programmes for women. This would have an improved, educational level of women.

The home science students develops social sensitivity towards a greater awareness of their own social status and thereby contribute constructivity to the social development of the nation as a whole. The home scientists should definitely be the initiators of social development and such social change as one finds desirable. The directions of development and change must be found in the cognitive as well as affective behaviours. Cognitively, the home scientists need to be especially knowledgeable about their social obligations, expectations, norms, responsibilities. The areas of knowledge may include methods of extension work among the rural and the urban deprived populations, and communication of knowledge about nutrition and food science child guidance, resource management and clothing needs of the people.

The role of home science is first in equipping with up-to-date and relevant knowledge about these areas. The role in social development and change, then extends to our affective behavior of developing desirable interests attitudes, adjustments, appreciations and finally the whole spectrum of values, regarding discipline of home science and its contributions. If a home scientists has sound attitudes and values toward her discipline of home science, she will contribute further social development in such diverse areas as food habits, family planning, managing resources, in homes and elsewhere, and extending all relevant home science knowledge outside schools and colleges. The home scientists must place a greater emphasis on social development which is affecting home and family living which are congruent to contemporary national goals. The home science students are aware of their social responsibilities and are social alert and committed persons. These could be spreading social changes like small planned families, no to dowry, food adulteration, consumer rights, women's rights, legal education, protest against abuse of women's bodies. The role of home science encompasses the education of women in not only making them aware of their social obligations and rights but in also combating the undesirable social changes. The benefits of social development and change can be maximized only when women are aware of these. So the aim of home science education in the modern context needs to be the elevation of women's social conscious. All the social changes accompanying the technological changes can be maximized only when women are socially awakened. Home Science can widen its orbit of knowledge and skills to be imparted to its students in order to create the readiness in people to get the maximum benefits from social changes.

The falling moral and ethical standards have made the quality of our food, medicines, education, equipment, inferior. The extent of adulteration in food and drug is so profound that it is said to be crossing all limits. Home scientists as teachers, nutritionists, child psychologists and extension workers can help in bringing change and fight incorrect practices. Home Scientists can help in wiping out the evils concurrent with social development. As they have considerable women power to control some evils. There is the Indian Standards Institution to control the quality of goods and equipment but more important is to control the quality of social and moral standards of women. This act may be like a drop in an ocean, but home scientists can definitely be the agents of social development and empower women. More and more Indian women want to participate in economic programmes rather than literacy. The means have therefore to be found to develop income generating skills so that women can improve their every day life.

In order to integrate women into national development the following strategies are suggested to be taken into consideration.

1. Women need more power to control their lives to meet their practical and strategic needs and to shape the world in which they live in ways that are not themselves oppressive.
2. Women should be empowered by giving education. This is important as rate of school dropout and illiteracy is high amongst women. Education plays a critical liberating role in the lives of people and therefore, women should be put on board to benefit adequately through formal and non-formal education just like the men.

3. Governments should increase the participation of women in institutional and administrative life through the creation of ministries of women's affairs aimed at women's empowerment and development or through quotas for representation.
4. Entrepreneurship programmes could be put in place for women in the informal sector to engage in and be able to earn a living rather than for them to remain as housewives and be perpetually dependent on the men to provide for all their daily needs.
5. Life skills/Quality of life improvement Training (Women)
   1. Health and Hygiene
   2. Family Planning
   3. Pre-natal and Post Natal Care
   4. HIV/AIDS Prevention Education
6. Rural Development (Women at the focus)
   1. Agricultural Extension
   2. Drinking water and sanitation
   3. Watershed Management
   4. Forest Management
7. Many schemes and programmes need to be designed mainly for women of low income, 'low caste' groups, elderly women and women with disabilities.
8. Partnership between NGO's and GO's should be encouraged.
9. Women's welfare and development must have an integrated approach.
10. Reorient and sensitize the administrative machinery at all level.
11. All efforts should be made to fight and unravel the many mysteries of gender mechanism operative in our society.

Although, India is predominantly a rural country, its urban population, alone can be ranked among the largest, countries of the world. Urbanisation is generally associated with an increase in population which creates tremendous problems of providing jobs within the limits of a profit aiming economy besides the problems of housing, schooling, medical services, nutrition and other amenities. The large section of urban poor men and women live in darkness, despair and unthinkable poverty.

The urban women of low SES earn money mostly through domestic labour which is very inadequate as they lack vocational skills involving the use of technologies. Importance of gainful employment through income generating activities need to be stressed among the urban low SES women. The women need to be helped to learn income generating skills not only to raise their status, but also to collaborate with men on an equal footing in achieving national development goals.

REFERENCES

Agarwal, S., Status of Women, Print-well Publishers, Jaipur, 1988.

Asthana, P., Women's Movement in India, Vikas Publishing House, Delhi, 1974.

Awasthy, Indira, Rural Women of India, B. R. Publishing Corporation, Delhi, 1982.

Baig, T.A., Indian Women Power, S. Chand and Co., New Delhi, 1958.

Baker, M.A., and Others, Women Today, A Multidisciplinary Approach to Women studies, Broks/Cole Publishing Company, Monterey, California, 1984.

Boserup, Ester, Women's Role in Economic Development, London George Allen and Unwin Ltd., Ruskin House, 1970.

Buch, M. B., II and IV Survey of Research in Education, Society for Educational Research and Development, Baroda.

Cooper, I. Murthy, R. K. and Gade J. Gender and Development in Southeast Asia : Concepts and strategies for the gender sensitive development module, development management course, New Delhi PRIA (1996).

Dagupta, S. N., Religion and the Rational Outlook, Motilal Banarsidas, Delhi, Reprint 1974.

Department of Social Welfare, Towards equality, Report of the Committee on the status of women in India, New Delhi, Government of India, Ministry of Education and Social Welfare (1974).

Desai, M. Policy approaches to women and poverty eradication, The Indian Journal of Social Work 59 (1) (1998).

Desai, Neera, "Social Movements, A struggle for Indian Women's Emancipation", Survey of Sociological Research, Vol. 2, 1991.

Desai, Neera, Women in Modern India, Vora and Co., Publishers Pvt. Ltd., Bombay, 1957.

Dubey, Manisha, "When Home is not a Heaven", Indian Express, March 8, 1992.

Government of India, Women in Indian, A statistical Profile, Government of India, Department of Women and Child Development, Ministry of Human Resource Development, New Delhi, 1988.

17

Functional Literacy for Women

Education in general, and adult education in particular can assist and enable people and communities to deal with many challenges. It can provide women with the necessary faculties, skills, awareness and creative competencies to cope up as well as to transform their conditions. Education is that right which enable women to best exercise and advance their other rights. The major tool that could be used to break the backdrop of ignorance, perpetual dependence and unnecessary oppression, either at the individual or community level, is EDUCATION, which may not necessarily be acquired from the four-walls of the formal school system.

Education to-day has a tremendous challenge to face in a world of increasing complexity of life, in a market friendly society where wealth creation is becoming more dominant than achievement of peace of tranquility. Nevertheless for any society to achieve sustainable development a balance has to be achieved between well-being and development. As the UNESCO constitution states "Since wars begin in the minds of men, it is the minds of men that the defenses of peace must be constructed". Lifelong and Adult Education has an important role to play in the development of women.

The following are the objectives of the Development programmes :-

(1) Improvement of the status of the women in the family and the society.

(2) Organizing a community library and developing an institution through which skills training can be provided to be neo-literate women.

(3) Enabling the people to network with NGOs and government agencies for availing the services for improvement of the quality of life of the community especially the women.

The noted economist Prof. Amartya Sen in Delhi on December 29, 1997 said that road ahead of India would depend much on the integration of different concerns - preservation of democracy, rapid social progress specially in education, health care, land reforms and gender equity. India has suffered in the last 50 years from ignoring the need for such integration and the tendency to neglect social development in particular.

The University Grants Commission (UGC) policy frame of 1977 paved the way for the university system to get actively involved in the trinity of education viz. teaching research and extension. Though some universities and colleges were involved in adult and continuing education process as early as 1970, yet however, it was in 1978 that the universities got engaged in a substantial manner in the National Adult Education programme (NAEP), Kothari Commission reviewed the activities of adult education during 1980-83. Based on the Commission's report, the UGC renewed the process of spreading Adult Education.

Active participation of women in national development, as envisaged in our Five-year Plans since independence, is not possible as long as majority of our women are illiterate and ignorant. Half of our population comprises women and the grim reality is that not just their problems, but their very existence has been ignored despite the fact that majority of our labour force consists of women who produce a little less than 50 percent of our food. Their cases are overlooked whenever there is opportunity for being trained for skilled jobs. In general the position of women in our country is not a happy one as they are illiterate, and are ignorant of political, legal, social and economic issues and rights.

Considering the position of women in our society and the responsibility they shoulder, it is a know fact that they are not well-equipped to discharge these obligations. A large number of women are outside the reach of formal education and they could be educated through adult education programme. The adult education programme should be such that they motivate the illiterate women to join functional literacy classes and sustain their motivation to continue with the programme. Thus, it can help in creating social awareness of the importance of education in improving the quality of life. Adult education programme can create consciousness about realities of life, develop skills to help them increase their family income and reduce drudgery of life and make them literate so that they can help in development.

VITAL NATIONAL RESOURCE

Women constitute an important part of human resources of the country. For a developing country like ours, the contribution of women is as indispensable as that of men. It is widely recognized that the success of national development very much depends upon the active and useful participation of women in all developmental programmes. But when we cast our glance over the existing status of literacy among women of our country, we are greatly disappointed. It is because of inadequate expansion of education among women in India that they feel themselves unable to shoulder their responsibilities in different walks of life; and this has an adverse effect on their own development and the development of the society as well. The equal partnership between men and women is a must to fight against hunger, poverty, ignorance and ill health. We in India have accelerated the pace of educational expansion after independence, but due to rapid increase in population and for several reasons - social, economic and political - we have not been able to extend the benefits of education to the entire population of the country. Hence the huge number of illiterates among whom the number of women is much higher than that of men.

For full development of our human resources, for the improvement of our homes and for moulding the character of children during the most impressionable years of infancy, the education of women is of even greater importance than that of men. So, keeping these points in view, our Government has decided to impart education to women so as to equip them in performing their duties and for shouldering heavy responsibilities at home as well as outside. For the very purpose, the Government has started adult education programme for adult illiterates from October 2, 1978 all over the country, Now it is the duty of all the people to make efforts for the success of this programme. The essential pre-conditions for the success of adult education for illiterate women is that it is quite useful and effective from the point of view of fulfilling their immediate needs. Women would be interested in adult education if it assures them economic benefits. This is possible only by giving a practical bias to their education.

Empowerment is the need of the day, specially for women as they have no voice. Education helps in raising these voices. The Delors Commission's Report published by UNESCO "Learning : The Treasure Within" has identified the four pillars of education. Learning to know, Learning to Do, Learning to Live Together and Learning to Be. which can be taken up as a framework for rebuilding education. The report further points out that the concept of learning throughout life will be the key which will give access to the 21st century. Knowledge is for everybody's service, but in the search of knowledge one has to keep running - running continuously to update.

On the other hand Universities Institutions need to keep their doors open, allowing the wind to blow freely, giving opportunities to individuals to walk in and walk out. Particularly women need to be equipped to meet the challenges of life through several options, structures and opening of new fields of learning so that they can pursue their education within their role responsibilities in their own time.

NATIONAL ADULT EDUCATION PROGRAMME

The National Adult Education Programme, launched in 1978, while emphasizing acquisition of literacy skills was to be :

- relevant to learner's need
- flexible regarding duration, time, location, instructional arrangements etc.
- diversified in regard to curriculum, teaching and learning materials and methods.

The outline of NAEP suggested the following types of programme to be orgnaised under the scheme :

- Literacy with assured follow-up
- Conventional functional literacy in association with a dominant development programmes
- Literacy with learning-cum-action groups
- Literacy for awareness and formation of organizations of the poor

The programme was to cover by 1984 the entire illiterate population in the 15-35 age group. The programme consisting of literacy, functionality and awareness, with literacy comprising reading, writing and numeracy; functionality aiming at improvement in the learner's skills and capabilities to the discharge of one's function as wage earner as a member for the family and as a citizen; and awareness seeking to arouse a sense of social obligation and consciousness about the manner in which the poor are deprived of the benefits of the various laws, policies and facilities designed for them. A programme of 19 months was to be followed by post literacy and follow up activities. It was also intended to link up the programme with other development programmes of the Government. There should be 30 illiterate adults in each centre. In each centre there will be on instructor, three supervisors and a project officer.

According to the 1981 census, 243 districts out of 402 have literacy rates below the national average. The literacy rate is also very low amongst women, schedule castes, schedule tribes, migrant labourers and other weaker sections of the society. As comtemplated in the sixth Five-year Plan document, it was to be endavour of the Government to take steps for covering 100 percent adult illiterates in the age group of 15-35 by the year 1990.

FUNCTIONAL LITERACY FOR ADULT WOMEN

The programme of functional literacy for women has been provided in the Fifth Five-Year Plan to endow them with necessary knowledge and skills to perform the functions of a good housewife, efficient mother and a useful citizen. The scheme is a programme seeking to deliver a package of services to illiterate women in the country. Attention is confined to adult women in the productive age group of 15-45 years and special attention is given to women in the age group of 15-35, since the latter group is likely to be more receptive to the requirements of attitudinal change.

In order to give women their rightful position in the main stream of national development, it is essential they should be empowered psychologically, economically and politically. Women are socialized to be submissive, to serve and let the men take all major decisions. Psychological empowerment involves the reverse in the patriarchal order of doing things. It calls for developing competence in women to make decisions at personal and societal level. It means development of self confidence and self-esteem in women.

It has been experienced that financial dependence is one of the key sources of subordination of women. It is thus essential to provide support to them to have independent income. This could be possible if income generating activities are part and parcel of the educational programmes for women. They should also be provided financial facilities and management skills to be self reliant. So women's education, adult education and continuing education as a means of empowering women from grass root to managerial level. A change in the outlook of women is very important and this can be brought about by drawing their attention to the socio-economic political and cultural changes and developments taking place around them, in society in the country and in the world.

Adult education plays an important role in Women's Development in India in the following ways:

- Increase the rate of literacy among women
- Improve the general level of health and nutrition

- Enable women to raise their family income
- Improve the quality of local skills by providing vocational training in tailoring and embroidery, textile design and printing and machine knitting etc.
- Make them aware of new simple household techniques.
- Inform them about new governmental policies and privileges offered to female farmers for loans, seeds etc.
- Encourage them to lead a more hygienic and healthy life simply through cleanliness and other preventive methods.

Besides imparting instruction in simple but useful art and crafts, there are many other significant areas of which adult women can be imparted adequate knowledge. India is making sincere efforts to raise the standard of living of every citizen through planned development. For the immediate solution of the problem of rapidly increasing population, it is essential that the illiterate adult women are acquainted with the problems and know the need and importance of family planning and family welfare programmes. It would not only enhance their own happy lives but also the lives of their children who could be healthy and happy indeed.

Another factor relating to women's development is that they are able to know and understand their fundamental rights and duties in the existing social structure. It is seen that most of illiterate women often come to grips with superstitions and many other social evils of which there is an adverse effect upon their individual development. Such women cannot be expected to make their children's growth in the desired direction. With the spread of right education these women may get rid of superstitions, caste feelings and inferiority complex, etc. Adult Education programme tries to make use of leisure time of adult women. For this purpose, Mahila Mandals are organized where women take part in bhajan, kirtan, folk music and songs, stories and talks.

The Adult Education Programme is expected to benefit specially the weaker sections, but ironically, the weaker sections in India are the least concerned with education. When such learners dropout or keep away, the adult education programme obviously cannot succeed.

The Adult Education learners bring their individual problems to the Adult Education class. Many problems are beyond the scope of Adult Education. Both young and adult learners often face conditions which compel them to drop out of the adult education programme.

1. Lack of Interest

The learner's imaginary or assumed interest, their neglected economic needs, migration of learners and the men's negative attitude towards women's Adult Education, can cause failure of Adult Education Programmes.

2. Lack of Support

The adult education is always in danger of failure because it does not have the support of the men as far as women's education is concerned.

3. Family Problems

In some cases, the learners and their families are victims of socio-economic deprivation that they cannot even perceive the need for adult education. Even when the organizers try to reach them, they find ways to escape. The sheer ignorance of the deprived makes them impervious to the benefit of any form of education. Such learners even though they join the programme, under pressure, soon dropout and thus contribute to the failure of it.

4. Under estimation of Adult Education

The adult education programme is expected to benefit specially the weaker sections but ironically, the weaker sections in India are the least concerned with education. Such learners keep away from Adult Education programmes due to poverty, family quarrels and poor health.

5. Migration of the learners

Learners, mostly of lower socio-economic status migrate in search of jobs which are more stable than their present occupation. Their working hours change, their residence changes, infact their life gets so disrupted that they do not have any time for Adult Education. They need to put in more men in learning which again conflicts with their shifting life.

6. Job pattern and education

Many a times job pattern of the women may not coincide with the Adult Education Programme. Whenever there is a clash, naturally they drop education. Working women feel tired and exhausted after job hours to attend classes. Monetary gains through overtime allowance in the job, or supplementary job also discourage them from attending the classes. Thus, their employment issues are the most common factors in determining their availing of adult education.

7. Economic needs

Many women consider educational programme to be useless and a waste of time if they do not cater to raising the incomes of the learners. They do not view literacy and general self-development programmes as necessary or useful for them, which results in lack of motivation.

8. State of health

The poor women who form the majority of adult education learners, suffer mostly from illnesses and ailments, including the evil of too many children, who do not possess physical stamina or motivation to sustain themselves through a meaningful training for work.

9. Women and girls

Social and familial restrictions and responsibilities on women and girls, inhibit them from taking up adult education. They are brought up in such a way that they develop negative self concept and have no achievement motivation.

SOME EFFORTS TO MAKE ADULT EDUCATION CLASSES MORE MEANINGFUL FOR WOMEN

- The training programme for instruction that was provided was just for 21 days in term. Now that was considered as a vary short time span to train any person. But now-a-days the training of instruction is in 2 stage.

1. Training for 11 days
2. Training for 10 days

- In adult education the learners are inculcated with leadership qualities and are involved in decision making and develop the ability to form organizations. They are also involved in community welfare programmes.
- The adult education organizations are well managed by government and other agencies which was not taken care of before.
- Generating self reliance in instructor and in learners instructor motivates the learners and stimulates the instruction accordingly to the need and interest of learners.
- The adult education programme organizes cultural programme and advisory bodies at the village level and by doing so they obtained co-operation from the members of the advisory body and other members of the community and thus creates resource of the teaching learning process.
- The adult education classes organizes training programmes like ornaments, clothes, bags and hold exhibition in nearby areas and earns profit from it i.e. distributed among the members.
- Adult education imparts purposeful and job oriented education. It bridges the gap between learning and living. So that the learners are well equipped in her own profession. So this part motivates the women to attend the adult education programme again and again, till it makes their life better.
- Now the instructor have become participatory in nature and taking more interest in learners learning activities by making more teaching aids by using different types of methods. Thus, both the learners and teachers are equally participating in the teaching learning process.

- In respect to adult education programme great importance has been given to inspection. Though inspection is required throughout the adult education programme organization, its requirement is most essentials at the field level. Project officer spend most of his time on inspection and make personal contact with the instructors, supervisors or village representatives during the course of his inspections. He has been provided with separate vehicle with a view to making his inspection tour convenient and quick.
- The instructor makes alternative arrangements when electric bulbs or petromax goes out of order, so they do not suspend the classes and can carry out the programme well.
- The programme is recommended to other agencies to give loans to those women who have finished their training and now want to get engaged in some other activities.
- The government gives monetary incentives to women who go in for sterilization for limiting population growth.
- Follow up activities for neoliterate women are important. Infact neoliterate women now are employed after becoming literate, women are given jobs and some incentives are also given for the literacy training.

SUGGESTIONS

1. Preparation of posters, calendars, slogans and pamphlets.
2. Organizing Nukkad Natak, Mahila Sammelans.
3. Convergence with other departments.
4. Organising mass mobilization programme.
5. Publication of success stories and articles.
6. Broadcasting radio talks, discussions on rural programmes.
7. Organising seminars, workshops and training programmes.

8. Involving local people through cultural troupes.
9. Encouraging and facilitating access for women through use of methods suited for them.
10. Providing maximum flexibility in timetables and admissions to girls and women.
11. Providing different types of financial assistance.
12. Introducing second chance programmes specially for women.
13. Facilitating transition between school education and adult education by organizing them along similar lines in terms of study area.
14. Providing education for 'leisure and pleasure' across the levels and wherever relevant promote.
15. Girl's participation and participation of weaker sections of the society through rational incentive measures and empowerment programmes.
16. Different institutions must get involved in adult education such as colleges and universities, the libraries, museums and multitude of government and social agencies.
17. More participative methods like Role playing, group discussions and social action programmes.
18. The special needs like vocational education, skills retraining, health and nutritional needs, community social development programmes should be carried out.

REFERENCES

Ahmad Nasim, "Benefits of Literacy and Learning", Literacy Mission, Vol. XXI (1-54), 1997, pp 18-22.

APPEAL Manual for Planning and Management of Literacy and Continuing Education (AMPH) Monitoring and Evaluation of Literacy and Continuing Education, UNESCO Vol. 4, 1994.

Census of India (1991).

Dighe, Anita and Patel, Illa, "Gender Equality in Literacy in India Some Issues", Perspectives in Education Vol. 9 (1), 1993 pp. 3-14.

Evaluation of Literacy Campaign in India, Report of Expert Group, New Delhi, Directorate of Adult Education, 1994.

Grey Areas in Post-literacy BGVS, 1993.

Jan Chetna Kendra, A Guide Book SEARCH SRC, Haryana 1997.

Journal of Adult Environmental Education, Supplement of Adult Education and Development No. 47, 1996.

National Policy on Education, New Delhi, Ministry of HRD, Government of India, 1986.

Patel, Ila "Trends in Adult Education Research India", New Delhi, National Institute of Adult Education, 1994.

Pillai, Sadasivan, "From Three R's to Empowerment", Indian Journal of Adult Education, Vol. 58 (3), 1997, pp. 71-76.

Ramabrahan, Adult Education, Policy Performance, New Delhi, Gian Publications, 1988.

UGC, Guidelines for the Programmes of Literacy and Continuing Education in Universities and Colleges, 1992.

University Grants Commission (1982); Revised Guidelines on Adult and Continuing Education and Extension, New Delhi.

Index

E

F

G

H